GOD OF OU

God of our Fathers:
Classical Theism for the Contemporary Church

Proceedings of the 5th Annual Convivium Irenicum

Presented May 31–June 2 and August 17–19, 2017

Edited by Bradford Littlejohn

Moscow, ID

ISBN-13: 978-0-9995527-7-3

ISBN-10: 0-9995527-7-3

Front cover image taken from Benjamin West (1738–1820), *Joshua Passing the River Jordan with the Ark of the Covenant* (Art Gallery of New South Wales, Sydney, AU).

Cover design by Rachel Rosales, *Orange Peal Design*

"To whom then will you compare me,
that I should be like him? says the Holy One.

Have you not known? Have you not heard?
The LORD is the everlasting god,
the Creator of the ends of the earth.
He does not faint or grow weary;
His understanding is unsearchable."

—Is. 40:25, 28

CONTRIBUTORS

Dr. E.J. Hutchinson is Associate Professor of Classics at Hillsdale College (Hillsdale, Mich.), where he also directs the Collegiate Scholars Program. His research interests focus on the literature of Late Antiquity and the Neo-Latin literature of early modernity. He is the editor and translator of Niels Hemmingsen's *On the Law of Nature: A Demonstrative Method* (CLP Academic, 2018).

Dr. David Haines is Associate Professor of Philosophy and Religion at VIU, Associate Professor of Ethics at SEMBEQ, and has taught history of Christian Apologetics at FTE-Acadia. He is also the founding president of Association Axiome, an association of French Evangelical scholars, and the Centre de Philosophie et Apologétique Chrétienne. He has co-authored a book on Natural Law, and has published a number of articles and book chapters related to natural theology and the philosophy of religion. His academic research focuses on ancient and medieval metaphysics, C. S. Lewis, Thomism, and natural theology.

Dr. Steven J. Duby is Assistant Professor of theology at Grand Canyon University. He is the author of *Divine Simplicity: A Dogmatic Account* (T&T Clark, 2017), and his research interests focus on theology proper and Christology.

Dr. Alastair J. Roberts is a Fellow in Scripture and Theology with the Greystone Institute and a Teaching Fellow at the Davenant Institute. He is the co-author of *Echoes of Exodus: Tracing Themes of Redemption Through Scripture* (Crossway, 2018).

Gayle Doornbos is a Th.D. student at Wycliffe College/University of Toronto. Her research interests include the Doctrine of God, Herman Bavinck, and Missiology. She also teaches occasionally for Calvin Theological Seminary's distance M.Div. program and is an associate editor of the *Bavinck Review*.

Rev. Timothy G. Harmon is the lead pastor of Northeast Baptist Church in Portland, OR, an instructor and Assistant Dean of Academics at Western Seminary, a Ph.D. candidate in systematic theology (University of Aberdeen), and co-editor of and contributor to the forthcoming *T&T Clark Companion to the Doctrine of Providence.*

Rev. Dr. Christopher Dorn resides in Holland, Michigan. He currently serves as chair of Christians Uniting in Song and Prayer, an interdenominational organization in Holland dedicated to promoting and practicing worship that embodies sound liturgical principles. He preaches regularly at First Presbyterian Church in Ionia and Redeemer Presbyterian Church in Holland.

Joseph Minich is a Ph.D. candidate in Humanities at The University of Texas at Dallas, and the Editor-in-Chief of The Davenant Press. His research interests include modern atheism, the nature of modernity, and the role of late modern technology in the formation of religious beliefs. Some of his writing can be found at *The Calvinist International, Mere Orthodoxy,* and in several edited volumes published by Davenant.

CONTENTS

FOREWORD

Fred Sanders, Torrey Honors Institute, Biola University

THE CHRISTIAN doctrine of God is simply vast, and in some ways Christians can hardly be blamed for not grasping the whole theological bundle. It seems to be a teaching that, venerable as it is, exceeds our capacities, or at least the capacities of that legendary beast, the average, informed believer in an ordinary church. Professional theologians and other academics who devote years to grappling with some aspect of the doctrine of God sometimes look up from their books and wonder how their less scholarly friends are expected to keep up.

Yet surely the point of God's self-revelation is to be known. Surely one of the principal ends of the Father sending forth His eloquent Word and His articulate Spirit is to make possible, among all the redeemed and not just among a few professors, actual knowledge of God. And surely something has gone wrong when contemporary Protestants flail around, untethered from solid knowledge of the God they worship, lapsing in various ways into what Brad Littlejohn calls an idolatry problem. It must be possible to know the true God well enough to avoid worshiping a false God.

In my own teaching and preaching in service to the church, my normal approach is to teach the doctrine of God by expounding the greatness of the doctrine of the Trinity. My expectation is that the doctrine's sheer magnitude will have a tonic effect, drawing believers beyond themselves to the deep things of God. But the bigness and comprehensiveness of the doctrine of the Trinity has a downside as well. It's simply more than a mind can hold. So it occupies a place larger than the individual mind of the believer, and this fact must be reckoned with. We cannot all always be walking around with minds consciously turning over the material of the Trinitarian doctrine of God.

Indeed, to treat the amount of understanding of Trinitarianism as the index of spiritual maturity would be to run perilously close to some kind of doctrine of salvation by understanding of theology.

On the other hand, to concede too much to the average Christian's necessary ignorance is to lapse into the notion of salvation by implicit faith, which at its extreme form Calvin mocked as "ignorance plus docility." The extremes are both insupportable, and in practical church life it seems the way forward is to occupy a principled middle position with some clearly indicated pathways for making and marking progress in knowledge. The average church member is of course neither wholly learned nor wholly ignorant, but somewhere in the middle, knowing something. To set the standard too high may be crushing; but to set it too low is infantilizing. The Protestant Reformation, with its vernacular translations, commentaries, and catechisms, had as its goal a church come of age, set free from its self-imposed immaturity. One way of grasping the Reformation's educational objective is as an intention to raise the standard of the ordinary church member, to present a more mature, more informed, more doctrinally educated and biblically literate congregation of believers.

This volume, *God of Our Fathers: Classical Theism for the Contemporary Church,* takes up that central Protestant task with a fresh vigor and a renewed determination to spread abroad the knowledge of God.

Drawing on the profound resources of Protestant thought, the authors of this book presuppose the fundamental, underlying unity of the Christian confession of the triune God; but they also presuppose certain crucial distinctions which have been too often overlooked in modern times. Among the most important of these is a distinction among four processes of growth in understanding. The conflation of these four historical-cognitive processes has led to no end of disarray in contemporary theology. The four are:

1. *Progressive revelation,* wherein God carries out a series of communicative actions to make something known more fully bit by bit, over time, in an economy of revelation. Progressive revelation is a phenomenon within the structure of biblical theology, and can be traced between shorter arcs within the biblical history of God's economy of communication, as well as across the entire canon's unity. Progressive revelation presupposes a comprehensive unity which is capable of partial unveiling.

2. *Doctrinal development,* whereby the church, without any new revelation, unfolds its understanding of what has been revealed. Doctrinal development is frequently driven by apologetic and polemical needs. Doctrinal development has the character of deeper insight into a revealed datum, and especially into the relations among its parts, and the "good and necessary consequence" by which implications and applications can be drawn from what has been revealed. It is crucial that doctrinal development be propagated through public teaching, in plain view of the evidence and warrants being marshaled, and be subject to critical testing. While inspired insight may motivate development of doctrine, and legitimate authority may be invoked to promulgate it, neither inspiration nor authority can be the root of it.
3. *Catechetical transmission,* wherein one generation hands on to the next the content of the faith and the support systems that make that content receivable. This is tradition as it outlives one era and stretches across generations. It has the basic structure of elders teaching the younger.
4. *Personal growth,* wherein an individual learns new things, or comes to a much better grasp of them. This has the character of insight, and while it sometimes involves learning brand new things, it is primarily characterized by the new awareness of how information already inside the individual's cognitive structure belongs together, is joined up, and is mutually implicated. Personal growth is perhaps the phase of knowledge most comfortable to moderns; in our period it is the symbol and paradigm of all learning, throwing the others in the shade.

Speaking of our contemporary situation, I would hazard the diagnosis that we tend especially to drop the ball at step three. This is a shame, because this third step is where the classical doctrine of the Trinity shines: it is preeminently a catechetical doctrine. Of course the doctrine of the Trinity can be meaningfully discussed under each of the four headings, for there is much to know and to learn about it in every way. In phase one, God's tri-unity was hinted at and adumbrated throughout God's covenant ways with His people, but was unveiled in the Father's sending of the Son and Spirit. In phase two, the church reflected on their biblical monotheism in light of the undeniable identity of Jesus Christ, and labored forward to epochal moments of doctrinal development like Tertullian's "one being, three persons" language, or, more crucially, the confession of Nicaea. In phase three, the church has confessed the Trinity and handed down the doctrine about it with striking unanimity and agreement; it is a gem of orthodoxy and a hallmark of continuity in the tradition. Phase four is the illuminating moment preachers and teachers strive to evoke from maturing believers as they search the Scriptures together, and there discern the face of God as the Father, Son, and Spirit bless them, keep them, are gracious to them, and lift up the light of their countenance upon them.

All four phases are historical processes of deeper insight. But when they are not distinguished, deep confusions arise. Among evangelicals in the low church traditions, a lack of fluency with the traditional historic creeds may exacerbate the problem. A congregation that recites the ancient creed regularly has a constant reminder that there is more to the Christian faith than the handful of doctrinal points we happen to be consciously thinking about or preaching about on any given week. In a habitually creedless church life, it is easy for a Christian to get the feeling that whatever he knows right now is the extent of what is known in the church. Yet simply adding creeds to the weekly gathering of evangelicals is not an adequate solution. Conspicuously creedal congregation have more than their share of ignorant and gullible believers, who cannot distinguish the Christian God from rival claimants. The threat of idolatry is widespread in the church today, and churches whose liturgies and creeds should have forewarned them are nevertheless capable of missing the point.

The New Testament treats the people of God as a people who know something, and are engaged in learning more. Paul prays that the God of our Lord Jesus Christ, the Father of glory, may give believers a spirit of wisdom and revelation in the knowledge of Him (Eph 1:17). And even in delivering ethical exhortations, he admonishes them that they "did not learn Christ in this way, if they have heard him" (Eph 4:20). The health of the doctrine of God in our churches lies in this Ephesian direction of knowing, with all the saints, the length, height, breadth, and depth, of the love of God in Christ (Eph 3:18).

The Davenant Institute's motto, "*adtendite ad petram unde excisi estis*," is the exhortation of Isaiah 51:1 to "look to the rock from which you were hewn." In a general sense, the Institute recognizes in these words a summons back to the sources of Protestant Christian theology. But in this volume, with its careful attention to the classical doctrine of God, its vigilance to name defections and failures in worship and confession, and its patient tracing of the way back to theological normalcy, the motto resonates with its deepest possible significance: to look to God, our rock, in whom alone is our salvation.

INTRODUCTION

Bradford Littlejohn, The Davenant Institute

"So the king took counsel and made two calves of gold. And he said to the people, 'You have gone up to Jerusalem long enough. Behold your gods, O Israel, who brought you up out of the land of Egypt.'" (1 Kgs. 12:28)

"To whom then will you liken God, or what likeness compare with him?" (Is. 40:18)

PROTESTANTISM'S IDOLATRY PROBLEM

PROTESTANTISM TODAY has an idolatry problem. And by that I do not mean what countless Protestant preachers on both the left and the right can be heard thundering from pulpits every Sunday—that we have embraced the idol of Mammon, or of the State, or of personal freedom, or of gluten-free dieting, etc. This may all be true enough, and yet when we seek to make the pervasive biblical warnings against idolatry relevant to the modern world in this way, we manage to miss a central strand of the Bible's teaching on the subject: that we can make an idol of Yahweh, the Holy One of Israel.

We are accustomed to wring our hands uncomfortably about the fierce divine judgments visited on the pagan Canaanites in the Old Testament, but we cannot even bring ourselves to think about God's sometimes equally fierce judgments on His own people not simply for worshipping the gods of the nations, but for making an idol out of the one true God. In one of the more tragicomic moments in all of Scripture, the children of Israel can be seen falling into this wickedness almost as soon as they have left Egypt, *at the very moment* when Moses is receiving the Commandments from God in fire and smoke upon the mountain. There, with the powerful and terrible presence of Yahweh apparent to their very eyes, Aaron is able to persuade the Israelites to fashion a golden calf and worship it as the god "who brought you up out of the land of Egypt." Lest there were any room for confusion about whom this calf was meant to represent, we are told, "And Aaron made a proclamation and said, 'Tomorrow shall be a feast to Yahweh."

Absurd as it may seem, this sad scene is repeated time and time again throughout Israel's history, most crucially at the moment when the people of God divide into two, Israel and Judah. From that point onward, true worship of Yahweh is scarce in the Northern Kingdom, which is left to oscillate between, at worst, outright Baal-worship, and at best, golden calf worship, worshipping the God of Abraham, Isaac, and Jacob under a false image. Even when the Jews finally repudiate image-worship after the Exile, they fall back into their old habits of worshipping the true God in a false guise, when the true God takes on flesh and they refuse to recognize or honor Him.

And indeed, this is the key point. We are apt to miss the lesson of the Old Testament's many warnings against idolatry by chuckling at the benighted folly of those who needed some physical image with which to worship God. Indeed, some American evangelicals can be quite loud in their denunciation of more liturgical churches that use images or physical gestures in their services. Now is not the place to debate the merit of such denunciations. But what should be clear to us from the witness of Scripture is that what fundamentally concerns God is our tendency to worship the creature rather than the Creator—and this includes worshipping the Creator *as* a creature. The human heart is a "perpetual factory of idols," as John Calvin observed,[1] and there are two main production lines in this factory. One starts with a creature that we are particularly enamored of because it promises to meet our deepest desires and needs, and to elevate it into an object of worship. Of the two basic modes of idolatry, this is certainly the one we are still apt to hear sermons about. The other, however, starts with the Creator, the God of Abraham, Isaac, and Jacob, and shudders before His holiness and incomprehensibility; needing a God that can be put on a greeting card or in a praise song, our idolatrous hearts shrink this God down to size, and make Him more like us.

Thus we find ourselves faced with phenomena like *The Shack*, in which the protagonist is consoled in his grief over his daughter's death by a God

---

[1] John Calvin, *Institutes of the Christian Religion*, ed. John T. McNeill, trans. Ford Lewis Battles (Philadelphia: Westminster, 1960), 1:108.

who appears in the form of an African American woman (the Father), a Middle Eastern carpenter (the Son) and an Asian woman (the Spirit). More recently, renowned spiritual writer Fr. Richard Rohr has claimed to introduce his readers to the doctrine of the Trinity as "the Divine Flow": "whatever is going on in God is a flow, a radical relatedness, perfect communion between Three—a circle dance of love." It is a circle dance that is not complete even within itself, for, writes Rohr, "creation is thus 'the fourth person of the Blessed Trinity'! Once more, the divine dance isn't a closed circle—we're all invited!"[2]

It might be easy to dismiss such heterodox pop spirituality (although if we did so, we'd be dismissing the millions of evangelical readers who turned these books into runaway bestsellers), were it not that the basic ideas behind these blasphemies have long been appearing in somewhat tamer form among our academic theologians. A couple decades ago, the evangelical academy was roiled by disputes over "open theism," which cast aside the traditional doctrines of God's eternity and omniscience in favor of a God who lives, learns, and loves right alongside His creatures, hoping they will make good decisions and everything will turn out right in the end. Although evangelical theologians for the most part succeeded in closing ranks against open theism as just a bit too explicitly heterodox, they have been more than content to flirt with less overt denials of God's eternity, as Steven Duby's essay in this volume notes. At the same time, the classic attributes of divine simplicity, immutability, impassibility, and aseity have often been casually set aside if not openly rejected. In his bombshell recent book *All That is in God*, James Dolezal has identified these trends, comprising a new theology of "theistic mutualism," as pervasive among leading Reformed and evangelical theologians and biblical commentators of the later 20th and early 21st centuries. "In an effort to portray God as more relatable," Dolezal summarizes, "theistic mutualists insist that God is involved in a genuine give-and-take relationship with His creatures."[3]

---

[2] Richard Rohr, *The Divine Dance: The Trinity and Your Transformation* (London: SPCK Publishing, 2016), quoted in Fred Sanders, "Why I Don't Flow with Richard Rohr," *The Gospel Coalition*, December 2, 2016, https://www.thegospelcoalition.org/reviews/the-divine-dance/ (accessed April 12, 2018).

[3] James Dolezal, *All That is in God: Evangelical Theology and the Challenge of Classical Theism* (Grand Rapids: Reformation Heritage Books, 2017), 1-2.

At the same time, a radical revision of Trinitarian theology has been underway for several decades, with the fierce traditional insistence on divine unity replaced by a "social trinitarianism" in which a community of three persons—redefined as no longer the mysterious Greek *hypostases*, but in the modern English sense of individual subjects characterized by personality—either flow in and out of one another in a radical egalitarian dance (if you are socially and politically liberal) or exist in carefully-regulated structures of authority and submission (if you are socially and politically conservative). Such formulations are simply inconceivable from the standpoint of historical Christian orthodoxy, whether Orthodox, Catholic, or Protestant. Equally inconceivable is the fashionable modern talk of "the Father turning his back on the Son," of the "Trinity being broken" at Christ's crucifixion, language that originated in Jurgen Moltmann's radical theological revisionism of the 1960s and 1970s and took only a couple of decades to become domesticated into conservative evangelical orthodoxy.

We could identify many causes for the current chaos—from widespread historical illiteracy, to the appearance of new philosophical challenges or at least intellectual fashions (often Kantian and Hegelian in origin), to methodological biblicism or Christocentricism. At the more popular level, though, I think that much of what drives our theological revisionism is what has always lain behind the human heart's penchant for idolatry: a hunger for a God who is like me, a God who can relate to me, and meet me where I am, a God who is real enough to be there beside me in the midst of suffering. Whether it's the anguished search by modern theologians for a God who could make sense out of Auschwitz or the infinitely superficial spirituality of the evangelical condolence card remembering that God will help us "mount up with wings as eagles," the fundamental drive—emotivist and anthropocentric—is the same.

THE GOD OF THE GOSPEL

What this search for a God we can relate to forgets, however, is that the only reason that the Psalmist can cry to God in anguish for deliverance is because he knows that "Yahweh is a rock" before whom the earth reels (Ps. 18:2, 7). We all know the inspirational opening and closing verses of Isaiah 40, in which the Lord promises to comfort His people and lift them up on eagles' wings, but how often do we ponder the resounding verses in between:

Who has measured the Spirit of the Lord,
  or what man shows him his counsel?
Whom did he consult,
  and who made him understand?
Who taught him the path of justice,
  and taught him knowledge,
  and showed him the way of understanding?
Behold, the nations are like a drop from a bucket,
  and are accounted as the dust on the scales …

To whom then will you liken God,
  or what likeness compare with him? …

To whom then will you compare me,
  that I should be like him? says the Holy One.…

Have you not known? Have you not heard?
The Lord is the everlasting God,
  the Creator of the ends of the earth.
He does not faint or grow weary;
  his understanding is unsearchable.
  (Is. 40:13-15, 18, 25, 28).

It is precisely the incomprehensibility of God that makes Him able to comprehend our every struggle and grief, the unsearchability of His understanding that enables Him to search us out and know us from our mother's womb (Ps. 139), and His infinite incapacity to suffer change or grief that gives Him an infinite capacity to carry our griefs and be our anchor through every change. Indeed, amidst all of modern theology's desire to do justice to the radical truth of the Incarnation—that the Almighty stooped to our level and died in our place—we have found at the end of it all that we have cheapened the Gospel into a generic love-story. If the Almighty was already at our level—suffering, changing, yearning, and dancing—then it should hardly surprise us that He decided to manifest Himself amongst us so as to have a closer relationship and add one more partner to His circle dance. Fallen man always wants to retell the story of His deliverance in more relatable terms—"behold your gods who brought you up out of the land of Egypt!"—but idolatry always destroys the Gospel.

Once you put it this way and take a step back to consider the landscape of modern evangelical theology, it's a frightening prospect. Amidst our fervent and often well-meant efforts to hold the line on creation against Darwinism, on justification by faith against Rome, on the atonement against liberalism, on the sanctity of life and traditional marriage against a libertine culture of death, we have somehow allowed outright idolatry to sneak in our back door and take up residence amongst us, so that we casually tolerate blasphemy against the Lord of Hosts and have exchanged the Gospel for a mess of pottage. Of course, it is easy to minimize this danger: "Are you really accusing your evangelical brothers and sisters of heresy?" "Shouldn't it be clear that we're all on the same team?" "All these people sincerely love Jesus and His Word, and that's the main thing that matters." Of course we must distinguish false *teaching* from false *teachers*—Scripture reserves the latter harsh label for those who arrogantly and stubbornly persist in the former. And the point, in any case, is not to try to pass judgment on individuals, but simply to name such departures from Christian orthodoxy for what they are: idolatry. No doubt the prophets' raging condemnations of Israel's false worship seemed to many well-meaning Israelites like mad ravings—after all, how much harm could it really do to make Yahweh more accessible? Quite a lot, as the Scriptures go on to chronicle. Contemporary Protestantism today is running on fumes, on borrowed capital from an earlier era of robust orthodoxy that informed our worship and practice. We should not be so naïve as to imagine that we can continue to maintain a biblical witness on sex and marriage, or on greed and freedom, if we have ceased to preach a gospel anchored on the biblical God. "If the foundations are destroyed, what can the righteous do?" (Ps. 11:3)

A BLUEPRINT FOR RETRIEVAL

Still, we can hardly hope to rebuild these foundations merely by shrilly lamenting how far we have departed from them. We are Protestants, after all, and we are apt to self-identify in terms of William Chillingworth's famous words: "The Bible, I say, the Bible only is the religion of Protestants."[4] Our job, we will say, is to take the Bible at its word, and let the chips fall where they may. If that entails radical revision of the doctrine of God taught by our fathers in the faith, then so be it; we will at least be following the method of the Protestant Reformers, if not the content of their faith. Of course, the cranky historical theologian will object that this is *not*, in fact, the method of the Reformers, but of the anti-metaphysical, Scripture-only Socinians whom

---

[4] William Chillingworth, *The Religion of Protestants a Safe Way to Salvation* (London: Thomas Tegg, 1845 [1637]), 460.

they fiercely opposed. But it will probably make little difference. This particular train is too far out of the station, and when called to account at the bar of the Reformed tradition, many contemporary theologians may be apt to say, "Well, perhaps the Socinians were onto something."

Ultimately, the need of the hour is to show not merely that historic Protestantism is no friend to revision of the doctrine of God—although this is critical, and some of essays in this volume make crucial contributions along these lines. Nor is it merely to show that the philosophical assumptions and concepts that underlie classical theism are eminently defensible—although again this is critical, and I hope you will find some of the essays in this volume immensely helpful in this regard as well.

Beyond this, we must show that philosophy really can be a handmaiden to theology, not a competitor, that the rigorous conceptual distinctions formulated by our forefathers actually serve to illuminate the biblical text—a text which, left entirely on its own and uninterpreted, would degenerate into self-contradiction. Consider Christ's cry of dereliction from Ps. 22:1, so beloved of Moltmann and his many disciples in the theology of God's own God-forsakenness. While Ps. 22:1-2 reads, "My God, my God, why have you forsaken me? Why are you so far from saving me, from the words of my groaning? O my God, I cry by day, but you do not answer, and by night, but I find no rest," vs. 24 appears to contradict it: "For he has not despised or abhorred the affliction of the afflicted, and he has not hidden his face from him, but has heard, when he cried to him." There are four options when confronted with such a "contradiction": (1) unequivocally side with a "strictly literal" reading of the first passage and ignore the second; (2) unequivocally side with a "strictly literal" reading of the second passage and ignore the first; (3) let the contradiction stand, without attempting to reconcile, and "live in the tension"; or (4) do the hard work (and in some cases, really not all that hard work) of interpretation. This may involve hermeneutical tools of literary analysis as well as, when applied to the cry of dereliction, the philosophical tools of systematic theology that distinguish Christ's human experience and divine identity.[5] Or consider the juxtaposition of Jn. 1:18—"No one has ever seen God"—with Ex. 33:11—"the Lord used to speak to Moses face to face,

---

[5] I am indebted to Michael McClenahan's sterling lecture, "The Mystery of the Gospel" (delivered at New Saint Andrews College, April 6, 2018), for a wonderful exegesis of these passages and account of the proper understanding of the cry of dereliction.

as a man speaks to his friend." A wooden literalist might have some trouble here, but it does not take a great deal of reasoning ability to reconcile these two passages by privileging the more literal affirmation of John 1 with what we judge to be the more metaphorical affirmation of Exodus 33.[6] This is not "refusing to take Scripture seriously," as many modern theologians accuse classical theists of doing. Rather, it is taking Scripture very seriously, by insisting on taking it *as a whole*. When we take it as a whole, we are necessarily committed to distinguishing between statements about God that are to be taken unequivocally and thus serve a more regulative role, and statements that have a more contextually-specific meaning and require careful interpretation. It is this basic task of distinguishing, essential to all good reading, that over the course of centuries bore fruit in the Nicene Creed, Chalcedonian Definition, and the elaborate formulations of the classic doctrines of the unity of God and trinity of Persons.

Not, mind you, that the purpose of these distinctions and formulations is to render God philosophically intelligible and lucid to our gaze. On the contrary, at the heart of classical theism is the doctrine of divine incomprehensibility, the rhetorical question of Isaiah: "To whom then will you liken God, or what likeness compare with him?" It is this humble awe before the mystery of the Triune God that all idolatry fails to sustain, and that so much modern theology, with its false claims to humility before the Scriptural text, is too self-important to accept. As no less a philosopher than John Locke said, when confronted with the first wave of modernity's redefinition of the doctrine of God, "Perhaps it would better become us to acknowledge our ignorance, than to talk such things boldly of the Holy One of Israel, and condemn others for not being as unmannerly as ourselves."[7]

THE ESSAYS IN THIS VOLUME

It remains to offer a brief overview of the essays contained in this volume, and how each contributes to the larger task I have here outlined.

At the risk of frightening away casual readers, the volume begins with by far the longest and most historically detailed essay, E.J. Hutchinson's

---

[6] I am indebted to Fred Sanders for this particular example.

[7] John Locke, *Remarks Upon Some of Mr. Norris's Books, Wherein He Asserts P. Malebranche's Opinion, of Our Seeing All Things in God*, in J.A. St. John, ed., *The Philosophical Works of John Locke* (London: George Bell and Sons, 1894), II:469.

"Melanchthon's Unintended Reformation? The Case of the Missing Doctrine of God." But do not be scared off. The mystery case that Hutchinson sets out to solve is one of the greatest importance for understanding our Protestant tradition, and one could hardly ask for a livelier guide in the investigation than him. Hutchinson begins with the great 19th-century theologian Friedrich Schleiermacher, who in many ways stands at the headwaters of the great revision of modern theology in an anthropocentric direction, and considers his claim that to be a true and full reformation, the Protestant Reformation must involve a reformation of the doctrine of God—as well as doctrines like ecclesiology and soteriology. Inasmuch as the Reformers failed to comprehensively undertake this critical project, Schleiermacher aimed to bring their reformation to completion. At first glance, shows Hutchinson, it might seem that Luther's great colleague, Philipp Melanchthon himself, had intended such a revision, rejecting the sterile scholastic doctrine of God in favor of a more dynamic redemptive God. However, he goes on to show through close engagement with Melanchthon's work that this is a misreading of the reformer—*sterile* scholasticism that leads men to speculation rather than to salvation is indeed rejected, but for Melanchthon this never meant reworking the basic formulations of creedal orthodoxy; on the contrary, philosophical distinctions still had an appropriate place in securing the mysteries of the Trinity and Incarnation. This essay thus offers something of a programmatic sketch of a properly Protestant approach to the doctrine of God: one that eschews needless speculation and hews closely to the saving narrative of Scripture, but without despising the catholic inheritance of rigorous reflection on the identity and attributes of the God who saves us.

The second essay in the volume, David Haines's "Natural Theology and Protestant Orthodoxy," builds upon this foundation by showing that for Protestants historically, there has been a symbiotic, rather than competitive, relationship between biblical and philosophical reasoning about God. At the intersection of this symbiotic relationship was the crucial discipline of "natural theology," which clarified what God revealed about Himself through creation and conscience, prior to His more direct self-revelation in Scripture. Indeed, Haines goes beyond showing that there is ample warrant in the Christian tradition for natural theology, so much despised today; rather, a commitment to natural theology is itself part of the core of doctrines that constitute historic Christian orthodoxy, and is necessary for helping sustain other doctrines recognized as part of orthodoxy. A *purely* biblical theology, historic Protestant teaching recognized, was likely to become a heterodox theology.

Since contemporary Protestant readers may be understandably suspicious of this bold claim, the next two essays in the book tackle two issues where recent theology has frequently posited a sharp opposition between the biblical testimony and the categories of classical theism, said to be derived from Greek philosophy rather than Scripture. In "Divine Action and the Meaning of Eternity," Steven Duby engages the very difficult question of divine eternity—how can a timeless and transcendent God engage in history in the way that He is constantly said to do in Scripture? The problem, Duby shows, is not one of how to reconcile Scripture with extra-biblical philosophy, but of how to make sense of the full testimony of Scripture itself. The God of the Bible is one who both transcends and acts in time. How are we to understand this? Duby suggests that rather than casually caricaturing the earlier scholastic tradition, we seek to read it careful and retrieve its insights. If we do so, we may find that they are far more nuanced and fruitful than we could have imagined.

Alastair Roberts's consideration of recent debates on the eternal subordination of the Son, "'Arid Scholars' vs. The Bible? A Theological and Exegetical Critique of the Eternal Subordination of the Son," poses the problem of the supposed opposition of Scripture and scholasticism in even sharper terms. Surveying the unhealthy opposition between biblical and systematic theology that prevailed through much of that recent debate on the nature of the Trinity, Roberts points us back to a symbiotic rather than competitive relationship between the two. Roberts then applies this relationship to the case study of the subordination of the Son, effectively showing how scholastic categories, developed in conversation with the biblical text, can shed light back upon the text in a way that enables us to rightly understand Christ's saving work.

Gayle Doornbos's essay, "Can the Trinity Save Everything? Herman Bavinck, Missional Theology, and the Dogmatic Importance of the Doctrine of the Trinity," brings us back to historical theology, but at its point of intersection with contemporary theology. Noting how the doctrine of the Trinity has been abused in contemporary missiology in a way that collapses the Creator/creature distinction and brings God down to our level, Doornbos asks what the proper "use" of the doctrine of the Trinity is. Is it merely, as critics of classical theism charge, a self-inclosed and sterile mystery that fails to shape the rest of our theology, or does it help us make sense of the Christian doctrines of creation and redemption, as well as the church's mission? The great Dutch Reformed theologian Herman Bavinck, argues Doornbos, offers us a sterling example of how to answer this question responsibly; Bavinck does argue for "cosmological" and "soteriological" dimensions of the doctrine of the doctrine of the Trinity in addition to its "ontological" dimension, but by carefully parsing the distinctions and relationships between these dimensions, Bavinck helps us avoid many pitfalls of recent Missional Theology.

One of the greatest contemporary systematic theologians, responsible perhaps more than anyone else for putting the classical doctrine of God back on the agenda of modern theology, is John Webster. This essay collection would thus hardly be complete without a consideration of what we can learn from Webster's methodological prioritization of the doctrine of God. This Timothy Harmon undertakes in his essay, "Biblical Inspiration and the Doctrine of God, with Attention to the Example of John Webster." Here again we find that classical theism is not a sterile doctrine, but a richly generative one. Harmon surveys the seemingly overworked terrain of the doctrine of Scriptural inspiration and argues that we can gain a much richer understanding of Scripture itself if, instead of taking for granted the idea of "God" and asking what we mean by His "Word," we pause to consider how close reflection on the nature of God Himself can enrich our understanding of what Scripture is and does.

Lest the reader come away from this book with the notion that "older is always better," and that there is nothing to be done for modern theology but to leap back into the arms of the older Reformed masters, the final two essays explore ways in which our contemporary moment should compel a reconsideration of our approach to the doctrine of God. In "Encounter With the Triune God in the Reformed Liturgy for the Lord's Supper: Eucharistic Prayer or Communion Order?" Christopher Dorn argues that the richness of historic Reformed theology has not always been matched by its communion liturgies. These have often been insufficiently Trinitarian in their shape, and the reforms of the modern liturgical movement, he argues, can in fact help us more faithfully reflect the catholic doctrine of the Trinity in our worship.

Finally, Joseph Minich's concluding essay, "Classical Theism in a World Come of Age," boldly proposes that rather than taking the "disenchantment" of the contemporary world as cause for lament, we should embrace it as an opportunity. The absence of God so keenly experienced by faithful believer as well as stubborn atheist under the conditions of modernity, he contends, is an invitation to a fuller consideration of what divine transcendence means. The biblical and classical Christian doctrine of God, Minich argues, is not best attested by the sense of an enchanted creation order in which God presents Himself in every flower or sunset, but by the concept of history itself, the experience of radical contingency somehow secured within a purposive order being guided to its fulfillment. Accepting our place within this history, rather than yearning nostalgically for an era in which belief in God was "easier," is essential if we are to again come face-to-face with the God of Abraham, Isaac, and Jacob, and reveal Him again to our contemporaries as the desire of the nations.

ACKNOWLEDGMENTS

As I close this introduction, it bears emphasizing that no project of retrieval and reformation can happen through books alone. Indeed, the essays here presented to the world are almost an afterthought rather than the main show. That happens each summer (and with increasing frequency throughout the year in smaller gatherings) at the Convivium Irenicum which played host to these papers. Theology, I have become increasingly convinced, is an enterprise that depends at every point on friendship; and the renewal of the church today, and the renewal of our teaching on the Triune God, cannot happen without the cultivation of bonds of deep friendship, trust, and collaboration between all those who love the faith once delivered to the saints and hope to keep handing it on. The bonds of friendship formed and nurtured at last year's Convivium Irenicum (in both its East and West gatherings) will, I am confident, long outlast the shelf life of this book, and accomplish far more for the church. I thus want to recognize the contributions of others who presented papers or helped lead panel discussions at the 2017 Convivium—Fred Sanders, Paul Nedelisky, Joel Carini, Ben Miller, Jake Meador, Steven Wedgeworth, and Peter Escalante—as well as all those who attended and contributed by their vigorous discussion and thoughtful questions.

As always, we are profoundly grateful to those who undertook the labor of revising and polishing their papers for publication in this volume, rather than taking them, as in many cases they could have, to a more prestigious academic journal. Finally, we appreciate the tireless labors of Sarah Belschner, Dan Kemp, Brian Marr, and Josiah Roberts in helping to prepare this manuscript for publication.

I:
MELANCHTHON'S UNINTENDED REFORMATION? THE CASE OF THE MISSING DOCTRINE OF GOD[1]

E.J. Hutchinson, Hillsdale College

INTRODUCTION

ONE SOMETIMES gets the impression that there is among Protestants a strange felt need to have a "Protestant" version of everything: not simply the way in which the redemption accomplished by Christ's life, death, and resurrection is applied to believers, or the way in which human authority relates to divine authority within the church, but even the way in which one should think about and dogmatically formulate theology proper, that is, the doctrine of God as trinity in unity. Such reworking of the order and content of dogmatics can be traced back at least in part to fundamental alterations to the system of doctrine made by Friedrich Schleiermacher, Germany's most important theologian of the eighteenth and nineteenth centuries,[2] as is evident from his system as presented in *The Christian Faith*.[3] I shall treat some

---

[1] *In memoriam* John Webster, who taught the church to think more, and better, about the doctrine of God by retrieving the past for the edification of the present.

[2] For a brief introduction, see B.A. Gerrish, *A Prince of the Church: Schleiermacher and the Beginnings of Modern Theology* (Philadelphia: Fortress, 1984). See also his "Friedrich Schleiermacher (1768–1834)," in *Continuing the Reformation: Essays on Modern Religious Thought* (Chicago: University of Chicago Press, 1993), 147–77.

[3] *Der christliche Glaube nach den Grundsätzen der evangelishen Kirche*, usually referred to as the *Glaubenslehre*. The first edition was published in 1821–22; the second, in 1830–31. Citations of Schleiermacher herein come from Friedrich Schleiermacher, *The Christian Faith*, ed. H.R. Mackintosh and J.S. Stewart (Edinburgh: T&T Clark, 1986),

aspects of this work very briefly, in which it will emerge that the revision of the doctrine of God was seen, in Schleiermacher's own view, as ingredient to the Protestant dogmatic project. My analysis shall then turn to the question of Protestant antecedents, if any are to be found, for the move that he makes. That is to say, is Schleiermacher's revisionism on this point "Protestant" at its core, as he alleges? Walter E. Wyman Jr., for instance, demonstrates that "Protestantism" for Schleiermacher may be defined in the first instance negatively as not-Romanist, which is to say that areas of agreement with Rome (for example, theology proper and Christology) do not tell us anything about the fundamental quiddity of Protestantism; only her distinctives in opposition to Rome can do that. Only when opposing Roman Catholicism, then, do "the confessions come into their own as evidence of the distinctively Protestant religious experiences and beliefs."[4] B.A. Gerrish, too, stresses the oppositional, negative element in Schleiermacher's understanding of the Reformation.[5]

To determine whether Schleiermacher is right about what constitutes the kernel of Protesantism in contradistinction to its hidebound husk, at least part of the evidence must be taken from the self-conception and dogmatic

---

translated from the second edition; citations are to page numbers rather than section numbers.

[4] Walter E. Wyman Jr., "The Role of the Protestant Confessions in Schleiermacher's *The Christian Faith*," *Journal of Religion* 87 (2007): 355–85; the quotation is from 377.

[5] B.A. Gerrish, "Schleiermacher and the Reformation: A Question of Doctrinal Development," in *The Old Protestantism and the New: Essays on the Reformation Heritage* (London: T&T Clark, 2004), 186–87. At the same time, he highlights another "strand" of his view that allows to the Church of Rome vis-a-vis Protestantism an abiding and legitimate individuality notwithstanding what the Reformers identified as abuses and corruptions (187–89). The whole essay (179–95, 366–75) is relevant to the issues treated herein. (Despite the above, Schleiermacher has been accused, not frivolously in my view, of a fundamentally Catholicizing theological project by, e.g., Karl Gottlieb Bretschneider, Emil Brunner, and Karl Barth: see John E. Thiel, "Schleiermacher as 'Catholic': A Charge in the Rhetoric of Modern Theology," *Heythrop Journal* 37 [1996]: 61–82. For a discussion of Schleiermacher and modern Roman Catholicism, see Francis Schüssler Fiorenza, "Schleiermacher and the Construction of a Contemporary Roman Catholic Foundational Theology," *Harvard Theological Review* 89 [1996]: 175–94.) It will be argued in the course of this essay that the (arguably dominant) negative "strand" in the understanding of the Reformation, with a concomitant belief that the movement was primarily an enfranchisement of a spirit of freedom to be applied to first theology as well as to Rome's soteriological and ecclesiological aberrations, is far from the self-understanding of the Reformers themselves; see below.

formulation of the Reformers themselves.[6] And to do that, one ought to begin at the beginning—which is to say, with Philip Melanchthon and his *Loci communes*, or *Commonplaces*.[7] Melanchthon, it is sometimes said, gave Protestantism the impulse of wholesale revisionism at the outset, for which he has been now praised, now blamed, but in any case heralded as responsible for opening the possibility of just such innovation with respect to the doctrine of God. Why? Because he omitted its treatment from the first era of the *Loci*. My brief, then, is as follows: can Melanchthon legitimately be held accountable for opening the floodgates to the revision of theology proper, unleashing a wave that crests in Schleiermacher's thought? In other words, is the charge true?

It must be granted at the outset that Melanchthon did indeed omit the doctrine of God from the first era of the *Loci*. The question, however, is not one of fact, but one of interpretation. That is to say, what must be investigated and explicated is not *whether* he did so, but *why*. The answer to the latter question, it will be argued, has eluded many of Melanchthon's interpreters, among whose number the most important, for our purposes, is Karl Barth, perhaps the most important theologian of the twentieth century. If a theologian of Barth's stature and influence misinterprets Melanchthon on this important point, it is of great moment that the mistake be corrected.

---

[6] Such a procedure is obviously not *ipso facto* dispositive: they may, after all, have been inconsistently "re-formed," that is, inconsistent with their own principles, as Schleiermacher himself alleges (see below). But other theologians and historians, such as Ferdinand Christian Baur, *did* think that this revisionary impulse was there from the beginning. If it can be demonstrated, moreover, that it is the revisions themselves that are inconsistent with Protestant principles as enunciated by the Reformers, then that will go some way toward indicating that, whatever else revisions to the doctrine of God may be, they are not "Protestant" in any meaningful or historically responsible sense.

[7] The work will usually be referred to in this essay by the abbreviated title *Loci*. The bibliographies for both Schleiermacher and Melanchthon are enormous, and I make no pretense that my citations are exhaustive; they represent a mere selection of the literature.

FRIEDRICH SCHLEIERMACHER AND THE DOCTRINE OF GOD

The Traditional Placement of the Doctrine(s) of God and the Holy Trinity

First, by way of brief prologue: it is worth remarking, despite its obviousness, that, in the centuries previous to Schleiermacher (with the exception of Melanchthon!), the first article for discussion in a work of dogmatics consistently had been that which concerns God Himself. The impulse here goes back to the Decalogue ("I am the Lord your God.… You shall have no other gods before me"), or the *Shema* of Deuteronomy 6.4: "Hear, O Israel: The Lord our God, the Lord is one." That impulse is taken up in the Creeds ("I believe in God"; "We believe in one God"), with the crucial addition of the explicit confession of God's triunity as Father, Son, and Holy Spirit.

It is thus not surprising that this basic pattern is everywhere in evidence for several centuries thereafter, having given basic shape to Christian dogmatic reflection. Peter Lombard, for example, begins the *Sententiarum libri IV* with a discussion of the mystery of the Trinity after treating the Augustinian distinction between things and signs. Thomas Aquinas begins the *Prima pars* of the *Summa theologiae* with expositions of the one God and the blessed Trinity (after a brief discussion on "what sort of thing sacred doctrine is, and to what matters it extends").[8] Likewise, John Calvin begins his own *summa*,[9] the *Institutes of the Christian Religion*, with a treatment "Of the

---

[8] *Necessarium est primo investigare de ipsa sacra doctrina, qualis sit, et ad quae se extendat.* There are, of course, significant and deep structural differences between the approaches of Lombard and Aquinas, on which see W.J. Hankey, *God in Himself: Aquinas' Doctrine of God as Expounded in the* Summa Theologiae (Oxford: Oxford University Press, 1987), 19–35. Hankey notes that Aquinas "chang[es] the formal subject of theology from 'res et signa' to God" (23). My point above, however, is a general one: all the examples given are theological attempts at following the overarching creedal pattern of beginning with an explication of the one God who is triune.

[9] *Summa* is, after all, the work's fifth word, and is the first word of the work's first edition in 1536. Peter Fraenkel, Testimonia Patrum: *The Function of the Patristic Argument in the Theology of Philip Melanchthon* (Geneva: Droz, 1961), 29 n. 94, points out that Calvin titled his 1546 translation of Melanchthon's *Loci La somme théologique ou lieux communs reveuz et aumentez pour la dernière foys par Philippe Melanchthon.* This is not quite right: the work, for which Calvin wrote the preface, was published under the title *La somme de théologie* … (2nd ed. 1551). It is not absolutely certain that Calvin was the translator, though Richard Muller, *The Unaccommodated Calvin* (Oxford: Oxford University Press, 2002), 201 n. 80, notes that it is "probable" that he was. Cf. Matthew Oseka, "What the Emerging Protestant Theology Was About: The

Knowledge of God the Creator" and then proceeds to "the Knowledge of God the Redeemer."[10] So too the *Augsburg Confession*, the *Smalcald Articles*, and the *Thirty-Nine Articles*. Other Protestant confessions, such as the *Second Helvetic Confession* and the *Westminster Confession of Faith*, do much the same, though they first include articles on Scripture. These, however, can be considered prefatory to the main dogmatic task (in a way not entirely unrelated to the first *quaestio* of Thomas' *prima pars*): for, if we are to talk about God, it makes some sense first to delineate how we are to know about Him.[11] In any event, what one can say is common to the approach of all of the preceding confessions and dogmatic works is the following: they all begin with the objective truths of the faith, what is "out there": God Himself and His revelation that makes Him savingly known to us.

Schleiermacher's Placement of the Doctrine of God

Not so Schleiermacher—and this is the only point I wish to make about *The Christian Faith*, a point that is in the first instance descriptive rather than evaluative. After introductory remarks on the nature and method of dogmatics, Schleiermacher begins the "First Part of the System of Doctrine" with what he calls the "feeling of absolute dependence," originating

Reformation Concept of Theological Studies as Enunciated by Philip Melanchthon in His Prolegomena to All Latin and German Versions of the *Loci*," *Perichoresis* 15 (2017): 22, and Karl Bretschneider and Heinrich Bindseil, eds., *Corpus Reformatorum* 22 (Brunsvigae: Schwetschke, 1855), 667–70.

[10] With respect to the examples given above one is on shakier ground in the case of the *Institutes*, as its structural principles are debated: cf. B.A. Gerrish, "Theology within the Limits of Piety Alone: Schleiermacher and Calvin's Notion of God," in *The Old Protestantism and the New*, 198–201. If one accepts (as I do) that the Apostles' Creed forms the primary ordering principle of the work (while allowing for other subordinate ordering principles), the basic point I wish to make is secure, though one is well advised to heed Gerrish's warning that *Institutes* 1 does not contain a complete doctrine of God. Nevertheless, it is not without significance for the above that Book 1 proceeds in the following order: Scripture (1.6–10); idolatry and the distinction of the true God from idols (1.11–12); the unity of the divine essence in three persons (1.13). See also Benjamin Breckenridge Warfield, "Calvin's Doctrine of God," in *Calvin and Calvinism* (Grand Rapids: Baker, 1931; originally published in *Princeton Theological Review* 7 [1909]: 381–436), 133–85; Richard Muller, *Post-Reformation Reformed Dogmatics* (2nd ed.), vol. 1 (Grand Rapids: Baker, 2003), 103–105.

[11] And, particularly, how we are to know about God as Savior, taken as the main purpose of special revelation in Scripture.

subjectively and internally[12]—though for Schleiermacher universally, and thus in some sense "objectively" from his perspective[13]—which takes the place of what had long been the customary way of formulating doctrine.[14]

This move has, one must grant, some resemblance to characteristically Lutheran "existential" concerns (for instance, how one can assuage the troubled or terrified conscience). However, that resemblance is more superficial than real, for the characteristically Lutheran way of addressing the conscience is through an extrinsic or alien Word whose truth is founded on the classical doctrine of God in Himself, on which see below. There is as well a superficial similarity to John Calvin's famous opening to the *Institutes*:

> Our wisdom, in so far as it ought to be deemed true and solid Wisdom, consists almost entirely of two parts: the knowledge of God and of ourselves. But as these are connected together by many ties, it is not easy to determine which of the two precedes and gives birth to the other.[15]

---

[12] Though not currently in fashion, the criticisms of "subjectivism" lodged against Schleiermacher by Emil Brunner in *Die Mystik und das Wort: der Gegensatz zwischen moderner Religionsauffassung und christlichem Glauben dargestellt an der Theologie Schleiermachers* (Tübingen: J.C.B. Mohr, 1924/1928), as summarized by Christine Helmer, "Mysticism and Metaphysics: Schleiermacher and a Historical-Theological Trajectory," *Journal of Religion* 83 (2003): 517–38, still seem to me to have some force. Helmer levels several forceful critiques against Brunner's reading, but does not, in my view, rescue Schleiermacher from the charge of subordinating Christian faith to a generic religious self-consciousness immanent in the human experience. Regardless, I have attempted above to gloss his position fairly. Helmer treats the subject again in *Theology and the End of Doctrine* (Louisville, KY: Westminster John Knox Press, 2014), 23–58. See also B.A. Gerrish, *Tradition and the Modern World: Reformed Theology in the Nineteenth Century* (Chicago: University of Chicago Press, 1978), 13–48.

[13] Schleiermacher's use of the concepts of "feeling" (*Gefühl*) and "self-consciousness" (*Selbstbewusstsein*) is admittedly complex and cannot be engaged here; cf. Louis Roy, "Consciousness according to Schleiermacher," *Journal of Religion* 77 (1997): 217–32, and Julia A. Lamm, "The Early Philosophical Roots of Schleiermacher's Notion of *Gefühl*, 1788–94," *Harvard Theological Review* 87 (1994): 67–105. Roy too observes that for Schleiermacher the "feeling" under consideration "is by no means merely subjective" (218).

[14] See below.

[15] John Calvin, *Institutes of the Christian Religion* 1.1.1, in *Institutes of the Christian Religion*, vol. 1, trans. Henry Beveridge (Edinburgh: Calvin Translation Society, 1845). The quotation is from the final edition of 1559, but the idea is already present in the first edition of 1536.

Again, however, there is an objectivity present in Calvin, who arguably had a deep impact on Schleiermacher, with respect to the external modes by which knowledge of God comes to us in its chief part that is missing in Schleiermacher's dogmatic starting-point.[16] A closer parallel may be found in the internal mode (though it, too, has an external origin, that is, God) by which we are, for Calvin, first cognizant of the existence of God, namely, the *sensus divinitatis*, though even here there remain important divergences between Calvin's *sensus divinitatis* and Schleiermacher's "feeling of absolute dependence."[17]

In any case, the material difference made by Schleiermacher's move in the opening of *The Christian Faith* for the conceptualization of the dogmatic task should not be underestimated. And indeed, the placement of the *locus de Deo* can serve as an index of just how far-reaching Schleiermacher's modification was. Whereas the traditional place for the treatment of the doctrine of God as one and three had been first, Schleiermacher does not discuss the two doctrines together or consecutively. Schleiermacher intends, moreover, for his procedure to make such a decisive material difference. He

---

[16] For criticism, see Mark Husbands, "Calvin on the Revelation of God in Creation and Scripture," in *Calvin's Theology and Its Reception: Disputes, Developments, and New Possibilities*, eds. J. Todd Billings and I. John Hesselink (Louisville, KY: Westminster John Knox Press, 2012), 25–31, and especially 28.

[17] For a brief overview of the similarities and important differences between the two, see Abraham Varghese Kunnuthara, *Schleiermacher on Christian Consciousness of God's Work in History* (Eugene, OR: Wipf & Stock, 2008), 11–14. Husbands, "Calvin on the Revelation," 29–30, touches on this question as well: "Although there appears to be a significant parallel … between Schleiermacher's treatment of the feeling of absolute dependence and Calvin's affirmation that '[m]en of sound judgment will always be sure that a sense of divinity which can never be effaced is engraved upon men's minds,' the family resemblance is more apparent than real. The crucial difference between these two positions is this: Calvin resists appealing to the innate *sensus divinitatis* as a foundation upon which one might reasonably construct a dogmatic project…. Whereas Calvin regards Scripture as the *principium cognoscendi* of dogmatic work, insisting upon humility and obedience to 'the things which we know have come from God,' Schleiermacher takes a quite opposite view of the matter, protesting … that 'the authority of Holy Scripture cannot be the foundation of faith in Christ.'" For Calvin on the knowledge of God, see Benjamin Breckenridge Warfield, "Calvin's Doctrine of the Knowledge of God," in *Calvin and Calvinism*, 29–130 (originally published in *Princeton Theological Review* 7 (1909): 219–325); Warfield dates Calvin's first real development of his concept of the knowledge of God to the 1539 edition of the *Institutes* (29).

says so explicitly in his *prolegomena*; because he begins from the "religious affections," and primarily from the "feeling of absolute dependence," the doctrine of God can only be developed *in cursu* as a derivative from those affections and cognitively dependent on them:

> From this [that is, the fact that Christian dogmatics consists of reflection on the religious affections] it follows that the doctrine of God, as set forth in the totality of the divine attributes, can only be completed simultaneously with the whole system: whereas it is usually treated continuously and without a break, and before any other points of doctrine.... [I]t is in general undeniable that the usual arrangement is peculiarly apt to conceal the relation of those doctrines both to the feeling of absolute dependence in general and to the fundamental facts of the Christian religion....[18]

Because, then, our feeling of absolute dependence "takes the place"[19] of the proofs for God's existence (often one part of a doctrine of God, as in Thomas' *Summa*),[20] Schleiermacher begins with man and his consciousness rather than with God and revelation, these two customarily being theology's *principium essendi* and *principium cognoscendi*.[21] It is only after "A Description of our religious self-consciousness in so far as the Relation between the World and God is expressed in it"[22] that Schleiermacher comes to, not exactly a doctrine of God (he has already said that this cannot be treated in its totality as a doctrinal *locus*), but a discussion of the divine attributes (again, traditionally a part of the opening treatise on God).[23]

---

[18] Schleiermacher, *The Christian Faith*, 128.

[19] Schleiermacher, *The Christian Faith*, 133. Cf. Georg Behrens, "Feeling of Absolute Dependence or Absolute Feeling of Dependence? (What Schleiermacher Really Said and Why It Matters)," *Religious Studies* 34 (1998): 471–81.

[20] Thomas Aquinas, *Summa theologiae*, I-I, Q. 2, A. 3.

[21] For the distinction with particular reference to Reformed theologians, see Richard Muller, *PRRD*, vol. 1, 125–32, 430–45. There is an echo here in *The Christian Faith* of the way in which Calvin begins the *Institutes* (see n. above), but for Calvin the objectivity of the knowledge of God in general and special revelation, and not simply in the internal testimony of the *sensus divinitatis*, is foregrounded and, in fact, determinative.

[22] Schleiermacher, *The Christian Faith*, ix.

[23] Again, cf. Aquinas, *ST*, I-I, Q. 3–11, 20–21. From a confessional standpoint, compare *Westminster Confession of Faith* 2.1. For an argument that Schleiermacher

Schleiermacher's Placement of the Doctrine of the Trinity

The case is the same—only more drastic—with respect to the doctrine of the Trinity as such, which comes as the very last article of all and serves as his "conclusion."[24] The Trinity, it is true, receives brief notice in a couple of other places earlier in the work, but not as a doctrine used for constructive dogmatics—so much is that not the case, in fact, that it is presented in those instances as actually *hindering* the task of constructive dogmatics.[25] Again, whereas the conceptualizing of the task of dogmatics prior to Schleiermacher took the triune God as the foundation for everything that follows, from the *locus de creatione* through the rest of the standard dogmatic topics, Schleiermacher's method turns that ordering on its head. In treating the doctrine of creation fairly early in the work, he indicates to his readers why he does so: "Since the doctrine of the Trinity is neither presupposed in every Christian religious experience nor contained in it, these definitions [of God

---

stands in continuity with the Reformed Orthodox on divine simplicity and the attributes of God, see Daniel J. Pederson, "Schleiermacher and Reformed Scholastics on the Divine Attributes," *International Journal of Systematic Theology* 17 (2015): 413–31. Cf. also Gerhard Ebeling, "Schleiermacher's Doctrine of the Divine Attributes," in *Schleiermacher as Contemporary - Journal for Theology and the Church 7*, ed. Robert W. Funk (New York: Herder and Herder, 1970), 125–62; Bruce L. McCormack, "Not a Possible God but the God Who Is: Observations on Friedrich Schleiermacher's Doctrine of God," in *The Reality of Faith in Theology: Studies on Karl Barth. Princeton-Kampen Consultation 2005*, eds. Bruce McCormack and Gerrit Neven (Bern: Peter Lang, 2007), 111–39.

[24] Robert R. Williams, *Schleiermacher the Theologian: The Construction of the Doctrine of God* (Philadelphia: Fortress, 1978), treats Schleiermacher's doctrine of God and the Trinity at length. For Schleiermacher's sympathetic stance toward "Sabellianism," in contrast to the theology of Athanasius, see 139–59. Francis Schüssler Fiorenza, "Schleiermacher's Understanding of God as Triune," in *The Cambridge Companion to Friedrich Schleiermacher*, Jacqueline Mariña (Cambridge: Cambridge University Press, 2006), 173–74 (cf. also 180), argues that Sabellius was not to be the "end-point," but rather that both Athanasius and Sabellius were to serve as "a resource for future doctrinal progress," so that theology could "go beyond" them both (174). The placement of the doctrine at the end of the work is consistent with a rigorous outworking of Schleiermacher's own principles.

[25] Cf. Schleiermacher, *The Christian Faith*, 144–45, on the doctrine of creation and preservation (which he takes to be equivalent to each other), where it is noted that, if the "credal formulas" do not "satisfy our present need," they can be "completely abandon[ed]" (145); 395, on Christology.

from the *Gallican Confession*, the *Augsburg Confession*, and the *Quicunque vult*] do not belong to our present discussion."[26]

The Trinity is also treated in Schleiermacher's reworking of a kindred doctrine, Christology, specifically with reference to the traditional formula of "one person in two natures." He notes that this terminology is customarily used to relate the doctrines of Christ and the Trinity, but concludes that the employment of such vocabulary in Christology is "indefensible"[27] and does not in general find the traditional terms useful.[28]

These are the brief gestures toward the Trinity found in the bulk of the work. But, to repeat, explicit treatment of the doctrine of the Trinity is saved for Schleiermacher's concluding remarks. What is particularly interesting for the purposes of this paper is the justification—or, more precisely, an *additional* justification[29]—he gives for the freedom with which he treats this doctrine. He writes:

---

[26] Schleiermacher, *The Christian Faith*, 144. For the complex relationship between the Lutheran and Reformed confessions and Schleiermacher's own constructive dogmatics, see Wyman Jr., "Role of the Protestant Confessions," *passim*. He remarks on the "principle" in *The Christian Faith* "that the theology of consciousness trumps the confessions" (372). In his telling final footnote, Wyman Jr. notes that "a very different approach" to the confessions can be found in Charles Hodge's *Systematic Theology* (385 n. 49). For a positive appraisal of Schleiermacher on the Trinity in general, see Schüssler Fiorenza, "Schleiermacher's Understanding," 171–88, though it is worth remarking that the "Trinity" there in view can no longer be considered identical with the Trinity of the creeds and confessions of the Reformers themselves, as Schüssler Fiorenza is aware. For further reflection on Schleiermacher's relationship to the Reformation, cf. B.A. Gerrish, "From Calvin to Schleiermacher: The Theme and Shape of Christian Dogmatics," in *Continuing the Reformation*, 178–95.

[27] Schleiermacher, *The Christian Faith*, 395.

[28] For a sympathetic treatment of the relation of Schleiermacher's Christology to Chalcedonian orthodoxy, see Richard Muller, "The Christological Problem as Addressed by Friedrich Schleiermacher: A Dogmatic Query," in *Perspectives on Christology: Essays in Honor of Paul K. Jewett*, eds. Marguerite Shuster and Richard Muller (Grand Rapids: Zondervan, 1991), 141–62. For the argument that Schleiermacher's Christology is neither a modern "low" Christology nor basically Chalcedonian, but "a new synthesis of the mutually corrective Christological positions that Chalcedon brought together," see Lori Pearson, "Schleiermacher and the Christologies behind Chalcedon," *Harvard Theological Review* 96 (2003): 349–97 (the quotation is found on 350).

[29] The initial justification is simply his choice to begin all Christian reflection from the feeling of absolute dependence.

> We have the less reason to regard this doctrine as finally settled *since it did not receive any fresh treatment when the Evangelical (Protestant) Church was set up*; and so there must still be in store for it a transformation which will go back to its very beginnings.[30]

We should ponder the peculiar view of the Reformation in this statement, for it is one that is, one suspects, widely shared even among so-called "conservative" Protestants today. What is required for a doctrine to be treated as "finally settled"? "[F]resh treatment" at the time of the Reformation.[31]

Aside from the fact that this view is paradoxical—if "fresh treatment" is a *desideratum* as such, how can anything ever be "finally settled"?—there is a more basic point that should be highlighted with respect to the idea of "reformation." On Schleiermacher's reading, "reformation" entails that all dogmatic *loci* be revised and overhauled from their very foundations.[32] According to the gloss of a recent commentator, Schleiermacher believed that the Protestants of the sixteenth century "too uncritically took over earlier views without testing them against the Protestant spirit."[33] Schleiermacher is explicit in the work's final section that his placement of the doctrine of the

---

[30] Schleiermacher, *The Christian Faith*, 747 (emphasis mine). The affirmation that "fresh" or distinctive treatment should serve as a kind of Protestant doctrinal criterion thus bookends the work, for he says the same with respect to the doctrine of creation in the introduction to the First Section of the First Part (143).

[31] Schleiermacher had already enunciated his basic position in his *prolegomena* when discussing how he will deploy the concept of the "antithesis" in his treatment of Protestantism vis-à-vis Roman Catholicism: see *The Christian Faith*, 101–103.

[32] Thus: "[T]the Reformation was not simply a purification and reaction from abuses which had crept in, but was *the origination of a distinctive form of the Christian communion*" (*The Christian faith*, 103, emphasis mine). As a happy corollary, for Schleiermacher, such retooling can be useful for relating to Christianity's cultured despisers: "'[W]e ought not to feel too much surprise that anti-trinitarian opinions should ever and again emerge and should occasionally gain ground; nor ought we to be precipitate in condemnation. It is here as with the doctrine of God in general: many not merely profess to be but actually think they are opposed to every belief in God, when in fact they are simply repelled by ordinary presentations of the subject, but have by no means parted with all those spiritual affections which spring from the God-consciousness" (*The Christian Faith*, 749).

[33] Wyman Jr., "Role of the Protestant Confessions," 365.

Trinity is due to just such a desire for total overhaul.[34] The assumption lurking behind this viewpoint—and it is an assumption—is that there was a unifying drive broader than and undergirding particular Protestant theological revisions, that it ought to be generalizable to all doctrinal topics, and that if it has not been so generalized, it is due to a lapse on the part of the Reformers in carrying their *Grundsatz* all the way through. Thus Schüssler Fiorenza can gloss Schleiermacher's stance as follows: "The traditional doctrinal formulations [about the Trinity] fail to express [the] reformation impulse."[35]

Schleiermacher's basic position on this question became a hallmark of a certain style of Protestant theologizing in subsequent generations. For that reason, one is not surprised to find Adolph Harnack claiming, in the late nineteenth century, that the spirit of the Lutheran Reformation required something like what Schleiermacher desired, though it was impossible for a single man, Martin Luther, to carry it out; thus the "Catholic elements" in Luther's theology "belong certainly to the 'whole Luther,' but not to the 'whole Christianity' of Luther."[36] This latter required the wholesale reworking that Luther himself could not perform. Indeed, this tension between the new and the old led the Reformation to "*terminate … in a contradiction*," in that *"it gave to [the new Church, in addition to Pauline faith] at the same time the old dogma as the unchangeable cardinal article, together with a christological doctrine, which did not negate the fundamental evangelical interest, but which had received an entirely scholastic shape and had therefore the inevitable effect of confusing and obscuring faith."*[37]

---

[34] Schleiermacher, *The Christian Faith*, 749–50.

[35] Schüssler Fiorenza, "Schleiermacher's Understanding," 173.

[36] Adolph Harnack, *History of Dogma* (3rd ed.), trans. Neil Buchanan, 7 vols. (Gloucester, MA: P. Smith, 1976), vol. 7, 229–30. Harnack goes on to say that "Luther knew too little of the history of the Ancient Church and of ancient dogma to be really able to criticise them" (232); "Luther never felt strongly impelled to start from the innermost center of the new view of the whole of Christianity which he had obtained, and from thence to furnish a systematic statement of the whole, indicating exactly what remained and what had dropped away" (233); "[S]o far as Luther left to his followers a 'dogmatic,' there was presented in this an extremely complicated system: not a new structure, but a modification of the old Patristic-Scholastic structure" (238). It goes without saying, one may safely say, that Harnack does not intend his description of Luther's theology as "a modification of the old Patristic-Scholastic structure" as a compliment.

[37] Harnack, *History of Dogma*, vol. 7, 243–44 (emphasis original). It is striking that it is once again in the doctrines of the Trinity and Christology that Harnack, like

BUT IS IT TRUE? MELANCHTHON AND THE DOCTRINE OF GOD

The sketch above gives an indication of a common interpretation of the principles of Protestantism and the role of the Reformation in reconfiguring the dogmatic task. One question that must be addressed, however, is: Is that sketch an accurate description of the Reformers' own self-understanding? In the rest of this paper, I shall endeavor to show that, though the sentiment that the spirit of the Reformation requires complete overhaul as a *desideratum* to be achieved may have a superficial plausibility due to post-eighteenth-century developments in Protestantism, it is worlds apart from the thinking of the Reformers themselves, who would have been rather surprised at Harnack's contention that there was a contradiction at the very core of the Reformation. And this is so, it shall be argued, despite some apparent similarities between the revisionist position and the work of Philip Melanchthon—similarities that have (unjustly, I shall further argue) given cover to such a revisionist way of thinking. That is, Melanchthon is sometimes said to have had this same spirit, though it was (unfortunately, in the view of some latter-day revisionists) stifled or badly rectified later in his career.

The Preface of the First *Loci Communes*

Why does Melanchthon receive this distinction? The chief evidence rests on two facts: first, the omission of the *locus de Deo* in the first edition of the *Loci communes* in 1521[38] and, second, the reasons he gives for its omission. It is of

---

Schleiermacher, finds theology most restricted by the "old dogmas." It should be noted that Harnack does not credit Schleiermacher as his model here, and indeed he believes that Schleiermacher did not go nearly far enough in his revisionism (cf. 244 n. 1).

[38] Melanchthon's *Loci* went through three major "eras" of publication (1521, 1535, and 1543/44), though there were multiple editions within each era that introduced changes into the text. The editions of 1521, 1535, and 1559 (the final edition published during Melanchthon's lifetime), along with preliminary versions and sketches of the work and extensive editorial discussion of the various editions of the *Loci* and its publication history, can be found in *Corpus Reformatorum* 21, eds. Karl Bretschneider and Heinrich Bindseil (Brunsvigae: Schwetschke, 1854). For a very brief overview of the development of the *Loci* over its three major eras, see Sachiko Kusukawa, "Melanchthon," in *The Cambridge Companion to Reformation Theology*, eds.

course true that Melanchthon did not comment on the doctrine of God in the first iteration of the *Loci*, though he does comment on it in both the second and third eras. We shall now have to look quite closely at his reasoning as demonstrated by the preface to that first manifestation of the *Loci*, as it has often been misunderstood, including by two of the more important theologians of the modern period, Ferdinand Christian Baur and Karl Barth.[39]

Melanchthon says at the outset of the *Loci* that he is writing a *summa* of Christian doctrine.[40] He then contrasts the way in which the "ancients" (*veteres*) did this with "more recent" attempts (he singles out John of Damascus and Peter Lombard here). His criticisms of these two figures are brief. First, John of Damascus "philosophizes" (*philosophatur*) too much.[41] That is a key term for Melanchthon: it means that he tries to understand divine revelation and the gospel via a way of thinking that restricts divine freedom and binds God to human expectations.[42] It also means that he

---

David Bagchi and David C. Steinmetz (Cambridge: Cambridge University Press, 2006), 58–62.

[39] The literature on the question of Melanchthon's "development" is vast. In this essay, I am concerned with only one small aspect of it, namely, the question of "development" with respect to his adherence to traditional Trinitarian and Christological formulae. For a very brief overview of older scholarship on the question in general, cf. Fraenkel, Testimonia Patrum, 24–28. None of this should be taken as lumping Baur and Barth on the same "side" as Schleiermacher—and, indeed, both were critics of him (Thiel, "Schleiermacher as 'Catholic'," 63, 70–2). Barth interacted with Schleiermacher at some length: see Karl Barth, *The Theology of Schleiermacher: Lectures at Göttingen, Winter Semester of 1923/24*, trans. Geoffrey W. Bromiley and ed. Dietrich Ritschl (Grand Rapids: Eerdmans, 1982); *Protestant Theology in the Nineteenth Century: Its Background and History*, [trans. not named] (Valley Forge, PA: Judson Press, 1973), 425–73. (For the argument that Barth's criticisms of Schleiermacher were based on a misreading of his predecessor, see James Gordon, "A 'Glaring Misunderstanding'? Schleiermacher, Barth and the Nature of Speculative Theology," *International Journal of Systematic Theology* 16 [2014]: 313–30.) But they are both relevant here, as they both seem to have seen Melanchthon as making the kind of move that might have been amenable to Schleiermacher.

[40] The word *summa* occurs in the first sentence of the work. Cf. the title of the French translation of the *Loci*, noted above.

[41] Melanchthon, *Loci communes* (1521), praef. (*CR* 21: 83). His criticism of John of Damascus is muted in later iterations of the preface. Unless otherwise noted, all translations of Melanchthon are my own.

[42] In 1527, Melanchthon gave what he took to be correct definitions of the gospel and philosophy: "Philosophy contains the arts of speaking, physiology, and precepts

speculates in an unprofitable way beyond what has been revealed. Second, Lombard similarly heaps up "human opinions" (*hominum opiniones*) willy-nilly in preference to the judgment of Scripture.[43]

But Melanchthon does not wish students to get bogged down, as he believes they are liable to do while reading John of Damascus or Lombard. Readers rather need to understand on what topics the *summa* of doctrine depends in order for them to know how to direct their studies.[44] And so he gives a list of what are usually the "chief heads of theological matters" (*rerum theologicarum … capita*). It is absolutely essential to note that the first four are

---

concerning civic morals … Philosophy concerning morals is the very law of God concerning morals.… The gospel is not philosophy or law, but the remission of sins and the promise of reconciliation and of eternal life on account of Christ; concerning these things human reason by itself can apprehend nothing.… But that philosophy is the law of God can also be understood from the fact that it is the knowledge of natural causes and effects; since they are ordained by God, it follows that philosophy is the law of God, which is the teaching concerning that divine order" (*De discrimine evangelii et philosophiae*, in Karl Gottlieb Bretschneider, ed., *Corpus Reformatorum* 12 (Halle: Schwetschke, 1844), 689–91. The translation is my own, but an English version of the full text can be found, under the title "On the Distinction between the Gospel and Philosophy," in Philip Melanchthon, *Orations on Philosophy and Education*, trans. Christine F. Salazar and ed. Sachiko Kusukawa (Cambridge: Cambridge University Press, 1999), 23–25.

[43] Melanchthon, *Loci communes* (1521), praef. (*CR* 21: 83). Although Melanchthon singles out Lombard, he probably has later commentators on the *Sentences*, and particularly recent and contemporary scholastics, in mind. Hankey, *God in Himself*, 21, quoting Fairweather, who was in turn quoting and translating de Ghellinck (!), notes the comparative brevity and lack of speculative philosophical overlay in the *Sentences* of the *Sentences*: "There is very little or hardly any metaphysics [and] the philosophical data are fragmentary or badly assimilated.… [The work is] sufficiently impersonal to give free play to comment by other teachers." And in fact, Melanchthon makes it clear in the preface to the 1535 *Loci* that his real targets are Lombard's commentators: "But as to the fact that our opponents exclaim that we are at variance with the church, because we do not approve of this mob of recent interpreters, who have added a labyrinth of questions to Lombard, in which they have in part ineptly mixed philosophy and the gospel and in part have established superstitions and a mania for idols received from the masses without any authority of the ancients: their slanders move me not at all" (*Quod vero adversarii nostri vociferantur, nos dissentire ab Ecclesia, quia non probamus hanc turbam recentium, qui Labyrinthos quaestionum addiderunt Longobardo, in quibus partim inepte miscuerunt Philosophiam, et Evangelium, partim superstitiones et* εἰδωλομανίας *acceptas a vulgo, sine ulla autoritate veterum stabilierunt, non moveor calumniis*) (Melanchthon, *Loci communes* [1535], *praef.* [*CR* 21: 342]).

[44] Melanchthon, *Loci communes* (1521), praef. (*CR* 21: 83).

God, God as one, God as three, and creation (*Deus*; *Unus*; *Trinus*; *Creatio*), because the fact that Melanchthon actually begins his exposition with the fifth topic, *Homo*, can obscure the equally salient fact that he recognizes the customary importance of the first four. As Robert Kolb points out, "Melanchthon asserted that he had carried on the task of proper organization of biblical teaching just as John of Damascus and Peter Lombard had, *but with a better method.*"[45] That is the crucial point, though it is true that Melanchthon's own system of organization was also influenced by the structure of Romans.[46]

Why, then, does he gloss over these chief articles? There is a theological reason and a practical reason, and the two are related. They are, he says, "utterly incomprehensible" (*prorsus incomprehensibiles*)—which is, from the classical perspective, true—while Christ desired other topics to be known by the whole mass of Christians (he is presumably thinking here of sin and grace).[47] Could Melanchthon really mean, then, that Christ did not wish the doctrines of God and creation to be known to all people? The next sentence he writes has been read in just that way, as encapsulating an approach that minimizes the importance of discussing these doctrines: "We should more correctly adore the mysteries of the Godhead than scrupulously search them out" (*Mysteria divinitatis rectius adoraverimus, quam vestigaverimus*).[48]

Melanchthon obviously does not *deny* the mysteries of the Godhead in this statement; but neither does he deny their *significance*, as he has often been thought to do. He takes them for granted, but sees them in and of themselves as beyond our reach when considered in isolation from Christ. H. Ashley Hall has characterized Melanchthon's statement as "apophatic" and thus as demonstrating Melanchthon's Cappadocian *bona fides*;[49] and, as Hall has

---

[45] Robert Kolb, "The Pastoral Dimension of Melanchthon's Pedagogical Activities," in *Philip Melanchthon: Theologian in Classroom, Confession, and Controversy*, eds. Irene Dingel, Robert Kolb, Nicole Kuropka, and Timothy J. Wengert (Göttingen: Vandenhoeck & Ruprecht, 2012), 35 (emphasis mine).

[46] On this question as well as Melanchthon's relation to his antecedents, see Robert Kolb, "The Ordering of the *Loci Communes Theologici*: The Structuring of the Melanchthonian Dogmatic Tradition," *Concordia Journal* 23 (1997): 317–25.

[47] Melanchthon, *Loci communes* (1521), praef. (*CR* 21: 84).

[48] Melanchthon, *Loci communes* (1521), praef. (*CR* 21: 84). The sentence is already present in the first sketch for the *Loci*, the *Lucubratiuncula* (*CR* 21: 11–12).

[49] H. Ashley Hall, *Philip Melanchthon and the Cappadocians: A Reception of Greek Patristic Sources in the Sixteenth Century* (Göttingen: Vandenhoeck & Ruprecht, 2014), 129.

notes, "awe-filled silence in the face of the divine mysteries" and a willingness to receive them humbly in the context of worship has a long patristic heritage, indicating that this way of demurring from close treatment is neither anti-intellectual nor rationalistic.[50] It is rather a reflex of creaturely finitude and an application of the rule *finitum non capax infiniti.*

Melanchthon continues:

> *Immo sine magno periculo tantari non possunt, id quod non raro sancti viri etiam sunt experti. Et carne filium deus Optimus Maximus induit ut nos a contemplatione maiestatis suae ad carnis, adeoque fragilitatis nostrae contemplationem invitaret.*
>
> Nay, rather, these things cannot be attempted without great risk—a fact that not a few holy men have also learned by experience. And God the Best and Greatest clothed his Son in flesh in order that he might call us from the contemplation of his own majesty to the contemplation of our own flesh and even weakness.[51]

Melanchthon obviously does not do so because our weakness is something of greater dignity than the Godhead, but because it must be reckoned with to restrain our characteristic presumptions about our facility in understanding things too high for us.[52] His statement is therefore one of humility before the ineffability of God, as Paul teaches in 1 Corinthians:

> *Sic et Paulus ad Corinthios scribit, deum per stultitiam praedicationis, nimirum nova ratione velle cognosci, cum non potuerit cognosci in sapientia, per sapientiam.*
>
> Thus Paul too writes to the Corinthians that God wished to be known through the foolishness of preaching, namely, by

---

[50] H. Ashley Hall, *Melanchthon and the Cappadocians* (Bristol, CT: Vandenhoeck & Ruprecht, 2014), 129.

[51] Melanchthon, *Loci communes* (1521), praef. (*CR* 21: 84).

[52] Melanchthon makes it clear elsewhere that the purpose of the revelation of God in Christ is to lead us back to God and to teach us to consider him aright, in a way not dissimilar to Athanasius, *On the Incarnation of the Word*, 8–16.

> a new way of thinking, since he was not able to be known in wisdom, through wisdom.[53]

There follows a statement that subsequently has received some attention:

> *Proinde non est cur multum operae ponamus in* ***locis illis supremis****, de deo, de unitate, de trinitate, de mysterio creationis, de modo incarnationis.*
>
> Consequently, there is no reason to expend much effort on **those highest topics**, on God, on his unity, on his Trinity, on the mystery of creation, on the mode of the Incarnation.[54]

B.B. Warfield, in "Calvin's Doctrine of the Trinity," highlights the word *supremis* ("highest") here, and he is right to do so.[55] Melanchthon does not mean merely that these topics come first, but that they are the most exalted and dignified topics.[56]

The Foregrounding of the *Beneficia Christi*

But this still does not answer the question as to why he omits any discussion of them at all, even given their ultimate inscrutability to man. Melanchthon explains as follows:

> *Quaeso te quid adsecuti sunt iam* ***tot seculis*** *scholastici Theologistae cum in his* ***locis solis*** *versarentur? Nonne in disceptationibus suis, ut ille ait, vani facti sunt, dum* ***tota vita*** *nugantur de universalibus, formalitatibus, connatis, est nescio quibus aliis inanibus vocabulis…*

---

[53] Melanchthon, *Loci communes* (1521), praef. (*CR* 21: 84).

[54] Melanchthon, *Loci communes* (1521), praef. (*CR* 21: 84).

[55] Benjamin Breckenridge Warfield, "Calvin's Doctrine of the Trinity," in *Calvin and Calvinism* (Grand Rapids: Baker, 1931; originally published in *Princeton Theological Review* 7 [1909]: 553–652), 195–96 n. 15.

[56] Quirinus Breen, "The Terms 'Loci Communes' and 'Loci' in Melanchthon," *Church History* 16 (1947): 208 n. 34, claims Melanchthon also uses this phrase for the topics on which he focuses most—law, gospel, sin, and grace—in two unpublished works written before the 1521 *Loci*, but I have been able to find no evidence of this.

> I ask you, what have the scholastic theologians gained in **so many centuries** when occupying themselves with **these topics alone**? Haven't they become vain in their disputings, as [Paul] says, while they trifle away their **whole lives** on "universals," "formal distinctions,"[57] "congenital properties," and whatever other empty words...[58]

It emerges over the course of the preface, however, that Melanchthon is referring to a matter of emphasis, despite the absolutizing terms he employs. Indeed, in the next part of this very sentence, he writes:

> *[E]t dissimulari eorum stultitia posset,* ***nisi Evangelium interim et beneficia Christi obscurassent nobis illae stultae disputationes.***
>
> And their foolishness could have been papered over, **if those foolish disputations had not meanwhile obscured for us the gospel and the benefits of Christ.**[59]

Melanchthon thus has in mind a particular construal of scholastic theology that emphasizes first theology, conducted in an overly subtle mode, *to the exclusion of* the gospel: scholasticism, that is, that is not disciplined by the gospel and so misses the forest for the trees. Not only so, but, he adds, scholastic theologians often veer into the heretical even in their discussion of the topics they choose to address in detail instead of defending "catholic dogmas" (*catholicis dogmatis*: another clue that Melanchthon does not wish to re-tool theology proper or Christology); they do so when they produce arguments "from philosophy" (*e philosophia*) for dogmas of faith.[60]

---

[57] This remark makes his target clear and sharpens the sense of what he means by "scholastic theologians: the subtle discussion about distinctions, no longer limited to those that are "real" (*realis*) and "in the reason" (*ratione*), inaugurated by John Duns Scotus. Cf. Nunzio Signoriello, *Lexicon peripateticum philosophico-theologicum in quo scholasticorum distinctiones et effata praecipua explicantur* (2nd ed.) (Naples: Pignatelli, 1872), s.v. "formaliter-realiter-ratione" (131–33).

[58] Melanchthon, *Loci communes* (1521), praef. (*CR* 21: 84).

[59] Melanchthon, *Loci communes* (1521), praef. (*CR* 21: 84–85).

[60] *Pro fidei dogmatis*. It is just possible that Melanchthon intends *pro* to be ambiguous here: "arguments for (i.e. on behalf of) dogmas of the faith" or "arguments for (i.e. in place of) dogmas of the faith." Melanchthon, *Loci communes* (1521), praef. (*CR* 21: 85).

The words *e philosophia* are found in one edition of the 1521 *Loci* and not the others.[61] But this addition is implicit, whichever reading of the text is to be preferred. How do we know? We know because Melanchthon tells us later in the preface. In one of its most apparently problematic passages, Melanchthon writes:

> *Paulus in Epistola quam Romanis dicavit, cum doctrinae Christianae Compendium conscriberet, num de mysteriis trinitatis, de modo incarnationis, de creatione activa, et creatione passiva* ***philosophabatur?***
>
> In the letter that he dictated to the Romans, Paul, when he was composing a summary of Christian teaching, didn't **philosophize** about the mysteries of the Trinity, about the mode of the Incarnation, about active creation, or about passive creation, did he?[62]

Over a century ago, Warfield pointed out that the key word in this sentence is *philosophabatur*. "[W]e must not neglect the emphasis on the term 'philosophical disquisitions.' Melanchthon was as far as possible from wishing to throw doubt upon either the truth or the importance of the doctrines of the Trinity, the Incarnation, Creation. He only wishes to recall men from useless speculations."[63] In other words, Melanchthon advises a chaste dogmatics that tracks closely with revelation rather than one that builds speculative sandcastles. His emphasis is clear yet again when he contrasts his approach to the Scriptures with that of his opponents:

> *Plerique locos virtutum et vitiorum* ***tantum*** *in scripturis requirunt,* ***sed ea observatio philosophica magis est, quam Christiana.***
>
> Very many people seek in the Scriptures **only** the topics of the virtues and vices, **but this observation is more philosophical than Christian.**[64]

---

61 Melanchthon, *Loci communes* (1521), praef. (*CR* 21: 85 n. 8).

62 Melanchthon, *Loci communes* (1521), praef. (*CR* 21: 85).

63 Warfield, "Calvin's Doctrine of the Trinity," 196.

64 Melanchthon, *Loci communes* (1521), praef. (*CR* 21: 85).

To put it another way: what, in the end, is it that makes one a Christian in Melanchthon's view? Trust in Jesus as Savior. Melanchthon goes so far as to say that the knowledge of Christ depends on knowledge of "the law, sin, and grace" *alone* (*locis* ***solis***).[65] This expression is a deliberate echo of the one used in castigation of the "scholastics" quoted above, who, Melanchthon said, focused on speculations on the Trinity, Christology, and creation *alone* (*locis* ***solis***).[66] Danger of misreading is at the door again. Melanchthon is not so foolish as to think that those topics are in fact the only topics that scholastic theologians ever discussed. But if that is so, by parity of reasoning he must not mean the word in an absolute sense in the later passage, either. What does he wish to say, then? He wishes to say that the scholastics have erred in their emphasis and in their exposition,[67] and the evangelicals will now correct that misplacement of emphasis to meet the needs of the time. Melanchthon's position, in other words, is that one can be a Christian without the philosophical "arguments" to which he has referred; but one cannot be a Christian without the gospel. As he had already said:

> *Reliquos vero locos, peccati vim, legem, gratiam, qui ignorarit, non video quomodo Christianum vocem, nam ex his proprie Christus cognoscitur, siquidem hoc est Christum cognoscere, beneficia eius cognoscere, non, quod isti docent, eius naturas, modos incarnationis contueri.*
>
> But he who is ignorant of the rest of the topics—the power of sin, the law, grace—I do not see how I could call him a Christian, for Christ is properly known from these topics, since this is to know Christ: to know his benefits—not, as they teach, to look intently into his natures and the modes of the Incarnation.[68]

---

[65] Melanchthon, *Loci communes* (1521), praef. (*CR* 21: 85).

[66] Melanchthon, *Loci communes* (1521), praef. (*CR* 21: 84).

[67] Just before his remark about "the law, sin, and grace" quoted above, Melanchthon had listed those same topics together with the question as to how the afflicted conscience should be consoled, and had asked: *Scilicet ista docent scholastici?* ("Tell me, do the scholastics teach these things?") (Melanchthon, *Loci communes* [1521], praef. [*CR* 21: 85]). He obviously does not mean that scholastic theologians never discuss sin and grace; he means that they discuss them inadequately or badly.

[68] Melanchthon, *Loci communes* (1521), praef. (*CR* 21: 85).

Barth on Melanchthon's "Act of Rashness"

It is of course true that the last of these clauses, when read out of context, can sound particularly out of step with the mainstream of Christian reflection on these topics. Karl Barth, for instance, took Melanchthon to task for this preface, and for this statement in particular.[69] It is worth quoting Barth at length, if only to show why he is wrong:

> It was, therefore, an act of rashness, of which he rightly repented, when in his *Loci* of 1521 Melanchthon, the first dogmatician of the Evangelical Church, thought he should so suppress the special doctrine of God in order to turn at once to the statement of the *beneficia Christi*. He did this on the ground that: *mysteria divinitatis rectius adoraverimus, quam vestigaverimus. Immo sine magno periculo tentari non possunt*. To this we must say that surely the *beneficia Christi* also belong to the revealed *mysteria divinitatis* which are only to be investigated at some risk; that the *beneficia Christi* cannot be properly investigated if some consideration of the *mysteria divinitatis* as such has not been undertaken in its proper place; that the danger of every human *vestigare* of divine truth, here as well as elsewhere, is not to be avoided as such; that here as well as elsewhere it can be met in the fact that *vestigare* is not separated from *adorare*, i.e., that here as well as elsewhere attention is paid (only) to God's revelation.[70]

First of all, Barth misunderstands what Melanchthon means by *vestigare*, as the rest of the context in the preface to the 1521 *Loci* makes clear. Melanchthon intends by this word the subtle speculations of what he calls "scholastic theologians" whose reflections are not tethered to and bound by divine revelation but are instead led astray by abstruse philosophizing, a point that presumably should have been quite welcome to Barth.[71] Second, Melanchthon does not mean that the *beneficia Christi* can be understood

[69] For an overview of Barth's own Trinitarian theology and its place in the *Church Dogmatics*, see Alan Torrance, "The Trinity," in John Webster, ed., *The Cambridge Companion to Karl Barth* (Cambridge: Cambridge University Press, 2000), 72–91.

[70] Karl Barth, *Church Dogmatics* II.1, trans. T.H.L. Parker et al. and ed. G.W. Bromiley and T.F. Torrance (Edinburgh: T&T Clark, 1957), 259.

[71] This interpretation is corroborated by Hall, *Melanchthon and the Cappadocians*, 129.

without reference to God Himself. Robert Kolb has noted that his "point of departure" from man in this first edition "inevitably had led back to the doctrine of God when presented in the classroom."[72] The difference from Schleiermacher here is subtle but significant. It must be repeated that Melanchthon does not remove the *locus de Deo* from its place at the beginning of the traditional list of *Loci*, even if he opts not to treat it in 1521, and thus his theological perspective does not demand a fundamental reworking of the structure of Christian dogmatics. On the other hand, the *Loci* is in many respects a work of polemical theology as well as systematic theology, and so naturally Melanchthon focuses on the topics under dispute with Rome: free will, sin, grace, works, and justification. Thus his approach is occasional and strategic, while remaining situated within the broader dogmatic structure that had been accepted by theologians and teachers for centuries.

Melanchthon, moreover, himself makes clear what he means by the passage on the *beneficia Christi* quoted above that is, in Barth's view, so dangerously misguided:

> *Ni scias in quem usum carnem induerit, et cruci adfixus sit Christus,*
> ***quid proderit** eius historiam novisse?*
>
> If you do not know why Christ put on flesh and was fixed
> to the cross, **what does it profit** to know his history?[73]

This sentence is followed by a metaphor: what good does it do a doctor to know about the shapes and colors of plants if he does not know how to use them in healing? Melanchthon's point, then, is rather different from what Barth wants to say. Barth charges that the benefits of Christ do not make sense without the doctrine of God. Well and good; but Melanchthon wishes to say that the doctrines of God and Christology do you no good if you do not know the gospel. Thus he draws the inference:

> *Christum … oportet **alio quodam modo** cognoscamus, quam exhibent scholastici.*

---

[72] Kolb, "Ordering," 328. Though I disagree below with his general assessment of what Melanchthon intended by the omission of the "highest topics" in 1521, he is surely correct with respect to what must have occurred in the classroom.

[73] Melanchthon, *Loci communes* (1521), praef. (*CR* 21: 85).

> It is right that we know Christ **in some other way** than the scholastics present.[74]

For Melanchthon, the issue is, again, one of emphasis and manner of treatment in order to ensure that Christians know first and foremost the content of the gospel, namely, that Jesus Christ is the Savior of sinners. An overthrow of the traditional Christian doctrine of God is nowhere in view. As Peter Fraenkel remarks, Melanchthon was a steadfast opponent of innovation, an opposition he deployed against both Anabaptists and Roman Catholics.[75] In this respect he was typical of the magisterial Reformers, and any attempt to unmask the true "spirit of the Reformation" in Schleiermacherian mode that fails to account for this fact is historically untenable. Thus one must attenuate the judgment of Robert Stupperich with respect to the 1521 *Loci*: "Consciously [Melanchthon] departs from traditional dogmatics, even though he refers to them. He starts with the portrayal of man."[76] Though this seems *prima facie* to be an intimation of Schleiermacher's *The Christian Faith*, it is nothing of the kind: it is, as already noted, pragmatic, due to the exigencies of circumstance, rather than a fundamental and theoretical matter of principle.

Furthermore, given Melanchthon's criticisms of the "scholastics," a second caution should be entered here regarding the later use of this term as found in Schleiermacher, because superficial similarities between the two uses can lead the reader astray. For example, Schleiermacher writes of Christology:

> It must be remembered … that in the original construction of Protestant theology nothing was done for this article [Christology]—the old formulae were simply repeated.… And so, *if Dogmatics are to be ever more completely purged of scholasticism, the task remains of constructing a scientific statement of*

---

[74] Melanchthon, *Loci communes* (1521), praef. (*CR* 21: 85).

[75] Fraenkel, Testimonia Patrum, 14.

[76] Robert Stupperich, *Melanchthon: The Enigma of the Reformation*, trans. Robert H. Fischer (Cambridge: James Clarke, 2006), 48; and cf. 93, where the Melanchthon of the early 1530s supposedly "preferred the doctrine of man as his point of departure in theology" (Stupperich contrasts the position at this point in Melanchthon's life with that of 1521 because he has now removed predestination from its place of primacy, but that difference is not material to my argument).

> *this particular doctrine also....* We hope that above we have laid the foundation for such a revision, *which attempts so to define the mutual relations of the divine and the human in the Redeemer, that both the expressions, divine nature and the duality of natures in the same Person (which, to say the least, are exceedingly inconvenient) shall be altogether avoided.*"[77]

The superficial similarity lies in the criticism of the place of scholasticism in Christian teaching, a rhetorical and polemical gambit that is ubiquitous in the writings of the magisterial Reformers.[78] Nevertheless, Schleiermacher has in this instance maintained the letter of the Reformers but not the spirit—despite claiming to do the opposite in his *magnum opus*[79]—and deploys the rhetoric in a way that would have been completely unacceptable to Melanchthon. Schleiermacher takes the "purg[ing] of scholasticism" to require the reconstruction and reformulation of every doctrine. By this metric, Melanchthon himself would—paradoxically—have to be considered a scholastic,[80] because he keeps the "old formulae"—and this in spite of his explicit polemic against scholasticism! The difference from Schleiermacher is apparent when one considers that Schleiermacher, unlike Melanchthon, wished to "get rid of all traces of the Scholastic mode of treatment, by which philosophy (transformed as it was the by spread of Christianity) and real Christian Dogmatics were frequently mingled in one and the same work."[81] But from the vantage-point of sixteenth century theologians, at least, the "old formulae" that had been retained and expounded by scholastic theologians were not mindlessly repeated because these same theologians had neglected to take Reformation far enough. They were rather mindfully repeated because they agreed with them and thought them necessary for other *loci* of Christian teaching, as will shortly become clear. In other words, they did not mean by "Reformation" at all what Schleiermacher means, and did not think

[77] Schleiermacher, *The Christian Faith*, 396–97 (emphasis mine).

[78] For convenient comparanda, cf. Calvin, *Institutes* 2.2.6, 27; 2.8.56, 57, 58; 2.17.6; 3.2.2, 8, 24, 33, 38, 41; 3.4.1, 4, 17, 18, 26, 38; 3.11.15; 3.14.12; 3.15.7; 4.14.23; 4.17.13, 30.

[79] Cf. Schleiermacher, *The Christian Faith*, 101–118.

[80] This is, in fact, a charge of Barth. It may be appropriate to class Melanchthon with the "scholastics" in the sense just given, though not for the reasons Barth alleges—on which, see below.

[81] Schleiermacher, *The Christian Faith*, 122.

Reformation required the revision of every doctrine, but only those that were in dispute; and those very revisions (the result of their *Nein!* to Rome, to ventriloquize Barth) were in service to a broader positive program that, in their view, consisted not of protesting but of pro-testing: bearing witness to the truth of the Christian gospel in its orthodox Trinitarian and Christological context.

Baur and the "Standpoint of the Reformation"

For that reason, one also cannot accept Ferdinand Christian Baur's description of Melanchthon or the "standpoint determined by the Reformation." Baur writes that "[i]t is precisely with these doctrines [God, Trinity, creation, the mode of the Incarnation] which the dialectic spirit of speculation of the Scholastics regarded as its peculiar object, and on which it expended itself with the greatest subtlety and thoroughness."[82] So much is an accurate summary of Melanchthon. But Baur then goes on to say that "Melanchthon would have so little to do [with these topics], that he did not even make a place for them in his *Loci*, and that not on the ground that it did not belong to the plan of the first sketch of Protestant dogmatics to cover the whole system, but on the ground of the objective character of those doctrines, as they appeared to him from the standpoint determined by the Reformation."[83] However, as the foregoing analysis has shown, it was

82 "Gerade mit denjenigen Lehren, welche der dialektische Speculationsgeist der Scholastiker als sein eigentlichstes Object betrachtete, und über welche er sich mit der grösten Subtilität und Ausführlichkeit verbreitete…" Ferdinand Christian Baur, *Die christliche Lehre von der Dreieinigkeit und Menschwerdung Gottes in ihrer geschichtlichen Entwicklung*, vol. 3 (Tübingen: C.F. Osiander, 1843), 20, trans. Warfield, "Calvin's Doctrine," 195–96 n. 15. I have kept Baur's spelling rather than making it conform to modern usage (e.g. "Object" rather than "Objekt").

83 "[W]ollte Melanchthon [mit denjenigen Lehren] so wenig zu thun haben, dass er ihnen nicht einmal eine Stelle in seinen *Loci* einräumte, und nicht etwa nur aus dem Grunde, weil es nicht zu dem Plan jenes ersten Entwurfs einer protestantischen Dogmatik gehört hätte, das ganze System zu umfassen, sondern in der objectiven Beschaffenheit jener Lehre, wie sie ihm auf dem durch die Reformation bestimmten Standpunct erschienen." Baur, *Die christliche Lehre*, vol. 3, 20, trans. Warfield, "Calvin's Doctrine," 195–96 n. 15. In the case of Calvin, Warfield refers to Isaak August Dorner as one who saw in him an impulse toward revising the doctrine of the Trinity, though Warfield holds that "Dorner's account of Calvin's attitude to these questions is not quite exact either in the motive suggested, or in the precise action ascribed to him" (218 n. 47).

precisely "on the ground that it did not belong to the plan of the first sketch of Protestant dogmatics to cover the whole system" that Melanchthon did not include them: they did not need to be clarified in relation to the teachings of the Roman church. The "standpoint determined by the Reformation," insofar as there was such a thing in 1521, had to do with getting the gospel right and making Christian teaching clearer, simpler, and less encumbered with speculations that were unwarranted, in Melanchthon's view, by Scripture. It did not have to do with revising first theology. On the contrary, the "standpoint determined by the Reformation" required *maintaining* the core doctrines of first theology as they had been defined prior to the Reformation.

CORROBORATION: THE *ANNOTATIONES IN IOHANNEM* (1523)

The position just outlined may seem to be nothing more than a case of the sympathetic interpreter protesting too much, making excuses for Melanchthon that are not warranted. Such a suspicion might seem warranted, but it is unfounded. For what has been said above can be proved quite easily from nearly contemporaneous writings of Melanchthon himself.[84]

[84] In a related—and corroborating—vein, Fraenkel, Testimonia Patrum, 29, points out that in the years leading up to the first edition of the *Loci communes* Melanchthon had devoted himself to the study of patristic theology, and that "these interests reached something of a climax during the very year in which the Theological Commonplaces first went into print." Indeed, Melanchthon's edition of the first *Theological Oration* of Gregory of Nazianzus came out "at the very time when the first version of the Commonplaces was being published" (Fraenkel, Testimonia Patrum, 36). Far from being the product of a flight from history and traditional Christian teaching, then, the *Loci* come from Melanchthon's studies taking him deeper in history.

Melanchthon's Approach to Dogmatic Christology

In the preface to a set of annotations on the gospel of John first published in 1523,[85] but based on lectures that began in February of 1522[86] (by way of comparison, the complete edition of the *Loci communes* had come out in December of 1521),[87] Melanchthon takes aim at heretics such as the Ebionites who had denied the divinity of Christ, which he defends by the implicit use of classical Christology—one of the very subjects he had put on his list of topics not to be treated in the 1521 *Loci*—and yet with his characteristic caution about what this should and should not mean. Melanchthon writes:

> *Hic nobis* **non hoc satis est**, *discere, quod Christus sit Deus et homo, et quomodo naturae illae coniungi potuerint, et huiusmodi multa arguta. Sed hoc potius est consyderandum, cur oportuerit eum qui remissionem peccatorum erat praedicaturus, deum esse. Ebionitae sunt, qui negant Christi divinitatem. Bis Ebionitae sunt, qui cum Christo divinitatem tribuant,* **ea tamen non utuntur**.
>
> Here **it is not enough** for us to learn that Christ is God and man, and how those natures are conjoined, and many subtle things of this kind. But this rather ought to be considered: why it was right that he who was going to preach the remission of sins be God. Those who deny the divinity of Christ are Ebionites. Those who, although they attribute

[85] It was printed several times already in 1523. The primary edition I have consulted is: Philip Melanchthon, *Annotationes in Iohannem, castigatiores quam quae ante invulgatae sunt* (Nürnberg: [no pub.], 1523). Timothy J. Wengert, *Philip Melanchthon's* Annotationes in Johannem *in Relation to Its Predecessors and Contemporaries* (Geneva: Droz, 1987), 261, gives Johannes Petrejus as the printer. The text, which includes a prefatory letter by Martin Luther, is included in *Corpus Reformatorum* 14, ed. Karl Gottlieb Bretschneider (Halle: Schwetschke, 1847), 1043–1220. Wengert, *Melanchthon's* Annotationes, studies the commentary in detail in its relation to patristic and medieval sources, as well as in its relation to Wittenberg evangelical theology.

[86] Timothy J. Wengert, "The Biblical Commentaries of Philip Melanchthon," in *Philip Melanchthon (1497–1560) and the Commentary*, eds. Timothy J. Wengert and M. Patrick Graham (Sheffield: Sheffield Academic Press, 1997), 62; Wengert, *Melanchthon's* Annotationes, 49.

[87] *CR* 21: 59–60.

> divinity to Christ, **nevertheless make no use of it**, are Ebionites twice.[88]

It is not *sufficient*, Melanchthon says, to know about two-natures Christology—but this implies that one does in fact need to know about it in order not to be an Ebionite. It is just that one needs something more than this: one needs to *make use of* this knowledge by reflecting upon why Christ must be God come in the flesh. The pattern Melanchthon suggests reflects the one that he attributes to the Apostle John who, when "he was going to write the history of Christ, first expounded who he is; next, why he came; finally, what he did."[89] Recall here his comment from the 1521 *Loci* preface cited above: "If you do not know why Christ put on flesh and was fixed to the cross, what does it profit to know his history?"[90]

Shortly afterwards, the divinity of Christ underwrites a comment Melanchthon makes about Romans 8:

> *Atque ita nihil dubitent de voluntate patris erga se qui Christo credunt, sed simpliciter sciunt, quod sicut Christi, ita patris sint, quia Christus deus est. Ro. octavo. Si Deus pro nobis, quis contra nos?*
>
> And thus let those who believe in Christ doubt nothing at all about the will of the Father toward them, but simply know that, as they belong to Christ, so they belong to the Father, because Christ is God. Rom. 8: "If God is for us, who is against us?"[91]

---

[88] Melanchthon, *Annotationes in Iohannem*, sig. A3v.

[89] *historiam de Christo scripturus, primum quis sit exponit, deinde cur venerit, postremo quid gesserit.* Melanchthon, *Annotationes in Iohannem*, sig. A3v.

[90] Cf. Wengert, *Melanchthon's* Annotationes, 148–50: it is this soteriological focus that accounts for Melanchthon's divergences from traditional exegesis of John: the question of divergences in this respect is one of application rather than doctrine *per se*, and in this Melanchthon is like Luther.

[91] Melanchthon, *Annotationes in Iohannem*, sig. A3v.

This too relativizes his earlier comment about Romans in the 1521 *Loci* preface[92] and validates the reading already suggested:[93] Melanchthon warns against overly subtle philosophical speculation about classical doctrine, while nevertheless not seeking to undermine its importance. He makes this clear in the preface to the *Annotationes*, in which he cautions, in relation to "things divine and incomprehensible" (*ad res divinas et incomprehensibiles*), against trying to peer too curiously into the Holy of Holies (*ne quis curiosius Sancta sanctorum specularetur*). He goes on to offer a suggestion lest the reader fall afoul of the vice of curiosity to which he has just gestured:

> *Quare et hic de aeternitate, de Verbi genitura, deque huiusmodi mysteriis dicendum est paucis, ne qua humana cogitatione subvertantur curiosi.*
>
> Therefore, one should also say only a few things here about eternity, about the generation of the Word, and about [other] mysteries of this kind, in order that the curious may not be destroyed by any human thought.[94]

One should speak of them, then; but one should do so chastely and with a view to practical Christian profit.

The foregoing argument is confirmed once more in a comment that echoes his famous statement from the 1521 *Loci,* "We should more correctly adore the mysteries of the Godhead than scrupulously search them out." In this preface he says:

> *Haec cum ita habent, suo cuique spiritui relinquenda sunt haec sublimia mysteria, experiunda potius quam dicenda.*

---

92 "In the letter that he dictated to the Romans, Paul, when he was composing a summary of Christian teaching, didn't philosophize about the mysteries of the Trinity, about the mode of the Incarnation, about active creation, [or] about passive creation, did he?"

93 Even more telling is the fact that Melanchthon later says that Paul himself spoke about the two natures of Christ in Romans 1: *Duas naturas in Christo sic discrevit Paulus* ("Thus Paul distinguished the two natures in Christ" (Melanchthon, *Annotationes in Iohannem*, sig. a6r); he goes on to cite Rom. 1.3–4.

94 Melanchthon, *Annotationes in Iohannem*, sig. A4r.

> Since these things are so, these sublime mysteries should be left to each one's own spirit, to be experienced rather than spoken about.[95]

We now know that speaking about the mysteries is not absolutely forbidden, because he has just told us that a few things must be said about them; and this additional context helps us to interpret his words here (and, therefore, in the 1521 *Loci* preface) correctly. Moreover, his final proof for his method in the *Annotationes* is the same chapter that he used in the 1521 preface, 1 Corinthians 1.21—which is to say, the foolishness of the cross relativizes, or rather voids, human wisdom, and so one must not try to come to the Father by his own reason or thoughts or in any other way but through Christ.[96]

The congruity between these two prefaces in chronology and content indicates that their similarity is not fortuitous. They should instead be read as mutually illuminating and explicating each other. When they are read in this way, one can only conclude that Melanchthon had no desire, as Warfield already pointed out so long ago, to quietly elide the fundamental importance of Christology or classical Trinitarian doctrine, despite what Baur thought. With respect to Christology, the preface itself shows as much. The *Annotationes* proper prove the same about the Trinity. One is therefore not surprised to find that the opening of the *Annotations* proper begins with the Trinity.

Mysterium Trinitatis

In fact, one might put an even finer point on it: the very first words of the *Annotationes* are *Trinitatis mysterium*, the "mystery of the Trinity." And what does Melanchthon say about it? That Scripture teaches it in both testaments:

> *Trinitatis mysterium, et incarnationem filii Dei, scriptura Veteris Testamenti passim indicavit, sed exposuit clarius Novi testamenti.*

> The Scripture of the Old Testament everywhere pointed out the mystery of the Trinity, and the Incarnation of the Son

---

[95] Melanchthon, *Annotationes in Iohannem*, sig. A4r.

[96] Melanchthon, *Annotationes in Iohannem*, sigs. A4r-v. In a prefatory letter to the *Annotationes*, Luther had invoked the same text (sig. A2v).

> of God, but [the Scripture] of the New Testament expounded it more clearly.[97]

And then, the characteristic caution:

> *Et sicut haec una confessio est Novi testamenti, ita una blasphemia est, negare Christum filium Dei esse, hoc est, non credere peccatum sibi remitti per Christum.* ***Nihil prodest*** *posse personas trinitatis recensere,* ***Confessio prodest****, hoc est, fides, qua credimus nos in nomine patris, et filii, et spirtus sancti baptizatos esse: hoc est, in potentiam et virtutem patris, filii et spiritus sancti, qua potentia renascimur per baptismum, et efficimur filii Dei.*
>
> And just as it is the one confession of the New Testament, so it is the one blasphemy, to deny that Christ is the Son of God, that is, not to believe that one's sin is remitted through Christ. **It profits nothing** to be able to list the Persons of the Trinity; **confession brings profit**, that is, the faith by which we believe that we were baptized in the name of the Father, and of the Son, and of the Holy Spirit; that is, in the power and might of the Father, the Son, and the Holy Spirit, the power by which we are born again through baptism and made the sons of God.[98]

Melanchthon uses the same word that he employed in the 1521 *Loci* preface: *prodest*, "it profits." Melanchthon is consistently concerned to say that mere knowledge of the things of God brings the sinner no profit unless he believes that his sins are forgiven through Christ by the God of whom classical Trinitarianism speaks.[99] But he is so far from denying or minimizing the necessity of the personal distinctions within the Trinity that he goes on to

---

[97] Melanchthon, *Annotationes in Iohannem*, sig. A5r. As an index of Melanchthon's distance from Schleiermacher, one might observe that his friend and ally Friedrich Lücke defends Schleiermacher's theological innovations in theology proper by arguing that "the immanent Trinity is not biblically grounded, not even in John's gospel" (Schüssler Fiorenza, "Schleiermacher's Understanding," 183).

[98] Melanchthon, *Annotationes in Iohannem*, sig. A5r.

[99] Cf. Wengert, "Biblical Commentaries," 62: "[Melanchthon]...borrowed heavily from Luther to construct a soteriological approach to texts that had traditionally been exploited only for their christological information." The "only" is important: Melanchthon does not deny the Christological import of his text, but he also wants to stress its relation to the salvation of sinners.

give a Scriptural explanation of what the word "person" means, to assert the inseparable actions of the Persons, and to cite Hilary of Poitiers in support of his explanation.[100] One could not give a much stronger statement of allegiance to the doctrine than Melanchthon does at the end of this section:

> *Nos stulti arripiamus confessionem Trinitatis, et in illa gloriemur adversus portas inferi. Et haec de mysterio Trinitatis.*
>
> Let us, though fools, seize upon the confession of the Trinity, and let us boast in it against the gates of hell. And thus far concerning the mystery of the Trinity.[101]

All is summed up in the passage under examination: the dynamic of human foolishness over against divine wisdom; confession rather than mere knowledge; man's salvation. These are the things that matter to Melanchthon. The verb he uses (*arripiamus*), moreover, brings with it the sense of securing and maintaining that confession. Why? Because, in God's wisdom, the confession of the Trinity secures our salvation. It is that "soteriological slant," as Wengert calls it, that characterizes Melanchthon's scant but orthodox use of Trinitarian exegesis in John's gospel;[102] his relative "silence stems from neither a rejection of the Fathers nor a rejection of the early church's dogma. It arises instead from an unspoken acceptance of of their dogma and from a hermeneutical principle which Melanchthon invokes on the first page of his commentary and to which he adheres rigorously throughout the work."[103] Precisely this practical angle was to have a positive influence in later Reformed Orthodox reflection on the doctrine of the Trinity, particularly when combined with a more thorough exposition of the doctrine itself such as Melanchthon carried out after the early 1520s (to be discussed below).[104]

---

[100] Melanchthon, *Annotationes in Iohannem*, sigs. A5r-A6r. His account is echoed extremely closely in the *fragmenta* of the *Loci* of 1533 (*CR* 21: 258–59), which demonstrates that Melanchthon had settled convictions about the doctrine of God for a decade before he added sections on it to the *Loci*.

[101] Melanchthon, *Annotationes in Iohannem*, sig. A6r.

[102] Wengert, *Melanchthon's* Annotationes, 149.

[103] Wengert, *Melanchthon's* Annotationes, 92.

[104] Andreas J. Beck, "Melanchthonian Thought in Gisbertus Voetius' Scholastic Doctrine of God," in *Scholasticism Reformed: Essays in Honour of Willem J. van Asselt*, eds. Maarten Wisse Marcel Sarot, and Willemien Otten (Ledien: Brill, 2010), 124–25. For Melanchthon's influences on Voetius' doctrine of God more generally, see 107–126.

AN OMISSION IN SEARCH OF (FURTHER) EXPLANATION

But if that is the case, why did Melanchthon not devote even more attention to an unfolding of the doctrine of God in the first place, in addition to expounding its practical significance? In the first instance, the doctrine was omitted quite simply because, as has already been noted, it was not in dispute with the Church of Rome, and so there was no need to belabor it.[105] This fact is reflected even in later documents. For example, Luther's *Smalcald Articles* of 1537 open with the confession of the triune God. This confession contains standard-fare, if brief, classical Trinitarianism and Christology, to which he appends the following comment: "Concerning these articles there is no contention or dispute, since we on both sides confess them. Therefore it is not necessary now to treat further of them."[106]

The same was true of the *Augsburg Confession* seven years earlier (1530), which begins with a classical statement of the doctrine of God. In his *Defense of the Augsburg Confession*, also written in 1530, Melanchthon writes:

> The First Article of our Confession our adversaries approve, in which we declare that we believe and teach that there is one divine essence, undivided, etc., and yet, that there are three distinct persons, of the same divine essence, and coeternal, Father, Son, and Holy Ghost. **This article we have always taught and defended, and we believe that it has, in Holy Scripture, sure and firm testimonies that cannot be overthrown. And we constantly affirm that those thinking otherwise are outside of the Church of Christ**, and are idolaters, and insult God.[107]

Note what Melanchthon says here: "[W]e have always taught and defended this doctrine"; it has "sure and firm testimonies in Scripture";[108] it is required

---

[105] Cf. Hall, *Melanchthon and the Cappadocians*, 130–1; G.R. Evans, *Problems of Authority in the Reformation Debates* (Cambridge: Cambridge University Press, 1992), 4–5.

[106] The translation is cited from the online *Book of Concord*: http://bookofconcord.org/smalcald.php#firstpart.

[107] The translation is cited from the online *Book of Concord*:

http:// bookofconcord.org/defense_1_god.php.

[108] The *leitmotif* of the Reformation is evident: mere historicity does not prove a doctrine; only the warrant of Scripture can do that.

for being a Christian. One might note in this connection what Adolph Harnack says about Luther: "Luther would at any moment have defended with fullest conviction the opening words of the Athanasian Creed: 'Whosoever will be saved, before all things it is necessary that he hold the Catholic faith.'"[109] Given what we have now seen from the 1523 *Annotationes* on the gospel of John, we can be sure that this protestation that the Lutherans have always taught the doctrine of the Trinity is not merely rhetorical on Melanchthon's part. He simply does not belabor it in the first edition of the *Loci* because, as these two quotations make clear, the doctrines were not in question and furthermore because, as was noted above, they had been given such close attention in the context of "philosophical" or speculative elaboration that the truth of the gospel had, in Melanchthon's view, been obscured by comparison.

What, then, changed after the 1520s? The rise of a new anti-Trinitarianism, which found representatives in Francis Stancarus and John Campanus, but which was typified in the case of Michael Servetus, whose work *De trinitatis erroribus libri VII* was published in the year following Augsburg and whom Melanchthon singles out by name in the *locus de Deo* of the second era of the *Loci communes* in 1535.[110] Suddenly the early Reformers had opponents not only in the Church of Rome over the doctrines of

[109] Harnack, *History of Dogma*, vol. 7, 174–75. Harnack goes on to refer to both confessional documents just quoted, and concludes: "Of this also there can be no doubt—that the gospel was for [Luther] 'saving *doctrine*, *doctrine* of the gospel' ('*doctrina* salutaris, *doctrina* evangelii'), which certainly included the old dogmas; the attempt to represent the matter otherwise has in my opinion been a failure: the gospel is sacred *doctrine*, contained in the Word of God, the purpose of which is to be learned, and to which there must be subjection" (175, emphasis original). Harnack shows a firmer grasp of the mentality of the Reformers than that on display in George Cross, *The Theology of Schleiermacher: A Condensed Presentation of His Chief Work, "The Christian Faith"* (Chicago: University of Chicago Press, 1911), 67–72 and 75, who maintains that their classical orthodoxy was only a matter of state domination, in which the church was inconsistently complicit, and hidebound conservatism. Tellingly, he claims that the Anabaptists "were the nearest representatives of the revived religious spirit that made the Reformation a possibility" (74). Harnack's view also contrasts with that of B.A. Gerrish, *A Prince of the Church*, 39, who holds that "an authentic Reformation motive lay behind Schleiermacher's quest for new [Trinitarian and Christological] formulas altogether."

[110] Melanchthon, *Loci communes* (1535), *De tribus personis divinitatis* (*CR* 21: 359). He had already named Servetus as an opponent in the surviving *fragmenta* of the *Loci* of 1533 that precede the publication of the revised *Loci* in 1535 (*CR* 21: 262).

salvation and the church, but also in men like Servetus over the doctrine of God. Hall, who remarks upon the similarity between the anti-Trinitarians' view of the history of dogma and that of the Anabaptists, summarizes Servetus' program as follows: "His basic charge is that the pure Christianity of Jesus and his earliest disciples had been corrupted by the grafting of foreign Greek philosophical categories onto the pure Gospel."[111] Such a radicalizing of the rhetoric of the Reformation in Servetus has more in common with the Reformers' nineteenth century would-be heirs than it does with the Reformers themselves. Until this new anti-Trinitarianism had arisen, Melanchthon was content to focus his attention and energy on the soteriological application of the righteousness of God, but without contradicting the theological foundation on which it rested. As Wengert concludes of the *Annotationes*:

> Melanchthon assumes Trinitarian doctrine and never explicitly attacks it. He omits much of the traditional discussion of these problems and even some of the verses which most clearly raise them. Instead he focuses upon the soteriological implications of the text, putting flesh on the famous comment from the *Loci communes* that "to know Christ is to know his benefits." Until Trinitarian and Christological heresies arise among certain radical Reformers, Melanchthon is content to concentrate upon the power, function and benefits of Christ and not upon his essence or natures.[112]

MELANCHTHON GETS HIS GROOVE BACK—OR DOES HE?[113]

When the doctrine of God is included in the second era of the *Loci*, moreover, it is placed exactly where it had always been placed, just as it was in the confessions as well, and it is formulated in the traditional way. In other words, whatever the "spirit of the Reformation" may have been, it did not include

---

[111] Hall, *Melanchthon and the Cappadocians*, 123; the position Melanchthon attributes to the Anabaptists would later be taken up by Harnack. Melanchthon devoted an entire work explicitly devoted to the refutation of Servetus, where Servetus is grouped with the Anabaptists, his *Refutatio erroris Serveti et Anabaptistarum* (124).

[112] Wengert, *Melanchthon's* Annotationes, 150.

[113] The key word is "back."

innovation in this respect. Further evidence that this reading is correct, despite Melanchthon's early omission, is shown by a curious similarity in the prefaces of the 1521 *Loci* and the *fragmenta* of the 1533 *Loci*. In 1521, when he was about to list the chief heads of doctrine that are customarily included in a work of dogmatics, Melanchthon wrote:

> ***Sunt autem*** *rerum theologicarum haec* **fere** *capita*.
>
> **There are, moreover, generally** the following heads [i.e. categories] of [a work on] theology.[114]

In 1533 he writes:

> ***Sunt autem fere*** *loci, intra quos tota propemodum doctrina Christiana versatur.*
>
> **There are, moreover, generally** [the following] topics, around which nearly all of Christian teaching revolves.[115]

In the first instance, given what we know about Melanchthon's omission, one might be tempted to construe *fere* as follows: "Generally, this is what people have done, but I shall do differently, because I have a better way of organizing Christian teaching as a whole."[116] But the very similar wording in 1533 indicates something much more innocuous: "Generally, this is what people have done, and I shall do the same." Not only so, but he now says explicitly that nearly all of the Christian faith turns on (*versatur*) the *loci* that follow—and these include the doctrines of God and creation, both ostensibly criticized in 1521. Furthermore, in the published version of the *Loci* of 1535, Melanchthon says that it is "necessary" (*necesse est*) to hold to the judgments revealed by God and confirmed by the "judgment of the Christian church" (*Ecclesiae Christianae sententiam*) about the unity of the divine essence, the divine omnipotence, the natures of Christ, and the Holy Spirit.[117] In addition, his

---

114 Melanchthon, *Loci communes* (1521), *praef.* (*CR* 21: 83).

115 Melanchthon, *Loci communes* (1533), *praef.* (*CR* 21: 254).

116 Melanchthon certainly thought he had a better way of *explicating* Christian teaching in 1521, but that is not my point here.

117 Melanchthon, *Loci communes* (1535), *De Deo* (*CR* 21: 352). He makes this claim while (yet again) warning about the dangers of "speculation" and the "scholastics."

account of "person" in the *fragmenta*[118] echoes his discussion in the *Annotationes* extremely closely, demonstrating that Melanchthon had settled, not simply casual, convictions about the doctrine of God for a decade before he added sections on it to the *Loci*, and that those convictions remained consistent from the very beginning of his career as a theologian.

Barth on Melanchthon's "Disastrous Example"

Yet of Melanchthon's addition of the *locus de Deo*, Barth contemptuously says:

> The second mistake that Melanchthon committed later was if anything worse than the first. It consisted in this. When he later decided to take up again in his Loci the doctrine of God, he began to create it from another source than from the revelation of God, namely, from an independently formed and general idea of God. He therefore began to consider the *mysteria divinitatis* apart from their connexion with the *beneficia Christi.* In this he fell right into the *magnum periculum* of which he had been afraid in 1521, and was all the more guilty of the very error which in his first act of rashness he had had a right instinct to avoid as opposed to late medieval scholasticism, thus affording a disastrous example to the whole of Protestant orthodoxy. We must be at pains to avoid both these errors of Melanchthon.[119]

Given Barth's assessment, it is curious to discover that Melanchthon begins the *locus de Deo* as follows in the *fragmenta* of 1533:

> *Nullum invenio exordium aptius huic loco, in quo de natura dei aliquid dicendum est, quam id quod Christus ait ad Philippum cupientem videre patrem. Philippe qui videt me videt et patrem meum. An non credis quod ego in patre sum et pater in me? Hanc gravissimam admotionem teneamus, ut discamus deum quaerere in Christo, in hoc enim voluit patefieri, innotescere et apprehendi.*
>
> I know of no fitter beginning for this topic, in which I am to say something about the nature of God, than what Christ

118 Melanchthon, *Loci communes* (1533), *De tribus personis* (*CR* 21: 258–59.

119 Barth, *CD* II.1, 259–60.

> said to Philip when he wanted to see the Father. "Philip, he who sees me sees my Father also. Or do you not believe that I am in the Father and the Father is in me?" Let us hold to this most weighty warning, so that we might learn to seek God in Christ; for in him did he will to be revealed, made known, and apprehended.[120]

And indeed, though Barth charges him with having abandoned his opposition to "late medieval scholasticism," nothing could be farther from the truth. All of his characteristic language and concerns are still present from 1521. Thus he follows the remark just quoted by saying:

> *Quoties igitur tumultuantur in mentibus nostris* **speculationes** *cum de natura dei tum de voluntate dei, reiiciamus nos in Christum, et sciamus hunc nobis propositum esse, et in ipso quaeramus deum, iuxta illud. Nemo venit ad patrem nisi per filium.*
>
> Therefore, as often as **speculations** both about the nature of God and about the will of God are stirred up in our minds, let us cast ourselves on Christ and know that he has been made known to us, and let us seek God in Him Himself, according to that remark [of his]: "No one comes to the Father except through the Son."[121]

Melanchthon is at pains to insist that as soon as one allows one's thinking about God's nature and will to be sundered from the revelation of God in Jesus Christ, things go awry; such "Christocentrism," one might have thought, Barth would have considered amenable.[122] In this Melanchthon is absolutely consistent with his perspective in 1521. His authorities at the beginning of this section are, moreover, the Gospel of John—and so we see the influence of the *Annotationes* on John from a decade prior at work again—and 1 Corinthians 1, also used a decade earlier. Melanchthon's method is *a Christo* rather than *a priori*, as he himself says:

---

120 Melanchthon, *Loci communes* (1533), *De Deo* (*CR* 21: 255).

121 Melanchthon, *Loci communes* (1533), *De Deo* (*CR* 21: 256).

122 It would be worthwhile to discuss how Melanchthon could employ this "Christocentrism" while retaining a place for natural theology, in contradistinction to Barth, though it is beyond the scope of this paper.

> *Haec methodus non progreditur a priore, hoc est, ab arcana natura dei ad cognitionem voluntatis dei, sed a cognitione Christi et misericordiae revelatae ad cognitionem dei.*
>
> This method does not progress *a priori*, that is, from the secret nature of God to knowledge of the will of God, but from the knowledge of Christ and His revealed mercy to the knowledge of God.[123]

Anti-Scholastic Scholasticism?

And yet his actual doctrinal positions (which, to repeat, he claims to be "necessary" [*necessaria*]),[124] are consistent with the Western Christian tradition, including the scholastics. How to account for this? First, by way of his basic stance from 1521, as it happens. One remark from 1533 about "speculations" has already been noted, but it is not the only one. In addition, Melanchthon continues to castigate "philosophizing" about God's hidden nature (*philosophari de arcana natura dei*),[125] because detaining oneself in matters of speculation does not "profit" (once again, the verb is *prodest*).[126] Though historical circumstances called for renewed attention to the doctrine of God, because it had been brought into question by Servetus and others, Melanchthon still demands simplicity and straightforwardness of treatment, which he denies to "the disputations of the scholastics" (*scholasticorum disputationes*)[127]—though this continued polemic should not obscure the fact that he still would have shared, and did share, their basic doctrinal formulations, because those formulations were not original to them, but were rather the heritage of the ancient church.

This point brings me to the second way in which Melanchthon's standard-fare orthodox doctrine of God can be accounted for despite his rhetorical and, in certain respects, methodological rejection of the scholastics.

---

123 Melanchthon, *Loci communes* (1533), *De Deo* (*CR* 21: 256).

124 Melanchthon, *Loci communes* (1533), *De Deo* (*CR* 21: 257).

125 Melanchthon, *Loci communes* (1533), *De Deo* (*CR* 21: 256).

126 *Semper autem meminerit lector non esse resistendum in his speculabilibus, ac ne prodest quidem in eis commorari.* Melanchthon, *Loci communes* (1533), *De Deo* (*CR* 21: 256).

127 Melanchthon, *Loci communes* (1533), *De Deo* (*CR* 21: 257).

That is to say, it can be accounted for by way of the authorities Melanchthon predominantly employs: Scripture and the church fathers.[128] (One might suggest, however, that this move itself savors something of the scholastic, since medieval theologians regularly did the same; Lombard's *Sentences* are more or less a compendium of Augustine.) In the preface, Melanchthon had already referred to the Creed and Origen (noting that the church does not approve of him),[129] in addition to Cyprian and Augustine, as well as John of Damascus and Peter Lombard. It is the last who comes in for extended criticism for all of the reasons just noted (somewhat surprisingly, perhaps, because of the summary nature of Lombard's work;[130] incidentally, Melanchthon has, just before his criticism, referred to the little known pseudo-Augustinian work *De fide ad Petrum* also cited by Lombard in *Sentences* 2.2.3).[131] Melanchthon thus draws a sharp rhetorical line between the fathers and the scholastics and employs the former to the exclusion of the latter. In the treatment of the doctrine itself, he refers favorably to Gregory of Nazianzus,[132] Basil,[133] Irenaeus,[134] Tertullian,[135] and Origen (*On First Principles*, the same work he noted in the preface as having been censured by the church!),[136] while disparaging the Arians, Valentinus, Mani, Paul of Samosata, and Servetus.

Even so, Melanchthon's treatment of the order and content of the doctrine in the *fragmenta* might usefully be glossed as a modified and abbreviated Thomism, albeit disencumbered of what he viewed as the excrescences of the scholastic method of treatment. For after the section on Christ, titled *De Deo*, as the necessary principle for reflection on the Godhead,

---

[128] *[E]t certa scripturarum testimonia et veterum autorum sententias ostendere*. Melanchthon, *Loci communes* (1533), *De Deo* (*CR* 21: 257). Hall, *Melanchthon and the Cappadocians*, 126, also notes this pattern and discusses its use elsewhere in Melanchthon's writings.

[129] Melanchthon, *Loci communes* (1533), *praef.* (*CR* 21: 253).

[130] Once again, it is most likely that Melanchthon's real target is the tradition of long and diffuse scholastic commentaries on Lombard's *Sentences*.

[131] It is actually by Fulgentius of Ruspe.

[132] Melanchthon, *Loci communes* (1533), *De tribus personis* (*CR* 21: 258).

[133] Melanchthon, *Loci communes* (1533), *De tribus personis* (*CR* 21: 259).

[134] Melanchthon, *Loci communes* (1533), *De tribus personis* (*CR* 21: 263, 266).

[135] Melanchthon, *Loci communes* (1533), *De tribus personis* (*CR* 21: 263).

[136] Melanchthon, *Loci communes* (1533), *De tribus personis* (*CR* 21: 263–64).

he treats the unity of God (*Quod unus sit deus*) first, followed by a section on the God's threeness (*De tribus personis*).[137]

Two examples will show Melanchthon's advocacy of the classical doctrine of God in this work. First, in the section on the divine unity Melanchthon denies the presence of accidents in God and thus affirms absolute divine simplicity. He writes:

> *Sapientia, bonitas, iustitia, misericordia, non sunt accidentia in deo, sed sicut potentiam non divellimus a substantia, sic nec sapientiam nec bonitatem a substantia separamus. Nam potentia est ipsa sapientia, bonitas, etc.*
>
> Wisdom, goodness, justice, [and] mercy are not accidents in God, but just as we do not tear his power away from his substance, so we separate neither his wisdom nor his goodness from his substance. For his power is his very wisdom, goodness, etc.[138]

Second, the section on the three περσονσ affirms the ὁμοούσιος in traditional terms and cites Gregory of Nazianzus and Basil for support, along with Chalcedonian two-natures Christology.[139] It is true that Melanchthon does not go into great detail, but his brief references use enough of the key terminology to make it clear that his positions are classical ones. In short, he affirms the same basic positions as his medieval predecessors, even though he leapfrogs over them with respect to the use of authorities. He affirms them not *because* they are medieval, but because they are the possession of the catholic church in accordance with Scripture and patristic theology.

The same order of treatment is maintained in the full published text of the second era dating from 1535. The *locus de Deo* begins with Christ and is

---

[137] One mark of his abbreviation is that he does not insert a treatment of the divine operations between the sections on God as one and God as three, as Aquinas does.

[138] Melanchthon, *Loci communes* (1533), *Quod unus sit Deus* (*CR* 21: 257).

[139] Melanchthon, *Loci communes* (1533), *De tribus personis* (*CR* 21: 258–63). Hall, *Melanchthon and the Cappadocians*, 131–38, documents the growing presence of the Cappadocians in successive editions of the *Loci communes*. The source in Gregory's writings for Melanchthon's 1533 reference is *Oration* 21.35. The reference to Basil relating to baptism in the Triune Name as a proof of the Trinity finds its inspiration Basil's *On the Holy Spirit* (134).

followed by a section on the unity of God that affirms simplicity, which in turn is followed by a discussion of the three Persons.[140] Indeed, it is present even in the last "era" of the *Loci* (the final edition of which was published in 1559), which yet again begins substantively with Christ, though a few preliminary remarks are added[141]—thus causing one to wonder what, after all, Barth had in mind in his criticism.

A (SOMEWHAT) POLEMICAL CONCLUSION

What can we conclude from all of this evidence when set next to the different perspectives represented in the nineteenth century by Friedrich Schleiermacher and Ferdinand Christian Baur? First, Schleiermacher and Baur both, in their own ways, seem to have thought that the original impulse of the Protestant Reformers demanded a total "Protestantizing" of theology, from first to last, even if they had not fully carried through such a project. Second, Schleiermacher correctly recognized what must be the consequence of completing this purported "intended Reformation":[142] a complete revision of the systematic treatment of dogma. Thus there are two different—but related—elements in play, one historical and the other theological.

For the first: it is quite manifest from a close reading of the preface and the *locus de Deo* in the several eras of the *Loci*, particularly when viewed in relation to other works of Melanchthon, that the original impulse of the Reformers—what Baur calls the "standpoint of the Reformation"—had nothing to do with revising, let alone minimizing the principial position of, the doctrine of God. In light of what was argued above, this seems to be beyond doubt. As Peter Fraenkel remarks, "[T]he role that [Melanchthon] attributed to theological 'tradition' remained substantially the same throughout his career. The increasingly significant place it came to occupy in later years was no more than an elaboration and expansion, called forth by circumstances, of what he had previously been largely content either to assume and assert in more general terms, or, at the most, to work out in some

[140] Melanchthon, *Loci communes* (1535), *De Deo*, *Quod unus sit Deus*, *De tribus personis Divinitatis*, and *De Spiritu sancto* (*CR* 21: 351–67).

[141] Melanchthon, *Loci praecipui theologici* (1559), *De Deo*, *De tribus personis Divinitatis*, *De Filio*, and *De Spiritu sancto* (*CR* 21: 607–637).

[142] To turn on its head Brad S. Gregory's hypothesis in *The Unintended Reformation* (Cambridge, MA: Harvard University Press, 2012).

particular context."[143] More closely, Fraenkel reaches a conclusion similar to that reached here against the readings of Baur and Barth, though he mentions neither by name:

> "Melanchthon's formulae in [the preface of] the Commonplaces of 1521 should be interpreted to mean that he saw in these dogmas an incontrovertible basis for the teaching of the Reformation; that he never thought that these dogmas needed in any way to be critically examined or justified afresh; that he conceived of the Reformers' doctrine of grace as a practical application of truths, of which credal orthodoxy provided the theoretical formulations; and that this attitude was one of the permanent factors in Melanchthon's theology from beginning to end."[144]

The use of "tradition" by Melanchthon and others was not an accidental oversight; without the doctrine of God as traditionally understood, they believed, there could be no grounding for the Reformation's articulation of the gospel. Their perspective on what "Reformation" means is not compatible with that of Schleiermacher.

For the second: it is for the reader to judge the effects of Schleiermacher's removal of the doctrine of God and the Holy Trinity from its aforementioned principial position. What can be maintained, at the very least, is that the effects its removal and replacement by a very different dogmatic starting-point are felt throughout Schleiermacher's system, such that theology is no longer talk primarily about God *per se*, and, secondarily, all things in relation to God, but rather by definition must be restricted to God-in-relation, given Schleiermacher's focus on the feeling of absolute dependence and the God-consciousness. The question that must then be addressed is whether Protestantism—as a body of concrete beliefs and affirmations, that is, as an articulation of the confession of God and the

---

143 Fraenkel, Testimonia Patrum, 29. Fraenkel also treats Melanchthon's relationship to tradition in "Revelation and Tradition: Notes on Some Aspects of Doctrinal Continuity in the Theology of Philip Melanchthon," *Studia Theologica* 13 (1959): 97–133. For further discussion, see Wengert, *Melanchthon's* Annotationes, 57–93.

144 Fraenkel, Testimonia Patrum, 36.

gospel[145]—can survive such a radical revision. If Protestant doctrines respecting the authority of revelation and justification by faith alone—to take only two, but two of the chief, Protestant principles—are in fact underwritten by the classical doctrine of God; and if those doctrines are required for the term "Protestant" to have an objective dogmatic meaning; then the answer to the question must be "no." If the answer is "yes," then "Protestantism," it would seem, is little more than a posture that prioritizes novelty and demands a distinctively Protestant view of everything, because that is what must follow from the (supposed) pre-reflective Protestant impulse that underlies and determines the contours of the Christian confession in this view. But this posture, paradoxically, results in the loss of what is distinctively Protestant in doctrinal terms with respect to the first alternative above. Again, readers must judge for themselves. But as a historical matter, one can say with confidence that a "yes" answer leaves one with a Protestantism in many respects unrecognizable to our first Protestant fathers.

Having said something by way of conclusion about Schleiermacher and Baur, I shall round out the discussion by saying something about my third modern interlocutor. Barth, it seems to me, wants to maintain both something of the tradition and something distinctively Protestant, or at least Christocentric, viz. the primacy of the doctrine of God, but one anchored in Christ and evacuated of abstruse speculation. Melanchthon, as is now clear, does both of these things, together with a strong rhetorical aversion to speculation. But even here one can perhaps mark a difference. Melanchthon's aversion to scholastic speculation in the texts examined throughout is above all a matter of emphasis, for he believed that the schoolmen had obscured the gospel and its subjective relation to sinners in need of forgiveness (and it is this concern for the subjective relation to God that Schleiermacher above all echoes). But this criticism does not prevent him from making use of the traditional formulations of divine simplicity and of Trinitarian unity within diversity—which are, after all, simply the explication of the ecumenical creeds, which in their turn are explications of divine revelation. If he is right, then Barth's worry is misplaced: while he restored the doctrine of God to its traditional and scholastic location in the second era of the *Loci*, he did so while avoiding over-curious speculation and thus, from his own perspective, emphatically did not fall into the scholastic trap as Barth avers. For that

145 Scheiermacher, of course, would contest this as a fundamental description of the Christian religion.

reason, Barth's worries can be addressed—as odd as it may sound—by doing what Melanchthon does, in just the way he does it: restoring emphasis on Christ as the revelation of God and forgiveness in His name, in reliance upon the classical doctrine of God as its necessary foundation.[146] In Melanchthon, then, one finds premonitions of the chief concerns of some modern theologians about the proper relation of Protestantism to ecclesiastical tradition, and yet—another paradox—the way he finds best suited to addressing those concerns is through the rigorous appropriation, with respect to both the ordering of topics and their dogmatic content, of the catholic and creedal faith. Did Melanchthon have a doctrine of God, then? No—but not for the reasons Baur thought. Melanchthon didn't have a doctrine of God; the church did, and Melanchthon was happy to use it. For that reason, I must demur from the judgment of Robert Kolb that in the second era of the *Loci* Melanchthon "returned to the dogmatic tradition of the church" after the fashion of John of Damascus and Peter Lombard—and that because, in my view, he had never left it.[147]

---

146 Thus I disagree with Hall's remark (*Melanchthon and the Cappadocians*, 130) that Melanchthon viewed these doctrines as "not necessary for salvation" in 1521. Again, the question was one of emphasis, as Hall elsewhere notes.

147 Robert Kolb, "The Ordering of the *Loci Communes Theologici*," 328.

BIBLIOGRAPHY

Barth, Karl. *Church Dogmatics* II.1. Translated by T.H.L. Parke, W.B. Johnston, Harold Knight, and J.L.M. Haire and edited by G.W. Bromiley and T.F. Torrance. Edinburgh: T&T Clark, 1957.

——. *Protestant Theology in the Nineteenth Century: Its Background and History.* Translator not named. Valley Forge, PA: Judson Press, 1973.

——. *The Theology of Schleiermacher: Lectures at Göttingen, Winter Semester of 1923/24.* Translated by Geoffrey W. Bromiley and edited Dietrich Ritschl. Grand Rapids: Eerdmans, 1982.

Baur, Ferdinand Christian. *Die christliche Lehre von der Dreieinigkeit und Menschwerdung Gottes in ihrer geschichtlichen Entwicklung*, Volume 3. Tübingen: C.F. Osiander, 1843.

Beck, Andreas J. "Melanchthonian Thought in Gisbertus Voetius' Scholastic Doctrine of God." In *Scholasticism Reformed: Essays in Honour of Willem J. van Asselt*, edited by Maarten Wisse Marcel Sarot, and Willemien Otten, 105-126. Ledien: Brill, 2010.

Behrens, Georg. "Feeling of Absolute Dependence or Absolute Feeling of Dependence? (What Schleiermacher Really Said and Why It Matters)." *Religious Studies* 34 (1998): 471-481.

Book of Concord. http://bookofconcord.org/smalcald.php#firstpart.

Breen, Quirinus. "The Terms 'Loci Communes' and 'Loci' in Melanchthon." *Church History* 16 (1947): 197-209.

Brunner, Emil. *Die Mystik und das Wort: der Gegensatz zwischen moderner Religionsauffassung und christlichem Glauben dargestellt an der Theologie Schleiermachers.* Tübingen: J.C.B. Mohr, 1924/1928.

Calvin, Calvin. *Institutes of the Christian Religion.* Vol. 1. Translated by Henry Beveridge. Edinburgh: Calvin Translation Society, 1845.

Corpus Reformatorum 14. Edited by Karl Gottlieb Bretschneider. Halle: Schwetschke, 1847.

Corpus Reformatorum 21. Edited by Karl Bretschneider and Heinrich Bindseil. Brunsvigae: Schwetschke, 1854.

Corpus Reformatorum 22. Edited by Karl Bretschneider and Heinrich Bindseil. Brunsvigae: Schwetschke, 1855.

Cross, George. *The Theology of Schleiermacher: A Condensed Presentation of His Chief Work, 'The Christian Faith.'* Chicago: University of Chicago Press, 1911.

Ebeling, Gerhard. "Schleiermacher's Doctrine of the Divine Attributes." In *Schleiermacher as Contemporary - Journal for Theology and the Church 7*, edited by Robert W. Funk, 125-75. New York: Herder and Herder, 1970.

Fiorenza, Francis Schüssler. "Schleiermacher and the Construction of a Contemporary Roman Catholic Foundational Theology." *Harvard Theological Review* 89 (1996): 175-194.

——. "Schleiermacher's Understanding of God as Triune." In *The Cambridge Companion to Friedrich Schleiermacher*, edited by Jacqueline Mariña, 171-88. Cambridge: Cambridge University Press, 2006.

Fraenkel, Peter. "Revelation and Tradition: Notes on Some Aspects of Doctrinal Continuity in the Theology of Philip Melanchthon." *Studia Theologica* 13 (1959): 97-133.

——. Testimonia Patrum: *The Function of the Patristic Argument in the Theology of Philip Melanchthon.* Geneva: Droz, 1961.

Gerrish, B.A. *Tradition and the Modern World: Reformed Theology in the Nineteenth Century.* Chicago: University of Chicago Press, 1978.

——. *A Prince of the Church: Schleiermacher and the Beginnings of Modern Theology.* Philadelphia: Fortress, 1984.

——. *Continuing the Reformation: Essays on Modern Religious Thought.* Chicago: University of Chicago Press, 1993.

——. *The Old Protestantism and the New: Essays on the Reformation Heritage.* London: T&T Clark, 2004.

Gordon, James. "A 'Glaring Misunderstanding'? Schleiermacher, Barth and the Nature of Speculative Theology." *International Journal of Systematic Theology* 16 (2014): 313-330.

Gregory, Brad S. *The Unintended Reformation.* Cambridge, MA: Harvard University Press, 2012.

Hall, H. Ashley. *Philip Melanchthon and the Cappadocians: A Reception of Greek Patristic Sources in the Sixteenth Century.* Göttingen: Vandenhoeck & Ruprecht, 2014.

Hankey, W.J. *God in Himself: Aquinas' Doctrine of God as Expounded in the* Summa Theologiae. Oxford: Oxford University Press, 1987.

Harnack, Adolph. *History of Dogma*. 3rd ed. 7 vols. Translated by Neil Buchanan. Gloucester, MA: P. Smith, 1976.

Helmer, Christine. "Mysticism and Metaphysics: Schleiermacher and a Historical-Theological Trajectory." *Journal of Religion* 83 (2003): 517-538.

———. *Theology and the End of Doctrine*. Louisville, KY: Westminster John Knox Press, 2014.

Husbands, Mark. "Calvin on the Revelation of God in Creation and Scripture." In *Calvin's Theology and Its Reception: Disputes, Developments, and New Possibilities*, edited by J. Todd Billings and I. John Hesselink, 25-48. Louisville, KY: Westminster John Knox Press, 2012.

Kolb, Robert. "The Pastoral Dimension of Melanchthon's Pedagogical Activities for the Education of Pastors." In *Philip Melanchthon: Theologian in Classroom, Confession, and Controversy*, edited by Irene Dingel, Robert Kolb, Nicole Kuropka, and Timothy J. Wengert, 29-42. Göttingen: Vandenhoeck & Ruprecht, 2012.

Kolb, Robert. "The Ordering of the *Loci Communes Theologici*: The Structuring of the Melanchthonian Dogmatic Tradition." *Concordia Journal* 23 (1997): 317-25.

Kusukawa, Sachiko. "Melanchthon." In *The Cambridge Companion to Reformation Theology*, edited by David Bagchi and David C. Steinmetz, 57-67. Cambridge: Cambridge University Press, 2006.

Lamm, Julia A. "The Early Philosophical Roots of Schleiermacher's Notion of *Gefühl*, 1788-94." *Harvard Theological Review* 87 (1994): 67-105.

Melanchthon, Philip. *Lucubratiuncula*. In *Corpus Reformatorum* 21, eds. Karl Bretschneider and Heinrich Bindseil. Brunsvigae: Schwetschke, 1854.

———. *Loci communes*, ed. 1521. In *Corpus Reformatorum* 21, eds. Karl Bretschneider and Heinrich Bindseil. Brunsvigae: Schwetschke, 1854.

———. *Annotationes in Iohannem, castigatiores quam quae ante invulgatae sunt*. Nürnberg: [no pub.], 1523.

———. *Loci communes*, ed. 1533. In *Corpus Reformatorum* 21, eds. Karl Bretschneider and Heinrich Bindseil. Brunsvigae: Schwetschke, 1854.

———. *Loci communes*, ed. 1535. In *Corpus Reformatorum* 21, eds. Karl Bretschneider and Heinrich Bindseil. Brunsvigae: Schwetschke, 1854.

———. *Loci communes*, ed. 1559. In *Corpus Reformatorum* 21, eds. Karl Bretschneider and Heinrich Bindseil. Brunsvigae: Schwetschke, 1854.

———. *De discrimine evangelii et philosophiae*. In *Corpus Reformatorum* 12, edited by Karl Gottlieb Bretschneider. Halle: Schwetschke, 1844.

———. "On the Distinction between the Gospel and Philosophy." In *Orations on Philosophy and Education*, translated by Christine F. Salazar and edited by Sachiko Kusukawa, 23-26. Cambridge: Cambridge University Press, 1999.

McCormack, Bruce L. "Not a Possible God but the God Who Is: Observations on Friedrich Schleiermacher's Doctrine of God." In *The Reality of Faith in Theology: Studies on Karl Barth. Princeton-Kampen Consultation 2005*, edited by Bruce McCormack and Gerrit Neven, 111-39. Bern: Peter Lang, 2007.

Muller, Richard. "The Christological Problem as Addressed by Friedrich Schleiermacher: A Dogmatic Query." In *Perspectives on Christology: Essays in Honor of Paul K. Jewett*, edited by Marguerite Shuster and Richard Muller, 141-162. Grand Rapids: Zondervan, 1991.

———. *The Unaccommodated Calvin*. Oxford: Oxford University Press, 2002.

———. *Post-Reformation Reformed Dogmatics*. 2nd ed. Vol. 1. Grand Rapids: Baker, 2003.

Oseka, Matthew. "What the Emerging Protestant Theology Was About: The Reformation Concept of Theological Studies as Enunciated by Philip Melanchthon in His Prolegomena to All Latin and German Versions of the *Loci*." *Perichoresis* 15 (2017): 22.

Pearson, Lori. "Schleiermacher and the Christologies behind Chalcedon." *Harvard Theological Review* 96 (2003): 349-97.

Pederson, Daniel J. "Schleiermacher and Reformed Scholastics on the Divine Attributes." *International Journal of Systematic Theology* 17 (2015): 413-31.

Roy, Louis. "Consciousness according to Schleiermacher." *Journal of Religion* 77 (1997): 217-32.

Schleiermacher, Friedrich. *The Christian Faith*. Edited by H.R. Mackintosh and J.S. Stewart. Edinburgh: T&T Clark, 1986.

Signoriello, Nunzio. *Lexicon peripateticum philosophico-theologicum in quo scholasticorum distinctiones et effata praecipua explicantur*. 2nd ed. Naples: Pignatelli, 1872.

Stupperich, Robert. *Melanchthon: The Enigma of the Reformation*. Translated by Robert H. Fischer. Cambridge: James Clarke, 2006.

Thiel, John E. "Schleiermacher as 'Catholic': A Charge in the Rhetoric of Modern Theology." *Heythrop Journal* 37 (1996): 61-82.

Torrance, Alan. "The Trinity." In *The Cambridge Companion to Karl Barth*, edited by John Webster. Cambridge: Cambridge University Press, 2000.

Kunnuthara, Abraham Varghese. *Schleiermacher on Christian Consciousness of God's Work in History*. Eugene, OR: Wipf & Stock, 2008.

Warfield, Benjamin Breckenridge. *Calvin and Calvinism*. Grand Rapids: Baker, 1931.

Wengert, Timothy J. *Philip Melanchthon's* Annotationes in Johannem *in Relation to Its Predecessors and Contemporaries*. Geneva: Droz, 1987.

———. "The Biblical Commentaries of Philip Melanchthon." In *Philip Melanchthon (1497-1560) and the Commentary*, edited by Timothy J. Wengert and M. Patrick Graham. Sheffield: Sheffield Academic Press, 1997.

Williams, Robert R. *Schleiermacher the Theologian: The Construction of the Doctrine of God*. Philadelphia: Fortress, 1978.

Wyman Jr., Walter E. "The Role of the Protestant Confessions in Schleiermacher's *The Christian Faith*." *Journal of Religion* 87 (2007): 355-85.

II:
NATURAL THEOLOGY AND PROTESTANT ORTHODOXY

David Haines, Veritas International University

INTRODUCTION

THE LAST century of Christian theology and Apologetics has seen quite a bit of discussion, primarily in protestant circles, concerning what we will label as "the orthodoxy of Natural Theology." Theological giants such as Karl Barth, and influential apologists such as Cornelius Van Til, have made claims that either explicitly, or implicitly (by denying, for example, that man is actually capable of coming to true knowledge of the true God by any other means than Holy Scriptures), refused to allow any room for what is commonly known as Natural Theology.[1] In what follows we wish to ask a

[1] The most noted opponents to Natural Theology in recent times have been Cornelius Van Til, and the Van Tillian school of presuppositionalism, and Karl Barth and his followers. It should be noted that Van Til does not deny Natural Theology entirely, but claims that it is only possible if one first presupposes the truth of divinely inspired Christian scriptures (becomes a Christian), and is divinely guided by the Holy Spirit (Cornelius Van Til, *An Introduction to Systematic Theology*, vol. 5 of *In Defense of the Faith* [1974; Phillipsburg, NJ: P & R Publishing Co., 1982], 12, 13, 44, 54, 57, 61, 63, 66, 69, 71, 84, 197). Karl Barth claimed that, "The possibility of a real knowledge by natural man of the true God, derived from creation, is, according to Calvin, a possibility in principle, but not in fact, not a possibility to be realised by us. One might call it an objective possibility, created by God, but not a subjective possibility, open to man. Between what is possible in principle and what is possible in fact there inexorably lies the fall. Hence this possibility can only be discussed hypothetically: *si integer stetisset* Adam (*Inst.*, I, ii, I). Man does not merely in part not have this possibility; he does not have it at all. (Karl Barth, *NO!*, in *Natural Theology*, ed. John Baillie [Eugene, OR: Wipf & Stock Publishers, 2002], 106. Cf. Barth, *NO!*, 108).

very simple, yet very important, question: What place does Natural Theology have, or not have, in orthodox Protestant theology?[2]

In order to answer this question, we must, first of all, attempt to attain some comprehension of what we mean by "orthodox" and "unorthodox." We will then attempt to provide a very clear explanation of what we mean by "Natural Theology." With these two notions clearly defined, we will then attempt to answer the proposed question.

The answer that we will give to this question will carry with it some very important consequences. For example, if we determine that it is unorthodox to engage in Natural Theology, then those who do so, are unorthodox. On the other hand, if we determine that Natural Theology is necessary for orthodox Christian belief, then those who either deny it's possibility, or refuse to allow any room for it in their understanding of theology, should be considered unorthodox. It is always touchy to discuss the orthodoxy, or unorthodoxy, of a person's beliefs, as nobody wishes to be told that they are so theologically in error as to be considered outside of true Christian faith. Yet, if the limits of orthodoxy are not clearly defined, then anybody can determine their own limits, and either include, or exclude, anybody who does not fit inside their self-determined limits of orthodoxy. As such, this question should be of the utmost importance for Christian theologians and philosophers alike. Let us begin with the question of Orthodoxy.

ORTHODOXY

Definitions and Nuances

There is much talk of theological orthodoxy, but those who talk about it the most are often the same who take the least amount of time to define it. In other words, the terms "orthodox" or "unorthodox" are often used to either discredit or approve a theological or philosophical claim; yet, we rarely see

---

[2] Though we could certainly include Catholicism in our query, it does not seem necessary to ask this question, as it seems evident that Natural Theology is a necessary part of orthodoxy Catholic belief. I suppose that it is possible to debate this claim, but it doesn't seem all that likely that anyone could/would seriously debate the place of Natural Theology within that church which explicitly claims Thomas Aquinas as it's doctor. As such, we will be concerned with the place of Natural Theology within orthodox Protestant theology.

those who use these terms offer any explanation of the basis upon which they cast the judgment, "orthodox" or "unorthodox." If we are going to succeed in analyzing the orthodoxy or unorthodoxy of Natural Theology, we are going to need to make some very clear claims about just what we mean by "orthodox."[3]

As is commonly known, the word *orthodox* comes from two Greek words which mean, respectively, "right or proper" "belief, opinion, or teaching."[4] As such, the general notion of *orthodoxy* could be summarized as follows: a thinker is considered orthodox when he/she possesses right or true beliefs in that domain of thought concerning which he/she possesses these beliefs or opinions. In Muller's terms, "Orthodoxy consists in the faithful acceptance both of the fundamental articles and of those other, secondary doctrines, that sustain and serve to secure the right understanding of the fundamental doctrines."[5] Thus, a Christian thinker would be considered orthodox when they hold to those true doctrines/beliefs/opinions which are taught by true Christianity—when they hold to be true those doctrines which are truly Christian. When discussing orthodoxy, we also need to keep in mind that it is possible to be *partially orthodox*. A person would be considered partially orthodox when they adhere to a portion (greater or smaller) of those doctrines that are considered necessary for true Christian belief, but deny a portion (greater or smaller) of those same doctrines. Thus we can say that a

[3] "Unorthodox" would simply be the opposite of "orthodox."

[4] Cf. T.W. Chambers, "Orthodoxy and Heterodoxy," in *The Concise Dictionary of Religious Knowledge and Gazeteer*, 2nd ed., ed. Samuel MacAuley Jackson, Talbot Wilson Chambers, and Frank Hugh Foster (New York: The Christian Literature Company, 1891), 668. William Staunton, "Orthodox and Orthodoxy," in *An Ecclesiastical Dictionary*, 4th ed. (New York: The General Protestant Episcopal Sunday School Union and Church Book Society, 1875), 519. "Orthodox," in *Dictionary of Doctrinal and Historical Theology*, 2nd ed., ed. John Henry Blunt (London: Rivingtons, 1872), 531–32. Charles Buck, "Orthodoxy," in *Fessenden & Co.'s Encyclopedia of Religious Knowledge*, ed. J. Newton Brown (Brattleboro, VT: Brattleboro Typographic Company, 1837), 894–95. Walter Farquhar Hook, "Orthodoxy," in *A Church Dictionary*, 6th ed. Ed. anonymous (Philadelphia: E. H. Butler, Co., 1854), 418. James D. Davidson and Gary J. Quinn, "Theological and Sociological Uses of the Concept 'Orthodoxy,'" *Review of Religious Research* 18, no. 1 (Autumn, 1976): 74. Francis Brown, "What is Orthodoxy?," *The North American Review* 168, no. 509 (Apr., 1899): 409. Richard A. Muller, *Scholasticism and Orthodoxy in the Reformed Tradition: An Attempt at Definition* (Grand Rapids, MI: Calvin Theological Seminary, 1995), 2, 19.

[5] Muller, *Scholasticism and Orthodoxy in the Reformed Tradition*, 21.

person is, for the most part, orthodox, but unorthodox in relation to some one or another doctrine.[6]

The Protestant Problem

Our definition of orthodoxy, however, seems to cause significant problems for Protestantism as a whole. The problem could be explained as follows: (1) The definition of "orthodoxy" seems to imply that there is an official list containing a minimum of true Christian teachings to which a person must adhere in order to be considered orthodox. (2) As has been frequently noted, it would appear that Protestantism (through the doctrine of *Sola Scriptura* and the doctrine of the priority of individual interpretation as led by the Holy Spirit) makes impossible any official list containing a minimum of true Christian teachings to which a person must adhere in order to be considered orthodox. (3) If it turns out that (2) is true, then it is pointless to talk about Protestant Orthodoxy. Alister E. McGrath and Darren C. Marks state in the Blackwell Companion to Protestantism that "The 'Protestant problematic' (Karl Rahner) is that it places priority on individual conscience in response to revelation—in the Bible and the experience of salvation—as its defining characteristics. As such it must create the possibility, but not the necessity, of interpretative difference in doctrine, practice and polity."[7] They have rightly noted the major problem. How can we determine just what is to be considered orthodox Christian belief when the only authority for theology is the Bible, as interpreted by the reader who is, we hope and pray, guided by the Holy Spirit? Experience demonstrates even those men who are looked upon, by Protestants in general, as being the most knowledgeable in matters of doctrine, and the most indwelt and guided by the Holy Spirit, also tend to disagree the most about some of the most important Christian doctrines (such as the role of the human will in salvation, the nature of the church, the nature of the Eucharist, the role of works in the preservation or loss of salvation, etc.). This question, is, in itself, of the utmost importance, but we

---

[6] An example of a partially orthodox theologian would be Pelagius, who affirmed, without hesitation, the Nicaean Creed, but who denied some theological claims which, though not in the creed, were held by all Christians to be true.

[7] Alister E. McGrath and Darren C. Marks, "Introduction: Protestantism – the Problem of Identity," in *The Blackwell Companion to Protestantism*, ed. Alister E. McGrath and Darren C. Marks (Oxford: Blackwell Publishing, 2004), 14.

can address it only briefly here, by considering how Protestants have traditionally solved this problem.

Standards of Protestant Orthodoxy

There have been at least three traditional ways in which Protestants have determined orthodoxy. We will not, here, be debating the relevance, coherence, or relative importance of these ways. For the purposes of this article it is only necessary to name and explain them. They are: (1) *Via* close to undebatable interpretation of some biblical text(s), such that other possible interpretations are either demonstrably false or overly strained, and a clear doctrine can be drawn out of the passage(s) in question; (2) *Via* Confessions, Catechisms, and Creeds, which were purported to represent, at best, the doctrinal claims which are proposed as orthodox for certain denominations of Protestantism; and (3) *Via* close to unanimous teaching amongst the great theologians about some one doctrine, whether this be throughout the entire history of the church (c. 100AD to the present) or just since the Reformation. It is my humble opinion that, to these three tests of orthodoxy, which have frequently been explicitly mentioned in Protestant writings of different sorts, we may add a fourth test, (4) *Via* close to undebatable interpretation of some natural truths, such that other possible interpretations are either demonstrably false, overly strained, incoherent, or otherwise fallacious, and such that a true conclusion can be drawn out of the observations in question.

Some Protestant denominations have put more emphasis on one or another of these different ways of determining orthodoxy. For example, many Baptist denominations have tended to reject all forms of Confessions, Creeds, and Catechisms—claiming that the Bible alone could be authoritative. Many Presbyterian, or broadly Reformed, churches have tended to create confessions and catechisms in order to determine that which would be considered right belief. Most theologians are familiar with the Fundamentalist movement of the early 1900s which sought to establish and defend a list of authoritative doctrines which were necessary for orthodoxy belief, regardless of denomination.

In this article we will not attempt to argue that one or another of these ways should be given precedence in determining orthodoxy. We propose that, that if some doctrine passes all four tests, then it is a necessary part of Christian orthodoxy. Thus, accepting all four of these tests, we will ask the following question: What is the status of Natural Theology when judged according to these standards? Before we can answer this question, however, we must be clear about what we mean by "Natural Theology," and it is to this that we now turn.

NATURAL THEOLOGY

One would think that providing a definition of Natural Theology should be fairly straight-forward. Unfortunately, there is much confusion about just what is meant by Natural Theology. As such we will begin by providing a general definition of what we mean by Natural Theology, followed by an explanation of what we do not mean by Natural Theology.

Natural Theology, broadly defined, is that part of philosophy which explores that which man can know about God (his existence, divine nature, etc.) from nature *via* His divinely bestowed faculty of reason, and this, unaided by any divinely inspired written revelation from any religion, and this, without presupposing the truth of any one religion.

We must distinguish our definition of Natural Theology from a number of other concepts. Natural Theology, so defined, is not co-extensive with what some have called *Natural Revelation.* Natural Revelation is to Natural Theology as the Bible is to Biblical Theology. That is, Natural Revelation is, as John Calvin says, what God does when He manifests "his perfections in the whole structure of the universe," and, so manifests Himself daily, "in our view, that we cannot open our eyes without being compelled to behold him."[8] *Natural Revelation* is made up of the traces or footprints of God as they are seen by all men (regenerate and unregenerate) in creation.[9] Natural Revelation is the material with which Natural Theology works, just as the Bible is the material with which Biblical Theology works.

---

[8] John Calvin, *Institutes of the Christian Religion*, trans. Henry Beveridge (2007; repr., Peabody, MA: Hendrickson Publishers, 2012), 16.

[9] See the French edition of the *Institutes* that was republished in 1888 (Jean Calvin, *Institutes de la religion chrétienne*, nouvelle édition, éd. Frank Baumgartner [Génève : E. Béroud & Cie, éditeurs, 1888]), t.1, c.5, s. 6. In French we read, « Je voulais seulement observer ici qu'il y a une voie commune aux païens et aux croyants de l'église de rechercher Dieu, en suivant ses traces, comme ils sont esquissée dans le firmament et sur la terre, comme les peintures de son image. » Calvin here says, my translation, "I just wanted to note here that there is a way to seek God that is common to pagans and to believers of the church, by following in his footsteps, as they are outlined in the heavens and on earth, as paintings of his image."

Natural Theology, so defined, is also not co-extensive with what some have called *Natural Religion.*[10] Natural Religion was, historically, the attempt by a number of Deistic philosophers to make that which can be known of God *via* Natural Revelation into a Religion in its own right.[11] The ambiguous conflation of Natural Theology and Natural Religion has caused many people to reject Natural Theology, thinking that they were rejecting (as they should) Natural Religion. We distinguish, in this article, Natural Theology and

---

[10] This is the case in spite of the fact that some theologians have erroneously equated these two concepts. Cf. John Macpherson, *The Westminster Confession of Faith with Introduction and Notes*, in *HandBooks for Bible Classes*, ed. Marcus Dods and Alexander Whyte (Edinburgh: T.&T. Clarke, 1881), 29. Another writer who demonstrates some confusion concerning these terms is David Foster, "'In Every Drop of Dew': Imagination and the Rhetoric of Assent in English Natural Religion," *Rhetorica: A Journal of the History of Rhetoric* 12, no. 3 (1994): 293–325. In his article "Concerning Natural Religion," W. W. Fenn notes the difficulty of defining this term, in light of the fact that "since the term is variously understood by 'divines and learned men.'" (W.W. Fenn, "Concerning Natural Religion," *The Harvard Theological Review*, vol. 4, no. 4 (1911): 460.) The fact that this term is given so many different meanings may be partially due to those who, being card-carrying orthodox Christians, were also seeking to engage in Natural Theology. In order to be clear on what we mean by Natural Theology, though, we will need to clearly distinguish it from Natural Religion. Even John Henry Blunt's article on Natural Religion seems to conflate Natural Religion and Natural Theology ("Religion, Natural," in *Dictionary of Doctrinal and Historical Theology*, 2nd ed., ed. John Henry Blunt (London: Rivingtons, 1872), 630).

[11] Cf. "Deism," in *Dictionary of Doctrinal and Historical Theology*, 2nd ed., ed. John Henry Blunt (London: Rivingtons, 1872), 194–96. Edmund Gurney, "Natural Religion," *Mind* 8, no. 30 (1883): 198–221. Fenn, "Concerning Natural Religion," 461. William Warren Sweet, "Natural Religion and Religious Liberty in America," *The Journal of Religion* 25, no. 1 (1945): 45–55. A. Owen Aldridge, "Natural Religion and Deism in America before Ethan Allen and Thomas Paine," *The William and Mary Quarterly* 54, no. 4 (1997): 835–48. Aldridge notes a confusion between Natural Theology and Natural Religion, but proposes a distinction which seems, to us, a distinction without a difference. He says, "Another confusion exists between the terms 'natural religion' and 'natural theology.' The first was used by Jean Bodin in the late sixteenth century and the second by Gottfried Wilhelm Leibniz early in the eighteenth. In the strictest sense, natural religion comprises mainly cosmic evidence to prove the existence and providence of God, whereas natural theology forms one of the branches of metaphysics dealing with the deity" (Aldridge, "Natural Religion and Deism in America," 836). We propose that it is better to understand Natural Theology as that part of philosophy which "interprets" natural revelation (whose observations are integrated into a properly Christian Systematic Theology), and that Natural Religion should be understood as that attempt to worship the God of the Philosophers which eventually turned into Deism.

Natural Religion. Natural Theology is not a religion in and of itself. It is, rather, a part of philosophy which is integrated into Christian Systematic Theology; and, which, if separated from that theology which is acquired through the right reading of Holy Scriptures, tends to turn into that monster which became known as Natural Religion. However, it is not, as defined above, Natural Religion in the technical sense of the term.

Natural Theology is not the claim that all the truths of Christianity can be proved *via* human reasoning, without the aid of divinely inspired scriptures. Rather, Natural Theology, properly understood, does not venture to say anything about that which can be known only through divine revelation, such as, that Jesus was born of a virgin, that Jesus is God, that God is Triune, etc. Having made these distinctions, we are now in position to ask if Natural Theology, understood as that which can be known about God *via* rational human observations of our Universe (including ourselves), is a necessary part of protestant orthodoxy.

TESTING THE ORTHODOXY OF NATURAL THEOLOGY

Having defined Natural Theology, we will now attempt to test the orthodoxy or unorthodoxy of Natural Theology with the four ways of testing orthodoxy that we outlined above. We will first consider what the Bible says about Natural Theology, or, at least, the notion of Natural Theology that we see in our definition. We will then look, briefly, at what some of the greatest theologians of the church have said about the notion of Natural Theology that we see in our definition. We will continue with a brief glance at how some of the most important Protestant creeds approach Natural Theology, as defined above; and we will finish with some comments concerning how Natural Theology provides us with knowledge of God, and the coherency of Natural Theology in Christian Theology

The Bible of Natural Theology

When we consult the Scriptures, we find a number of verses that have traditionally been understood as saying that all men (regenerate and unregenerate) are able to know something about God by their simple, rational, observation of the universe. These verses include, but are certainly not limited to, Psalm 19:1-5; Acts 14:16-17 and 17:26-27; and Romans 1:19-

20, and 2:14-15. We cannot discuss each of these passages, so we will simply make some comments about Romans 1:19-20, where we read,

> "For what can be known about God is plain to them, because God has shown it to them. For his invisible attributes, namely, his eternal power and divine nature, have been clearly perceived, ever since the creation of the world, in the things that have been made. So they are without excuse."

Now, though to some the interpretation of these verses may seem fairly straightforward, their interpretation has been contested (though to be fair, not by very many). Cornelius Van Til, the father of Presuppositionalism, says, concerning Romans 1:19-20,

> Accordingly, it must now be added, as Calvin points out so fully on the basis of Paul's words, that God is displayed before men in the works of his hands. This means that God, not some sort of God or some higher principle, but God, the true God, is displayed before men. That is the fact of the matter, whether men recognize it or not. Paul does mention the power of God in particular as the attribute that comes most prominently to the foreground, but he also says that men have the divinity (Theiotes) displayed before them. This does not mean that God is as fully displayed in nature as he is in the gospel of Christ … All too often it has been argued that on the basis of nature or by natural theology man should be able to establish the existence of a God, while it is only by Christ and through grace that we can know anything more fully about the nature of this God. Now it is true that we have the fullest revelation of the nature of God in Christ. On the other hand, it is also true that when man was created in paradise [i.e., the Garden of Eden], he knew not merely of the existence of God, but he knew the nature of God as far as it had been revealed to him. It is for the loss of this actual knowledge of the nature of God that man, when he became a sinner, must be held responsible. If this is not done, men will be looked upon

> merely as unfortunates who have not had the good fortune of having had the right information about God.[12]

For Van Til, the rejection of the knowledge of God to which Romans 1:18-21 refers, for which men are held responsible, happened at the Fall of Adam and Eve in the Garden of Eden. Is this the traditional interpretation of Romans 1:18-21?

Note, first of all, that for John Calvin these verses apply to all mankind, and are true of all men (regenerate and unregenerate) of all time.[13] John Calvin says, for example, "When he says that *God made* it [His own existence, power and eternal nature] *manifest to them*: the meaning is, that mankind was created to this end, that he be the contemplator of this excellent work, the world: that his eyes were given to him in order that seeing such a beautiful image, he would be brought to know the author himself that made it."[14] Calvin goes on to say that "But he [humankind] does not deduce, by himself, all the things that can be considered in God, but he shows that we come to know his power and eternal divinity. For it is of necessity that he who is the author of all things, be without beginning and consist of himself. "[15] He goes on to state that though such knowledge should bring us to worship the one true God, due to our blindness it does not. Rather, though we come to know of the existence and power of the one true God (in spite of our blindness), we cannot come to know this true God so as to worship Him (because of our blindness).[16] Thus, humans are guilty. But which humans? One final quote from Calvin's commentary on Romans should suffice to make this

---

[12] Cornelius Van Til, *An Introduction to Systematic Theology*, vol. 5 of *In Defense of the Faith* (1974; repr., Phillipsburg, NJ: Presbyterian and Reformed Publishing, 1982), 100.

[13] Jean Calvin, *Commentaires sur l'épîstre aux Romains*, dans *Commentaires de Jehan Calvin sur le Nouveau Testament* (Paris: Librairie de Ch. Meyrueis et co., 1855), 3:25–27.

[14] Calvin, *Commentaires*, 26. My translation. In French we read, "Quand il dit que *Dieu* le *leur a manifesté* : le sens est, que l'homme a esté créé à ceste fin qu'il fust contemplateur de cest excellent ouvrage du monde : que les yeux luy ont esté donnez afin qu'en regardant une si belle image, il soit amené à cognoistre l'autheur mesme qui l'a faite."

[15] Calvin, *Commentaires*, 26. My Translation. In French we read, « Or il ne déduit pas par le menu toutes les choses qui peuvent estre considérées en Dieu, mais il monstre qu'on parvient jusques à cognoistre sa puissance et Divinité éternelle. Car il faut nécessairement que celuy qui est autheur de toutes choses, soit sans commencement, et consiste de soy-mesme. »

[16] Calvin, *Commentaires*, 26.

point quite clear, "*Because they knew God.* He declares here, quite obviously, that God made a knowledge of his majesty flow down into the spirits of all men: which is to say that he has shown himself so much, by his works, that they are forced to see that which they do not seek by themselves, that is, that there is a God."[17] There can be no doubt as to how John Calvin thought these verses should be interpreted. But perhaps some would not consider him "up-to-date"? Let us consider, in closing, the thoughts of one of the most well-known contemporary Reformed commentators, Douglas Moo, thinks about the proper interpretation of Romans 1:18-21.

Douglas Moo answers the very question that we are asking here by noting the traditional answer, "Whose experience does Paul describe in these verses? Traditionally, it has been assumed almost without argument that Paul is depicting the situation of Gentiles."[18] He notes that some recent scholarship has attempted to argue that Paul was talking about Adam and Eve, and the experience of the Fall, but states that the evidence falls overwhelmingly in favour of the traditional interpretation,[19] with the qualification that these verses may also include the Jews (and, thus, be referring to all humanity).[20] Moo notes that there are some important elements in this text that force us to accept the interpretation by which these verses apply to all humans of all times: first of all, the Greek terms are in the aorist tense, and, "Scholars have long recognized that the Greek aorist tense does not, in itself, indicate 'one-time' action; it can depict action of all kinds, including continuous and repeated action. Some grammarians would go even further and claim that the aorist (even in the indicative mood) has, in itself, no indication of time of action either."[21] Therefore, it is better to understand this passage as being the experience of all men of all time. Secondly, "this view [the view espoused by Van Til: that these verses apply only to Adam

---

[17] Calvin, *Commentaires*, 26. My Translation. In French we read, « *Pource qu'ayons cognu Dieu.* Il déclare yci apertement, que Dieu a fait descouler dedans les esprits de tous hommes une cognoissance de sa majesté : c'est-à-dire qu'il s'est tellement démonstre par ses oeuvres, qu'il leur est force de veoir ce qu'ils ne cherchent pas d'euxmesmes, asçavoir qu'il y a quelque Dieu. »

[18] Douglas Moo, *The Epistle to the Romans*, NICNT (Grand Rapids, MI: Wm. B. Eerdmans Publishing, 1996), 96.

[19] Moo, *Epistle*, 96–98.

[20] Moo, *Epistle*, 97.

[21] Moo, *Epistle*, 98fn21.

and Eve] fails to explain the heart of this passage: the characterization of all those upon whom the wrath of God falls as those who possessed the truth of God but turned from it."[22] Moo concludes that, "Paul says more than that all people experienced the consequences of an original turning away from God, or even that all people shared such an original turning away. He insists that those who turned were also those who knew better, and who are consequently deserving of God's wrath. This, coupled with the obviously universal thrust of vv. 18 and 32, makes clear that this foolish and culpable rejection of the knowledge of God is repeated in every generation, by every individual."[23]

It seems, then, that one of the first Reformed theologians and Bible commentators (John Calvin), and at least one leading contemporary Reformed Bible commentator (Douglas Moo), agree, against Van Til, that Romans 1:18-21 is referring to the experience of all humans of all times—that is, that God's existence, power and divine nature is so manifest in the universe that all men know (at least in potency, if not in actuality) that God exists; but, because they reject this knowledge of God, they are reprehensible before God.[24] It would seem, then, that the notion of Natural Theology outlined above, is found clearly expressed in scriptures. It meets, therefore, the first standard of orthodoxy: close to undebatable interpretation of some biblical text(s), such that other possible interpretations are either demonstrably false or overly strained, and a clear doctrine can be drawn out of the passage(s) in question. We could stop at this point, and claim that, based upon the proper interpretation of a clear biblical passage, all those who affirm Natural Theology are orthodox, and all those who deny Natural Theology are unorthodox. Yet we think that it would be advisable to consider the other ways of determining orthodoxy.

The Great Theologians on Natural Theology

We have found that the notion of Natural Theology that we described above is overwhelmingly evident in the proper, and almost entirely undebatable,

---

[22] Moo, *Epistle*, 98.

[23] Moo, *Epistle*, 98.

[24] That this interpretation is the interpretation of the great majority of Biblical exegetes throughout the history of the Church (100 A.D. to the present) is evident to any who have taken the time to peruse the available commentaries.

interpretation of the Word of God; but what have the great theologians of the church thought about Natural Theology? We have already noted that at least two of the greatest contemporary theologians have denied the concept of Natural Theology that we have proposed above: Karl Barth and Cornelius Van Til. What do the others say?

There are so many important Christian theologians that it would be impossible to survey them all in this brief section. So, perhaps it would be admissible to mention the thoughts of just a couple fairly important Christian Theologians, such as Tertullian, Gregory of Nyssa, Thomas Aquinas, John Calvin, Francis Turretin, and J. Gresham Machen.[25]

Tertullian

According to Everett Ferguson, Tertullian taught (in *De Testimonio Animae*) that there are many truths that can be known naturally (from our observations of nature) by man, by reason alone, without the help of divine revelation, such as the existence of God, some divine attributes, the immortality of the soul, and the future judgment of man.[26]

---

[25] Be it noted that we could also consider the thoughts of, for example, Pietro Martyr Vermigli, *Loci communes*, caput 2, section 1, where he clearly says that Paul talks about that which is known of God, in Romans 1:19–20 "because many are the divine mysteries, to be attained naturally by anybody with small ability." (My translation. Pietro Martyr Vermigli, *Loci communes* [Genevae: Petrum Aubertum, 1624], 2). Benjamin Breckinridge Warfield, "The Idea of Systematic Theology," in *Studies in Theology*, vol. 9 of *The Works of Benjamin B. Warfield*, 49–87 (1932; repr., Grand Rapids, MI: Baker Book House, 2000). Benjamin Breckinridge Warfield, "The Task and Method of Systematic Theology," in *Studies in Theology*, vol. 9 of *The Works of Benjamin B. Warfield*, 91–114 (1932; repr., Grand Rapids, MI: Baker Book House, 2000). As well as, Charles Hodge, *Systematic Theology*, 3 vols (1940; repr., Peabody, Mass: Hendrickson Publishers, 2003). See especially the first 30 pages of volume 1. See also the Calvinist Baptist Theologian, A. H. Strong, *Systematic Theology*, 3 vols in 1 (1907; repr., Old Tappan, NJ: Fleming H. Revell Company, 1979). Herman Bavinck, *Reformed Dogmatics*, Abridged in one volume, ed. John Bolt (Grand Rapids, MI: Baker Academic, 2011), 159. I suppose we could go on for a long time, mentioning such Christian theologians as Anselm, Boethius, Norman Geisler, R. C. Sproul, Aristides, etc.

[26] Everett Ferguson, "Tertullian," in *Early Christian Thinkers: The Lives and Legacies of Twelve Key Figures*, ed. Paul Foster (Downer's Grove, IL: InverVarsity Press, 2010), 89–90. Cf. Justo L. Gonzalez, "Athens and Jerusalem Revisited: Reason and Authority in Tertullian," *Church History* 43, no. 1 (1974): 18.

As he is providing us with a description of God, in his *Apologeticus*, Tertullian makes some interesting claims, which, if we are to take his words seriously, sound very much like a somewhat confused attempt at a demonstration of the existence of God. In spite of the ambiguity of his argument, he very clearly claims that man is able to have some knowledge of the one true God *via* his observations of Nature (including himself and his own thoughts and sensations). He introduces us to his approach to the natural knowledge that man can have of God with a paradox that is found in Christian doctrine, "The eye cannot see Him, though He is … visible. He is incomprehensible, though in grace He is manifested. He is beyond our utmost thought, though our human faculties conceive of Him. He is therefore equally real and great."[27] Note that Tertullian thinks that this paradox demonstrates both the greatness and the existence of God. Tertullian thinks that even though God is invisible, intangible, and incomprehensible, He somehow appears to humans such that man can know of Him through the human faculty of reason.

How, then, does Tertullian think that God is known by human reasoning? We do not find here an argument which demonstrates, conclusively, the existence of God, but it is clear that Tertullian thinks that we can prove the existence and greatness of God from the things that are presented to our senses.[28] He explicitly mentions that both God's creation that surrounds human's, and the human soul itself, testify to the existence and great power of God. So much so that those who ignore this truth are guilty for their ignorance.

> This it is [the notion mentioned in the quote in the previous paragraph] which gives some notion of God, while yet beyond all our conceptions—our very incapacity of fully grasping Him affords us the idea of what He really is. He is presented to our minds in His transcendent greatness, as at once known and unknown. And this is the crowning guilt of men, that they will not recognise One, of whom they cannot possibly be ignorant. Would you have the proof from the works of His hands, so numerous and so great,

---

[27] Tertullian, *Apologeticus*, in *The Writings of Tertullian*, vol. xi of *Translations of the Writings of the Fathers*, ed. Rev. Alexander Roberts and James Donaldson (Edinburgh: T&T Clarke, 1869), 1:86.

[28] Tertullian, *Apologeticus*, 1:86.

> which both contain you and sustain you, which minister at once to your enjoyment, and strike you with awe; or would you rather have it from the testimony of the soul itself?[29]

Following this question is a brief argument, by which Tertullian seeks to show that the human soul itself testifies to the existence of God.[30] As such, Tertullian clearly thinks that all of creation, human-beings included, testify to the existence, of "the One God, He who by His commanding word, His arranging wisdom, His mighty power, brought forth from nothing this entire mass of our world, with all its array of elements, bodies, spirits, for the glory of His majesty."[31] Creation and the human soul also make manifest that God is the judge of all men.[32] This idea is clearly based upon his interpretation of Romans 1:19-20 and 2:14-16. In his articulation of this position we see the beginnings of a conception of God (conception which we have already seen in Irenaeus) which will become very popular in the church—that is, that God is the most perfect Being possible. This notion will find its clearest articulation in the writings of Anselm. It is interesting to note the *negative theology* of Tertullian, manifest, for example, in the following quote: "but that which is infinite is known only to itself. This it is which gives some notion of God, while yet beyond all our conceptions—our very incapacity of fully grasping Him affords us the idea of what He really is. He is presented to our minds in His transcendent greatness, as at once known and unknown."[33]

Gregory of Nyssa

In the *Great Catechism* of Gregory of Nyssa we get a glimpse at his approach to what is typically called Natural Theology. In the prologue to the *Catechism* Gregory explains that it is not the case that "the same method of instruction will be suitable in the case of all who approach the word."[34] Rather, "The

---

[29] Tertullian, *Apologeticus*, 1:86–87.

[30] Tertullian, *Apologeticus*, 1:87.

[31] Tertullian, *Apologeticus*, 1:86.

[32] Tertullian, *Apologeticus*, 1:87.

[33] Tertullian, *Apologeticus*, 1:87.

[34] Gregory of Nyssa, *The Great Catechism*, in Series 2 of the *Nicene and Post-Nicene Fathers*, ed. Philip Schaff (NY: Christian Literature Publishing Co., 1892), 5:474.

catechism must be adapted to the diversities of their religious worship."[35] Gregory explains that "The method of recovery must be adapted to the form of the Disease. You will not by the same means cure the polytheism of the Greek, and the unbelief of the Jews as to the Only-begotten God … It is necessary, therefore, as I have said, to regard the opinions which the persons have taken up, and to frame your argument in accordance with the error into which each has fallen, by advancing in each discussion certain principles and reasonable propositions, that thus, through what is agreed upon on both sides, the truth may conclusively be brought to light."[36] In other words, whenever one enters into dialogue with a person who holds a position other than the truth of Christianity, we must begin by discovering what authorities or beliefs we hold in common with the other person. Once we have discovered "what is agreed upon on both sides," then we may successfully bring them to recognize the truth of Christianity *via* "certain principles and reasonable propositions." Gregory, in what follows, discusses how to properly begin a discussion with people who hold different positions, from the Atheist to the Heretic.[37]

Turning to the question of the existence of God, for Gregory recognizes that some people deny that one God exists, Gregory says, concerning our interlocutor, that "Should he say there is no God, then, form the consideration of the skilful and wise economy of the Universe he will be brought to acknowledge that there is a certain overmastering power manifested through these channels."[38] In other words, Gregory thinks that we can prove the existence of God *via* an argument that is based upon our rational observations of nature, and which takes the form of Design or organisation argument. That is, we live in a world—a unified system of different beings—which demonstrates a certain order and planning. It is a platitude to say that planning and order, in a unified system of different beings, are the product of an intelligent Planner and Organizer. Therefore, our world is the product of an intelligent Planner and Organizer.[39]

---

[35] Gregory of Nyssa, *The Great Catechism,* 5:474.

[36] Gregory of Nyssa, *The Great Catechism,* 5:474.

[37] Gregory of Nyssa, *The Great Catechism,* 5:474.

[38] Gregory of Nyssa, *The Great Catechism,* 5:474.

[39] We could also note that Gregory of Nazianzus, another of the important Cappadocian Fathers, expressly states, in his well-known Homily *On Theology*, that man can know something of God from his observations of nature. He compares

Thomas Aquinas

It is well-known that Thomas Aquinas thought that Natural Theology, as we defined it above, was not only possible, but biblically supported by the clear reading of Scriptures. In the first article of the first question of the *Summa Theologiae*, Thomas Aquinas states that though humans could come to some knowledge of God *via* their thinking about their observations of nature (though it was a long process filled with many errors about God), it was necessary for God to divinely reveal those truths that were necessary for man's salvation.[40] It is important to note the context of this statement. The first article of the first question asks, "Whether is is necessary, over and above the philosophical disciplines, to have another doctrine?" This other doctrine is Sacred Theology (based upon Holy Scriptures). This question was necessary, for, as Aquinas notes in his *respondeo*, the philosophers have been able to come, *via* human reasoning alone, to knowledge of the nature of God, and of the fact that God exists. If man is able, by reasoning alone, to come to knowledge of the existence and nature of God, of the immortality of the human soul, and of a future judgement, then what is the purpose of sacred doctrine? To this question, Aquinas states that Sacred doctrine was necessary for the salvation of man. This could be considered as something of a precursor to Calvin's Creator/Saviour distinction.

We could certainly elaborate on Aquinas's view of what we have called Natural Theology, considering his other works (especially the *Summa Contra Gentiles*, and the *Commentary on the* De Trinitate *of Boethius*), but we think that most scholars are willing to accept that Aquinas held that Natural Theology, as we have defined it above, was both possible and necessary for Christian theology. Furthermore, we will not belabour Aquinas's approach, for the simple fact that we are trying to determine whether or not Natural Theology is necessary for orthodox Protestant belief, and many Protestants explicitly reject just about anything that Aquinas says, for the simple reason that

---

three sources of knowledge about God (Nature, Holy Scriptures, and the beatific vision), such that we might say that Natural Theology is like a candle, Holy Scriptures like a spot light (casting direct light on certain very important things that we must know about God), and the beatific vision like looking directly into the sun (or being absorbed by it). Cf. Gregory of Nazianzus, *On Theology*, in *Five Theological Orations*, trans. and ed. Stephen Reynolds (Toronto, ON: Trinity College, 2011), 13–44.

[40] Thomas Aquinas, *Summa Theologiae* I, q. 1, a. 1, *respondeo*.

Aquinas said it. Let's look, instead, at some more authoritative figures for contemporary Protestants.

John Calvin

John Calvin states, concerning human knowledge of God, first of all, that "By knowledge of God, I understand that by which we not only conceive that there is some God, but also apprehend what it is for our interest, and conducive to his glory, what, in short, it is befitting to know concerning him."[41] The question that we must now ask is, Can man attain to knowledge of God? To this Calvin's answer is a resounding "Yes!" Not only can the regenerated man attain to knowledge of God, but the unregenerate man can also attain some knowledge of God.[42] Indeed, as is well known and attested, Calvin claims that all men, regenerate or unregenerate, have within them the *sensus divinitatis* (the sense of deity). He states, for example,

> "That there exists in the human minds and indeed by natural instinct, some sense of deity, we hold to be beyond dispute, since God himself, to prevent any man from pretending ignorance, has endued all men with some idea of his Godhead, the memory of which he constantly renews and occasionally enlarges, that all to a man being aware that there is a God, and that he is their Maker, may be condemned by their own conscience when they neither worship him nor consecrate their lives to his service."[43]

Finally, Calvin states that God reveals Himself to man in nature, in three ways: (1) through creation itself, (2) through man's nature & man's history, and (3) through Gods providential control of the creation and man. Take, for example, this statement:

> "He [God] has been pleased, in order that none might be excluded from the means of obtaining felicity ["the perfection of blessedness [felicity] consists in the knowledge

[41] John Calvin, *Institutes of the Christian Religion*, trans. Henry Beveridge (2007; repr., Peabody, MA: Hendrickson Publishers, 2012), 7.

[42] Calvin, *Institutes*, 4.

[43] Calvin, *Institutes*, 9. Cf. Calvin, *Institutes*, 10.

> of God"], not only to deposit in our minds that seed of religion of which we have already spoken [the *sensus divinitatis*], but so to manifest his perfections in the whole structure of the universe, and daily place himself in our view, that we cannot open our eyes without being compelled to behold him. His essence, indeed, is incomprehensible, utterly transcending all human thought; but on each of his works his glory is engraved in characters so bright, so distinct, and so illustrious, that none, however dull and illiterate, can plead ignorance as their excuse."[44]

Here Calvin states that God has not only given to all men (regenerate and unregenerate) the *sensus divinitatis*, but, on top of that, He also gives to all men, in nature (in all the things He has created), the proof of his existence and glory. This knowledge of God, attained through the contemplation of creation, is available to all men, everywhere, regenerate or not.

Concerning the notion of "common ground" between the regenerate and the unregenerate, let us look at the very words of John Calvin, who, in his *Institutes of the Christian Religion*, states that the fact that humankind (regenerate and unregenerate) *can* know God through His creation just is common ground between the regenerate and the non-regenerate. Calvin explicitly states, "I just wanted to note here that there is a way to seek God that is *common* to pagans and to believers of the church, by following in his footsteps, as they are outlined in the heavens and on earth, as paintings of his image."[45] So, Presuppositionalism, by claiming that there is *no* common ground between believers and unbelievers, and by claiming that unbelievers are unable to come to some knowledge of the true God through their observations of nature, explicitly rejects a biblical teaching that John Calvin himself explicitly held to be true.

---

[44] Calvin, *Institutes*, 16.

[45] Calvin, *IRC*, t.1, c.5, s. 6. My translation. Italics are mine. In French we read, « Je voulais seulement observer ici qu'il y a une voie commune aux païens et aux croyants de l'église de rechercher Dieu, en suivant ses traces, comme ils sont esquissés dans le firmament et sur la terre, comme les peintures de son image. » Beveridge translates this line as: "I only wish to observe here that this method of investigating the divine perfections, by tracing the lineament of his countenance as shadowed forth in the firmament and on the earth, is common both to those within and to those without the pale of the church." (Calvin, *IRC*, trans. Beveridge, 20.)

Francis Turretin

Turning to one who is, without a doubt, one of the greatest Reformed theologians, Francis Turretin, we discover that Presuppositionalism should be considered as Unorthodox by all Reformed thinkers. Why is this? Turretin, in the first couple pages of his *Institutes of Elenctic Theology*, writes (in opposition to the heresies of the Socinians, who denied that the unregenerate people could acquire some knowledge of God from nature with the unaided reason and "who deny the existence of any such natural theology or knowledge of God")[46] that "The orthodox, on the contrary, uniformly teach that there is a natural theology, partly innate (derived from the book of conscience by means of common notions [*koinas ennoias*]) and partly acquired (drawn from the book of creatures discursively)."[47] It seems, then, that in so much as Presuppositionalism denies that the unregenerate can actually know something of the true God from their observations of nature, it is unorthodox. Indeed, Turretin explicitly refutes, in the name of orthodoxy, Van Til's claim that prior to the Fall humans could know something of the true God from their unaided observations of the universe, but that after the Fall they could not.[48] Turretin explicitly states that natural theology does not concern knowledge of God that man had prior to the fall, "Nor does it concern this as it was in Adam before the fall."[49] "[R]ather," Turretin goes on, "it concerns this as it remained after the fall."[50] Therefore, for Turretin, Natural Theology is knowledge of God that can be obtained by fallen humans, even in their fallen, unregenerate state. Later in the *Institutes*, Turretin lays forth a number of arguments by which he seeks to demonstrate that God exists. The various arguments are based upon subordinate causes, the newness of the world, the beauty of the universe, the tendency of each thing to its appropriate end (as in the 5th way of Thomas Aquinas), human conscience, and the religious nature of man.

---

[46] Francis Turretin, *Institutes of Elenctic Theology*, trans. George Musgrave Giger, ed. James T Dennison, Jr. (Phillipsburg, NJ: P&R Publishing: 1992–97), 1:6.

[47] Turretin, *IET*, 1:6.

[48] Cf. Cornelius Van Til, *An Introduction to Systematic Theology*, vol. 5 of *In Defense of the Faith* (1974; repr., Phillipsburg, NJ: Presbyterian and Reformed Publishing, 1982), 100.

[49] Turretin, *IET*, 6.

[50] Turretin, *IET*, 6.

J. Gresham Machen

What about the very school where Van Til (the undisputed founder of Presuppositionalism) taught for almost his entire teaching career? We find that the founder of Westminster Theological Seminary in Pennsylvania, J. Gresham Machen, disagreed entirely with Van Til on the possibility of demonstrating the existence of God. In his well-known book, *The Christian Faith in the Modern World*, Machen explicitly states that the first place where God reveals Himself to man in the universe that He created.[51] He explains that God's self-testimony in the universe that He created comes to different people in different ways, by: (1) the natural sciences and the complexity and order that they discover in the natural world, (2) philosophy and ontological arguments which begin with the very existence of the universe, and (3) the existential experience of transcendence.[52] Machen, indeed, thinks that the many philosophical arguments that demonstrate the existence of God provide good evidence, and that the Christian man, whether he has a detailed knowledge of them or not, should never devalue or regard them as being of no importance in the debate concerning the existence of God.[53]

We could continue but the interested reader can go read the rest for themselves. We think that we have sufficiently shown that the great majority of the great theologians, both in the entire history of the church, and since the Reform, have declared unashamedly that Natural Theology was both possible and a clear biblical doctrine. We have now shown, therefore, that based upon two of the three Protestant ways of measuring orthodoxy, those who deny Natural Theology are unorthodox, and those who accept Natural Theology are orthodox. There remains one way, via the major confessions, creeds and catechisms.

The Confessions, Creeds, and Catechisms

We need to keep this last section relatively short, so we will restrain our comments to two very important creeds: (1) *the French Confession of Faith*, written by John Calvin himself, and approved by Theodore Beza, and (2) the

---

[51] J. Gresham Machen, *The Christian Faith in the Modern World* (Grand Rapids, MI: Wm. B. Eerdmans Publishing, 1965), 15.

[52] Machen, *The Christian Faith*, 17.

[53] Machen, *The Christian Faith*, 16.

most popular and well-known Protestant confession, the *Westminster Confession*.[54]

The French Confession of Faith: Confessio Fidei Gallicana

The *French Confession of Faith* was prepared, according to Philip Schaff, by John Calvin and his pupil, De Chandieu, and approved by the 1559 synod of Paris.[55] It was delivered by Theodore de Beza in 1561 to Charles IX, and adopted by the Synod of La Rochelle in 1571.[56] This confession was translated into a number of languages, including German, Latin, and English.[57] The confession begins, "Confession de foi, faite d'un commun accord par les François, qui desirent vivre selon la pureté de l'évangile de notre Seigneur Jésus-Christ. A.D. 1559."[58] We see, then, that this confession is seen by Calvin, Beza, and the other great reformers of the 1500s as being both (1) in line with the Gospel of Jesus-Christ, and (2) a test for orthodoxy—in order to be seen as living according to the purity of the Gospel you must agree with this Confession. What, then, do they confess concerning the knowledge of God that man can gain from his rational consideration of Creation? Article 2 begins as follows, "This God so manifests himself to men, first by his works, as much through their creation as through their conservation and direction. Secondly and with greater clarity, through his Word, which being first revealed through oracles, was afterwards

---

[54] Be it noted that *the Baptist confession of 1689* (which was accepted and promoted by men such as Charles Haddon Spurgeon and Andrew Gifford, along with all of the leaders of the Reformed Baptist Churches of London), *the Belgic Confession, or La Confession de Foi des Églises Chrétiennes Évangéliques de Belgique* (which was also approved by, and used by, Theodore Beza, and accepted at the Synod of Dort), *the Confession of the Waldenses* of 1655, *A short Baptist confession of Faith from the Baptist churches of Amsterdam, one of the first General Baptist Confessions* from 1651, the *Canons of the Synod of Dort*, and a number of other confessions, all affirm, as clearly as the Westminster Confession (or clearer), that Natural Theology is a necessary element of true orthodox theology.

[55] Philip Schaff, *The Creeds of Christendom* (New York: Harper & Brothers, 1877), 3:356.

[56] Schaff, *CC*, 3:356.

[57] Schaff, *CC*, 3:356.

[58] Schaff, *CC*, 3:359. Schaff provides the following translation of this comment, "Confession of Faith, made in one accord by the French people, who desire to live according to the purity of the Gospel of our Lord Jesus Christ. A.D. 1559." (Schaff, *CC*, 3:359.)

written in those books which we call Holy Scriptures."[59] Note that this confession, written by Calvin and his colleagues, clearly states that God makes Himself known to men in two ways. The first is through His works, and this through the conservation of His works and by His providential direction of it. This claim is in direct accordance with Calvin's clear teaching in his *Institutes* about the knowledge that unregenerate men can have of God via human reasoning about Creation. He supports the claims in this article by referring the reader to Romans 1:20, where—think Calvin and the other Reformers—we find the proof that humans can acquire some knowledge of God (not sufficient for salvation) through the reasoned consideration of nature.

The Westminster Confession of Faith, 1647

The *Westminster Confession of Faith* is probably one of the most well-known Protestant confessions, and is taken to be the standard of faith by Reformed and Presbyterian churches and Seminaries around the world. Schaff notes that "The Westminster Confession sets forth the Calvinistic system in its scholastic maturity after it had passed through the sharp conflict with Arminianism in Holland, and as it had shaped itself in the minds of Scotch Presbyterians and English Puritans during their conflict with High-Church prelacy."[60] Concerning the purpose of the Westminster Confession, we are told by William Dunlop that one of the primary reasons for the composition of the Westminster Confession was, "to secure the purity of the *christian doctrine* from the many contagious *heresies* which in all ages have infested the *church*; to distinguish betwixt those who were infected by prevailing *error*, and such as persevered in the uncorrupted *faith* of the *gospel*, and so to discover who in this respect should be admitted into the *communion of saints*, or might without danger to religion and truth be ordained to, or continued in the sacred *office* of the *ministry*."[61] Note that this Confession was to be used to

---

[59] Schaff, *CC*, 3:360. My Translation. In French we read, « Ce Dieu se manifeste tel aux hommes, premièrement par ses œuvres, tant par la création que par la conservation et conduite d'icelles. Secondement et plus clairement, par sa Parole, laquelle au commencement révélée par oracles, a été puis après rédigé par écrit aux livres que nous appelons l'Ecriture sainte. »

[60] Philip Schaff, *The Creeds of Christendom* (New York: Harper & Brothers, 1877), 1:760.

[61] William Dunlop, *A Preface to an Edition of the Westminster Confession*, 2nd ed. (London: T. Cox, 1724), 43. Italics are in the original. Be it noted that the full title of this work

discern between who was orthodox and unorthodox, and, thus, who could be accepted into the communion of the Church, and allowed to serve in a ministerial office.[62] If someone disagreed with the statements of the Confession they were to be excluded from communion, and could not hold a ministerial office. Dunlop continues by noting that "*Creeds* and *Confessions* have been thus used as a test of orthodoxy in all ages and in all places."[63] Furthermore, when the Reform took place, the reformers "did not altogether reject *Creeds* and *Confessions*, but rectifying the great abuses of them, still continued them as a means of preserving the purity of christian doctrine, and preventing the spreading of *heresy*."[64]

Concerning the role of human reason in knowing God, Schaff notes that, "The confession gives to reason, or the light of nature, its proper place."[65] What is that "proper place"? Some might suggest that it is outside of the Church, but when we read the Confession, we find that the role of reason in acquiring some knowledge of the one true God is affirmed, "Although the Light of Nature, and the works of Creation and Providence do so far manifest the Goodness, Wisdom, and Power of God, as to leave men unexcusable; yet are they not sufficient to give that knowledge of God

---

is: *A Preface To An Edition of the Westminster Confession, &c. Lately publish'd at Edinburgh. Being a full and particular Account Of all the Ends and Uses of Creeds and Confessions of Faith: A Defence of their Justice, Reasonableness and Necessity,* **As Public Standard of Orthodoxy** *AND An Examination ot the Principal Objections brought by different Authors against them; especially such as are to be found in the Works of Ensconus and LeClerk; in the Rights of the Christian Church, and in the Occasional Papers.* The part of the title that I have highlighted in bold is in bold in the original title. Note that for those who both received and wrote the Westminster Creed, it was understood as a standard of Orthodoxy for all protestants. He who disagreed with this creed, in any point, was unorthodox (as far as that point was concerned). As unorthodox they were invited to return to True Christian Belief.

[62] Dunlop also points out that in the Acts of the General Assemblies of 1690 and 1700, it was stated that all church leaders were to subscribe to the Confession, in its entirety (Cf. Dunlop, *PEWC*, 64). He quotes the formula that all church leaders were to state prior to being allowed to serve in a church, "I do sincerely own and declare the above Confession of Faith, approven by former general assemblies of this church, and ratified by laws in the year 1690, to be the Confession of my Faith; and that I own the doctrine therein contained to be the true doctrine which I will constantly adhere to." (Dunlop, *PEWC*, 64–65.)

[63] Dunlop, *PEWC*, 43. Italics in the original.

[64] Dunlop, *PEWC*, 44. Italics in the original.

[65] Schaff, *CC*, 1:767.

and of his Will, which is necessary unto salvation."[66] This claim is supported, as we have already seen in the other confessions, by reference to Romans 2:14-15, 1:19-20, Ps. 19:1-3, etc. Note, again, that the group of Protestant scholars and pastors who wrote, discussed, and eventually produced this authoritative document saw fit to state that Nature, the works of Creation, and divine Providence over creation, manifest, clearly to all men, a number of the attributes of God: Wisdom, Goodness and Power. John Macpherson, writing an authoritative commentary on the Westminster Confession, notes, concerning this first article, that "Their whole system [the system of those who wrote the Westminster Confession] may be estimated by an examination of their first article."[67] Furthermore, they believed that this claim was based upon Scripture properly interpreted. Finally, they thought that adherence to this belief, which is the foundational claim for Natural Theology, is necessary for Orthodoxy.

According to Macpherson, "Full acknowledgement is made of the importance of natural religion within its own province. Apart from a divine revelation as an oral communication of God's will, man may arrive at a knowledge of God's being, and at least a partial perception of His character."[68] Note that what Macpherson means by "natural religion" is what we are referring to when we use the term "natural theology." According to the Westminster Confession, though one's salvation is not placed in doubt based upon their rejection of Natural Theology (that is, one may still be saved without accepting the biblical truth of Natural Theology), if you reject Natural Theology, then you are unorthodox. Macpherson notes that "The statement of our Confession sufficiently guards against errors [thus against unorthodoxy or heresy] in two extreme directions. On the one hand, some pious men were led to deny altogether the reality of natural religion … On the other hand, the English Deists started with the assertion that all true knowledge, that of religion as well as of science and philosophy, is derived from the same revelation,—understanding by revelation simply the discoveries of man in the exercise of his natural powers."[69] Thus, according

---

[66] Schaff, *CC*, 3:599, 600.

[67] John Macpherson, *The Westminster Confession of Faith with Introduction and Notes*, in *HandBooks for Bible Classes*, ed. Marcus Dods and Alexander Whyte (Edinburgh: T&T Clarke, 1881), 29.

[68] Macpherson, *Westminster Confession*, 29.

[69] Macpherson, *Westminster Confession*, 29–30.

to Macpherson, the purpose of the above noted statement in the Westminster Confession is to keep the believer from following into two equally unorthodox positions: (1) denying the reality of Natural Theology, and (2) Making Natural Theology the be-all and end-all of Christian Revelation—only Natural Theology being necessary. In other words, those who deny the reality of Natural Theology—that humans can know something of God via their reasoned observations of Nature—are, according to the *Westminster Confession*, Unorthodox.

In case there was any confusion as to what was meant by the above quoted statement from the first article of the *Westminster Confession*, we are able to support our interpretation of this statement by referring the reader to the *Westminster Larger Catechism*. The Catechism was designed as a way of teaching, dialectically, the doctrines that are affirmed in the Confession. Note the second question in the *Westminster Larger Catechism*,[70] "Q. *How doth it appear that there is a God?* A. The very light of nature in man, and the works of God, declare plainly that there is a God: but his Word and Spirit only do sufficiently and effectually reveal him unto men for their salvation."[71] Almost no comment is required here! How do we know that there is a God? By the very natural light in man, by the creation of God, which clearly manifest His existence. All men can know that God exists in this way, but this natural knowledge of God is not sufficient for salvation. It is, however, still true knowledge of the one true God.[72]

---

[70] This question does not appear in the *Shorter Catechism*.

[71] Schaff, *CC*, 3: 675.

[72] In support of our understanding of both the *Westminster Confession* and the article in the *Larger Catechism*, we point the reader to the work of Thomas Ridgley, *A Body of Divinity: wherein the Doctrines of the Christian Religion are explained and defended. Being the Substance of several lectures on the Assemblies Larger Catechism*. Here Ridgley first quotes the question, and answer, that we have noted above. He then asks the question, "*Why proofs of the being of God should be studied*." (Thomas Ridgley, *A Body of Divinity*, ed. John M. Wilson [New York: Robert Carter & Brothers, 1855], 1:9. Italics in the original.) To this question Ridgley provides four reasons, the first being that the existence of God is fundamental to both natural theology and revealed religion. After having provided three other reasons for studying the proofs of the existence of God, Ridgley moves on to consider the proofs of the existence of God. The first point that he treats, before even arriving at the arguments that show that God exist, is an explanation of the statement that the natural light of man clearly shows that God exists. Here he states that, "By this we understand that reason which he is endowed with; whereby he is distinguished from, and rendered superior to, all other creatures in this lower world; and whereby he is able to observe the connection of things, and

THE TESTIMONY OF CREATION AND NATURAL THEOLOGY

Turning to the fourth and final test of orthodoxy—close to undebatable interpretation of the created universe—we discover that some very important Christian teachings either depend upon natural knowledge of God, or can only be known through natural knowledge of God. For example, as was noted in the section on the biblical teaching concerning Natural Theology, Paul's entire argument, in Romans 1-3, by which he shows that all men are guilty before God, and rightly fall under the righteous wrath of God, depends upon the fact that Romans 1:19-20 is true of all mankind (or, at least, of all Gentiles). Paul's argument, in Romans 1-3, could be roughly outlined as follows: (1) There are three types of people in the world: Jews, righteous gentiles and unrighteous Gentiles. (2) All unrighteous Gentiles rightly fall under that righteous wrath of God (Romans 1:18-32). (3) All righteous Gentiles rightly fall under the righteous wrath of God (Romans 2:1-16). (4) All Jews rightly fall under the righteous wrath of God (Romans 2:17-3:8) (5) Therefore, all humanity falls under the righteous wrath of God (Romans 3:9-20). This entire argument depends on, first of all, the fact that all Gentiles come to some knowledge of God through their rational observations of the universe, and that they all have some knowledge of the immorality of the actions they approve (the Jews do not need this approach to knowledge of God, as they have the prophets and the Law); and, secondly, the fact that all Gentiles reject this knowledge of God, and this naturally known moral code. Thus, in the thought of Paul, Natural Theology, as we described it above, is the logical foundation for the doctrinal claim: "All of humanity rightly falls under the righteous wrath of God, and all of humanity is in need of the salvific act of Christ." Thus, Natural Theology, as described above, is necessary for orthodox Christian Theology.

Furthermore, and of equal importance, some of the most foundational of the divine attributes (such as Divine Simplicity, Immutability, and Impassibility) can only known through Natural Theology, and can only be

their dependence on one another, and to infer those consequences which may be deduced from thence. The reasoning powers of man, indeed, are very much sullied, depraved, and weakened, by our apostacy from God; but they are not wholly obliterated; for there are some remains of them, which are common to all nations,—whereby, without the help of special revelation, it may be known that there is a God" (Ridgley, *A Body of Divinity*, 1:10).

affirmed through the interaction of Natural and Biblical theology (we may turn to the *Summa Theologiae* for an example of how we come to know, *via* reason alone, that God exists, and is simple, immutable, impassible, eternal, perfect, good, etc.). The doctrines of divine simplicity, immutability, impassibility, and even divine eternity (which have come under attack in recent years, by those who claim to be Christian theologians), which also pass the 4 standards of Protestant Orthodoxy, are only known through Natural Theology. By rejecting Natural Theology, we also, at the same time, reject that which allows us to affirm these divine attributes (which we must affirm if we wish to affirm the traditionally orthodox doctrines concerning the nature of God). Reject one of these attributes, and we no longer have the God of traditional Christianity. Indeed, as many philosophers, both Christian and non-Christian, have noted, it is not only possible to demonstrate *that* God exists *via* reasoning based on observations of the natural world, but it is also possible to demonstrate, *via* reasoning, many of the divine attributes. These are just a couple of examples of how our rational observations of the created universe are necessary for Christian orthodoxy. Thus, we propose, Natural Theology also passes the fourth test of Christian orthodoxy.

CONCLUSIONS

Our research has shown, without a doubt, that by the application of all four Protestant ways for measuring orthodoxy, Natural Theology (as we defined it above) is a necessary element for complete orthodoxy. Though it may not be necessary for salvation to accept the truth that all men are able to know something about God via their rational observations of nature, it is necessary in order to be considered fully orthodox. We have seen that the Bible clearly teaches this doctrine, that the greatest theologians of the history of the church (both pre- and post-reformation) clearly teach this doctrine, and that the most important creeds and confessions of the Protestant church clearly teach this doctrine, that the traditional doctrine of God requires it, and that reason demands it. It follows, then, that in order to be considered fully orthodoxy, according to available Protestant standards for measuring orthodoxy, one must accept Natural Theology. Those who deny it, such as Karl Barth and Cornelius Van Til, must be considered, on this point, unorthodox.

Yet the question might be raised, why does this matter? Is this not just another case of theologians fighting over irrelevant questions? One might, of course, respond that it is important because it is clearly taught in the Bible, and this is certainly true. The fact that the doctrine of Natural Theology is based upon a proper interpretation of the Bible should be enough to convince anyone that it is important. However, as we saw when we discussed the coherency of Natural Theology within Christian theology, if we deny Natural Theology, we remove the very basis upon which Paul makes his case in Romans 1-3, that God is just when He condemns all humanity. The fact that humans can know something of God from their observations of nature, is the basis for the righteous judgement of God against all mankind—they knew, and can know, that God is the creator and provident sustainer of the created universe, yet they reject this truth and worship the creation. Furthermore, the fact that humans can know something of God from their observations of nature provides us with a starting point in our personal evangelism—drawing the attention of the unbeliever to the manifest evidence of the existence of a personal creator. Finally, Natural Theology provides us with, all at once, demonstrations of the existence of God, which have an *apologetic* value—defending the truths of the historic Christian faith; and knowledge of what God is not (for example, God is not temporal, God is not composed of parts, God is unchanging), which has a *theological* value—helping us to better interpret the scriptures when they talk about the nature of God, and bringing us to a greater appreciation of the majesty of the God we love, serve, and worship. In fact, these truths which can be known about God from nature also have a *practical or existential* value—bringing us ever before the provident God who wisely governs His creation, and reassuring us that if He takes cares of the flowers and the birds, He knows how to take care of us. These truths which can be known about God from nature have, finally, an *adorative* value—as, first of all, we only truly worship God when it is the true God we worship, but, secondly, when we are confronted with these truths about God we are compelled to fall to our knees in worship of the sovereign creator who transcends our world and our understanding.

Francis Brown writing in 1899 about the notion of Orthodoxy, stated:

> Orthodoxy is right thinking, or, by our usage, right thinking about religion. Nothing could be simpler. But as a matter of fact no one on earth knows, exactly and exhaustively, what right thinking about religion is. We have some right thoughts, perhaps many, but we have not all the right thoughts there are—we are ignorant about some things; nor are all our thoughts probably right—we are doubtless

> mistaken about some things. If we were exhaustively and exactly orthodox, there would be no religious truths of which we are ignorant, and all our thoughts about religious things would be right. We sometimes talk and act as if this were the case. But the case really is that only one Being is omniscient and all-wise … Although human orthodoxy is imperfect, we are not free from the obligation to be orthodoxy. Truth claims our allegiance.[73]

There is certainly much more that could be said about both Natural Theology and Protestant orthodoxy, but this much should be said: It is impossible to fully possess right opinion on Christian theology without affirming that all men are able to know something about God *via* their rational observations of nature.

[73] Brown, "What is Orthodoxy?," 409.

BIBLIOGRAPHY

Aldridge, A. Owen. "Natural Religion and Deism in America before Ethan Allen and Thomas Paine." *The William and Mary Quarterly* 54, no. 4 (1997): 835-48.

Barth, Karl. *NO!* In *Natural Theology*, edited by John Baillie. Eugene, OR: Wipf & Stock Publishers, 2002.

Bavinck, Herman. *Reformed Dogmatics*. Abridged in one volume. Edited by John Bolt. Grand Rapids, MI: Baker Academic, 2011.

Blunt, John Henry. *Dictionary of Doctrinal and Historical Theology*. Edited by John Henry Blunt. 2nd ed. London: Rivingtons, 1872.

Brown, Francis. "What is Orthodoxy?" *The North American Review*. 168, no. 509 (1899): 409-417.

Buck, Charles. "Orthodoxy." In *Fessenden & Co.'s Encyclopedia of Religious Knowledge*, edited by J. Newton Brown. Brattleboro, VT: Brattleboro Typographic Company, 1837.

Calvin, Jean. *Institutes de la religion chrétienne*. Nouvelle edition. Éd. Frank Baumgartner. Génève : E. Béroud & Cie, éditeurs, 1888.

——. *Commentaires sur l'épîstre aux Romains*. Dans *Commentaires de Jehan Calvin sur le Nouveau Testament*. Paris : Librairie de Ch. Meyrueis et co., 1855.

Calvin, John. *Institutes of the Christian Religion*. Translated by Henry Beveridge. 2007; repr., Peabody, MA: Hendrickson Publishers, 2012.

Chambers, T.W. "Orthodoxy and Heterodoxy." In *The Concise Dictionary of Religious Knowledge and Gazeteer*, edited by Samuel MacAuley Jackson, Talbot Wilson Chambers, and Frank Hugh Foster. 2nd ed. New York: The Christian Literature Company, 1891.

Davidson, James D. and Gary J. Quinn. "Theological and Sociological Uses of the Concept 'Orthodoxy.'" *Review of Religious Research* 18, no. 1 (1976): 74-80.

Dunlop, William. *A Preface to an Edition of the Westminster Confession*. 2nd ed. London: T. Cox, 1724.

Fenn, W. W. "Concerning Natural Religion." *The Harvard Theological Review* 4, no. 4 (1911): 460-476.

Foster, David. "'In Every Drop of Dew': Imagination and the Rhetoric of Assent in English Natural Religion." *Rhetorica: A Journal of the History of Rhetoric* 12, no. 3 (1994): 293-325.

Ferguson, Everett. "Tertullian." In *Early Christian Thinkers: The Lives and Legacies of Twelve Key Figures*, edited by Paul Foster, 85-99. Downer's Grove, IL: InverVarsity Press, 2010.

Gonzalez, Justo L. "Athens and Jerusalem Revisited: Reason and Authority in Tertullian." *Church History* 43, no. 1 (1974): 17-25.

Machen, J. Gresham. *The Christian Faith in the Modern World.* Grand Rapids, MI: Wm. B. Eerdmans Publishing, 1965.

Gregory of Nazianzus. *On Theology*, in *Five Theological Orations.* Edited and translated by Stephen Reynolds. Toronto, ON: Trinity College, 2011.

Gregory of Nyssa, *The Great Catechism.* In Series 2 of the *Nicene and Post-Nicene Fathers*, vol. 5, *Gregory of Nyssa: Dogmatic Treatises*, edited Philip Schaff, 469-509. NY: Christian Literature Publishing Co., 1892.

Gurney, Edmund. "Natural Religion." *Mind* 8, no. 30 (1883): 198-221.

Hodge, Charles. *Systematic Theology.* 3 vols. 1940; repr., Peabody, Mass: Hendrickson Publishers, 2003.

Hook, Walter Farquhar. "Orthodoxy." In *A Church Dictionary*, editor anonymous. 6th ed. Philadelphia: E. H. Butler, Co., 1854.

Macpherson, John. *The Westminster Confession of Faith with Introduction and Notes*, in *Handbooks for Bible Classes.* Edited by Marcus Dods and Alexander Whyte. Edinburgh: T.&T. Clarke, 1881.

McGrath, Alister E. and Darren C. Marks. "Introduction: Protestantism – the Problem of Identity." In *The Blackwell Companion to Protestantism*, edited by Alister E. McGrath and Darren C. Marks, 1-19. Oxford: Blackwell Publishing, 2004.

Moo, Douglas. *The Epistle to the Romans*, NICNT. Grand Rapids, MI: Wm. B. Eerdmans Publishing, 1996.

Muller, Richard A. *Scholasticism and Orthodoxy in the Reformed Tradition: An Attempt at Definition.* Grand Rapids, MI: Calvin Theological Seminary, 1995.

Ridgley, Thomas. *A Body of Divinity.* Edited by John M. Wilson. New York: Robert Carter & Brothers, 1855.

Schaff, Philip. *The Creeds of Christendom.* New York: Harper & Brothers, 1877.

Staunton, William. "Orthodox and Orthodoxy." In *An Ecclesiastical Dictionary.* 4th ed. New York: The General Protestant Episcopal Sunday School Union and Church Book Society, 1875.

Strong, A. H. *Systematic Theology.* 3 vols. in 1. 1907; repr., Old Tappan, NJ: Fleming H. Revell Company, 1979.

Sweet, William Warren. "Natural Religion and Religious Liberty in America." *The Journal of Religion* 25, no. 1 (1945): 45-55.

Turretin, Francis. *Institutes of Elenctic Theology.* Translated by George Musgrave Giger and edited by James T Dennison, Jr. Phillipsburg, NJ: P&R Publishing: 1992-97.

Tertullian. *Apologeticus*, in *The Writings of Tertullian.* Vol. 11 of *Translations of the Writings of the Fathers*, edited by Rev. Alexander Roberts and James Donaldson, 53-140. Edinburgh: T&T Clarke, 1869.

Van Til, Cornelius. *An Introduction to Systematic Theology.* Vol. 5 of *In Defense of the Faith.* 1974; Phillipsburg, NJ: P & R Publishing Co., 1982.

Vermigli, Pietro Martyr. *Loci communes.* Genevae: Petrum Aubertum, 1624.

Warfield, Benjamin Breckinridge. *Studies in Theology.* Vol. 9 of *The Works of Benjamin B. Warfield.* 1932; repr., Grand Rapids, MI: Baker Book House, 2000

III:
DIVINE ACTION AND THE MEANING OF ETERNITY

Steven J. Duby, Grand Canyon University

I. INTRODUCTION

IN CONTEMPORARY theology, the topic of divine eternity is hotly debated. All orthodox Christians confess that God is without beginning and without end, but, according to some authors, a biblical view of creation and divine action in time requires us to affirm that God is not "timeless" but rather "temporal," experiencing succession in His existence and activity. This essay will first briefly recount relevant biblical teaching on creation and God's providence and canvas how some recent writers have concluded from their reading of Scripture that God must be "temporal." Then I will make a case that the Christian theological tradition possesses resources that will help us account for the doctrines of creation *ex nihilo* and divine providence without suggesting that God is temporal or undergoes succession in His life.

II. CREATION, DIVINE ACTION, AND DIVINE ETERNITY

The psalmist declares, "From everlasting to everlasting you are God" (Ps. 90:2). It is not uncommon to hear biblical commentators emphasize that such a statement does not necessarily entail that God is "timeless" or "outside time."[1] The scriptural doctrines of creation *ex nihilo* and providence in particular are sometimes taken to imply that God is "temporal" or "in time" as He acts and interacts with His creatures in history. Unlike some other

[1] For example, see the comments on God's eternity in John Goldingay, *Old Testament Theology, Volume Two: Israel's Faith* (Downers Grove: InterVarsity Press, 2006), 32–34.

ancient accounts of the universe, Scripture teaches that the universe is not infinitely old. The history of the world extends back only to the point at which the triune God spoke the universe into being (e.g., Gen. 1:1; Ps. 33:6, 9; 148:5; Jn. 1:1; 1 Cor. 8:6; Col. 1:16; Heb. 11:3). In light of this, some recent theologians have argued that God must exist in some sort of time prior to the beginning of creation in order to uphold that God brought the world into being at a particular time in the past and that God was free in choosing to do so. Jürgen Moltmann, for example, argues that God's decision to create the world led to him existing in a certain kind of time ("God's time for creation") even prior to the beginning of the world. For without a pre-existing timeline on which to place the beginning of creation, creation would have been co-eternal with God and would have appeared to be a necessary counterpart to God.[2] T. F. Torrance emphasizes that "God is always Father, not always Creator." To elaborate, "While God was always Father and was Father independently of what he has created, as Creator he acted in a way that he had not done before, in bringing about absolutely new events—this means that the creation of the world out of nothing is something new even for God. God was always Father, but he *became* Creator." Hence God is "absolutely free to do what he had never done before, and free to be other than he was eternally." Therefore, "there is, if we may express it thus, a 'before' and 'after' in God's activity, which calls for a consideration of the unique nature of 'time' in the eternal Life of God." "God's kind of time" is "marked by distinct moments in it such as that before and after creation."[3]

Scripture also speaks often of God acting in history and interacting with His creatures. For example, He speaks to Abraham and Moses at particular times and is even willing to engage them in dialogue (Gen. 18:17-33; Exod. 32:7-35). He is always with His people, leading them by a pillar of cloud and fire in their flight from Egypt (Exod. 13:17-22). We could multiply examples, but the point is that God acts and interacts at diverse times and brings about diverse effects, which has led some to conclude that God cannot be "atemporal." Garrett DeWeese observes that a "ubiquitous complaint against the atemporal view is that it cannot make sense of God's causal

---

[2] Jürgen Moltmann, *God and Creation: A New Theology of Creation and the Spirit of God*, trans. Margaret Kohl (Minneapolis: Fortress Press, 1993), 83–86, 116–17.

[3] T.F. Torrance, *The Christian Doctrine of God: One Being, Three Persons* (London: T&T Clark, 1996), 207–209, 241.

activity in the actual temporal order, if time is dynamic."[4] Nicholas Wolterstorff insists that because God "has a history of acting and responding" He is a "being among whose states there is temporal succession."[5] If God is an agent—"not an impassive factor in reality"—then He is a God who changes and has a "felt temporality in [his] experience."[6]

Similarly, Alan Padgett makes a case that though God is not in our physical, "measured" time, He is "temporal" in that He "really changes in relationship with the world." Padgett writes, "The occurrence of an effect (which is itself a change) implies a change in the cause of the effect." God could timelessly will that different effects take place at different times, but God's "power-to-act" could not be timeless and still produce effects at different times. Since God is not "absolutely timeless," "the traditional doctrine of eternity must be abandoned."[7] Padgett's mention of the "traditional doctrine of eternity" is significant because it expresses a common belief that traditional authors like Augustine, Anselm, Boethius and Thomas Aquinas believed that God was "absolutely timeless." In a moment we will examine whether such theologians' statements about God's eternity imply that God is unable to produce diverse effects at diverse times. We will also explore how resources within the catholic theological tradition can help us to affirm that God created the world *ex nihilo* and acts in the world to produce different effects at different times, without implying that God is "temporal." Before we do that, however, we ought to consider why readers of Scripture would be interested in the first place in holding that God is without succession and not "temporal."

---

[4] Garrett J. DeWeese, *God and the Nature of Time* (Aldershot: Ashgate, 2004), 159. For summaries of the different theories of the nature of time, see, e.g., William Lane Craig, *Time and Eternity: Exploring God's Relationship to Time* (Wheaton: Crossway, 2001), chs. 4–5; R. T. Mullins, *The End of the Timeless God* (Oxford: Oxford University Press, 2016), ch. 2. Without delving into the technical language on time, I should clarify that I assume in this article that only the present moment truly exists (not the past or the future) and that this view was held by traditional Christian authors like Augustine, Boethius and others.

[5] Nicholas Wolterstorff, "God Everlasting," in *Inquiring about God: Selected Essays, Volume I*, ed. Terence Cuneo (Cambridge: Cambridge University Press, 2010), 133–34, 150, 153; "Unqualified Divine Temporality," in *Inquiring about God*, 157, 173, 178.

[6] Wolterstorff, "God Everlasting," 145, 153–55; "Unqualified Divine Temporality," 158, 160–2.

[7] Alan G. Padgett, *God, Eternity and the Nature of Time* (New York: St. Martin's Press, 1992), 60, 62–66, 122, 130–31, 146.

III. DIVINE ETERNITY AND DIVINE ACTION IN SCRIPTURE

To anticipate some of the material to be discussed below, Boethius' definition of eternity has become a classic formulation in the Christian doctrine of God: "the whole, simultaneous and perfection possession of interminable life."[8] With its talk of God possessing His life as a whole and all at once, such a view of divine eternity rules out the claim that God undergoes succession in His existence and activity and is "temporal" in that sense. The burden of this section is to indicate why scriptural teaching would compel Boethius (and us) to think of God's eternity in that manner.

Here it is possible to offer only a brief account of relevant biblical teaching, and this section will focus on the Bible's description of the fullness of God's life and His way of acting both in Himself and toward us. The God of Scripture is the source of all that is good and satisfying in creation. David proclaims this when He and the Israelites give their treasures for the building of the temple to be completed by Solomon. David says that "the greatness and the power and the glory and the victory and the majesty" belong to the LORD, for the heavens and the earth belong to Him. Wealth and glory come from the LORD, for He rules all things. The abundant offerings of David and the people are ultimately not their own, for everything is from the LORD's hand (1 Chron. 29:11-16). Many of the psalms also speak of God's plenitude and generosity: the sons of men find refuge in Him and feast and drink from His abundance, for with Him is the fountain of life (Ps. 36:7-9). Among the LORD's mighty works are His provision of the earth's waters for His creatures and His special supply of sustenance and gladness to human beings (Ps. 104:5-18). When God opens His hand with good gifts, creatures are satisfied, and when God sends forth His creative Spirit, the face of the earth is renewed (Ps. 104:27-30). Generation after generation therefore celebrates God's rich goodness (Ps. 145:7). God can thus tell His people in their hypocrisy that He has no need of their sacrifices: "If I were hungry, I would not tell you, for the world is mine, and all that is in it" (Ps. 50:12).

The Gospel of John calls attention to the fact that it is not because of an outward relationship to creatures that God possesses fullness of life. Rather, God enjoys that fullness spontaneously and in Himself, even without

[8] Boethius, *Philosophiae Consolationis*, in *The Theological Tractates, The Consolation of Philosophy*, trans. S.J. Tester (Cambridge: Harvard University Press, 1973), V.6, 422–23.

reference to creatures. From this prevenient richness God gives physical and spiritual life to creatures (Jn. 1:1-5; 5:24-26; 11:25-26; 17:5). In His plenitude God is active in both creation and redemption. He is not served by human hands as though needing something but instead is the one who bestows life, breath and all good things upon His creatures (Acts 17:24-25; cf. Rom. 11:35-36). By His might God accomplished the resurrection and heavenly exaltation of Christ, a surpassingly great power also operative toward believers now as Christ, who "fills all in all," shares His "fullness" with the church (Eph. 1:19-23). By that "fullness" Christ rose from the dead and is the firstborn of the new creation, and in view of that fullness dwelling bodily in Christ the church must not look elsewhere for spiritual fulfillment (Col. 1:19; 2:9). God is thus called the "blessed God," for He enjoys in Himself all that is good and requisite to happiness and contentment (1 Tim. 1:11; 6:15). Having fullness of life in and of Himself, God is God "from everlasting to everlasting," the one for whom a thousand years are like a single day (Ps. 90:2, 4), which signals that God is not only without beginning and without end but also relates to the passage of time in a manner radically different from creatures. It is not just that the LORD's years have no end but also that He, unlike the passing created order, remains "the same" (Ps. 102:25-27). As Thomas Aquinas describes it, God is called the "Ancient of Days" (Dan. 7:9-22) because He is prior to all times, but, though He is "old" as one who always exists, He is "youthful" as one who suffers no deficiency or fading into the past, "remaining immovable in himself."[9]

Furthermore, according to Scripture, the God of Israel is not idle: "he who keeps Israel does not slumber or sleep" (Ps. 121:4). The Father is always sustaining the world through His Son and always working to accomplish His plan of salvation through His Son (Jn. 5:17; Col. 1:17; Heb. 1:3). His word is living and "energetic," piercing and judging the human heart (Heb. 4:12). Of course, there are biblical texts that call God to action. The psalmist asks, for example, "Why do you sleep, Lord" (Ps. 44:23)? Yet the book of Habakkuk teaches us that human ignorance of God's working is no reason to deny that He is at work. Habakkuk asks the LORD how long he must cry out to Him about the violence surrounding him. Why does the LORD "look idly" upon wrongdoing? But the LORD responds that, even though it may not appear

[9] Thomas Aquinas, *In Librum Beati Dionysii De Divinis Nominibus Expositio*, ed. Ceslai Pera (Rome-Turin: Marietti, 1950), X.2.860 and 864, 324.

to be so, He is in fact working, doing something among the nations that Habakkuk could hardly have imagined (Hab. 1:2-5, 13).

Moreover, God is eternally active in His own triune being. The Father eternally gives life and glory to the Son and loves the Son, while the Son proceeds from the Father and lives in eternal fellowship with the Father and the Holy Spirit—the "eternal Spirit, who is not just sent economically but "proceeds from" the Father and the Son eternally (Prov. 8:22-31; Jn. 1:1; 5:26; 7:29; 15:26; 16:14-15; 17:5, 24; Heb. 9:14). While various authors in the Christian tradition have (justifiably, in my estimation) gleaned from general revelation that God is "pure act" (never inactive or having any unrealized potential in Himself) the doctrine of the Trinity secures this claim in a powerful way. It clarifies that God's knowing, willing, and loving are eternally fulfilled in the triune processions, problematizing any claim that God would exist in idleness and need to transition to actuality in creating the world or acting in it. Since this triune God is already in act in perfect love before the foundation of the world, He accomplishes His works without exertion or labor. God simply commands, for example, that the entire universe should come into being *ex nihilo* (Ps. 33:6-9; 148:5; Rom. 4:17; Heb. 11:3). In the work of regeneration too the word of God is efficacious without exertion, for the Son by His mere voice raises the dead (Jn. 5:25).

This fullness and actuality of God attested in Scripture ultimately stands behind Boethius' definition of divine eternity and ought to make us pause before asserting that God's life involves a succession of moments (or is that sense "temporal"). Still, it is important to consider whether the traditional authors operating with something like a Boethian definition of eternity can do justice to the Bible's teaching of creation *ex nihilo* and its insistence on God's presence and action in time. In order to explore that question, we will next look at some material in the works of Augustine, Boethius, Anselm and Thomas.

IV. DIVINE ETERNITY AND DIVINE ACTION IN SOME TRADITIONAL AUTHORS

In Augustine's musings on divine eternity, he can say, on the one hand, that God is "above all times" and that God's knowing, willing, seeing, moving, speaking, and resting do not occur "temporally."[10] Yet Augustine clearly believes that God is present with creatures in time and that God acts in time. He can trace the providential hand of God in his pre-conversion experience, for example, discerning God working through human teachers who shaped his youth.[11] He can similarly recognize that God worked through human authors to produce the Scriptures.[12] Not all of God's effects themselves are simultaneous and eternal. For example, the speech of God the Father at the baptism of Jesus ("This is my beloved Son…") is determined by God's eternal will but "made temporal," thus having a distinct beginning and end in time.[13] In short, for Augustine, God is both "immutable" and actively "changing" and "renewing" all things.[14]

Along with offering his aforementioned definition of eternity, Boethius claims that God "presides" over created life so that no one is outside His care. Indeed, God "keeps together" the "diversity of natures" in the world; the "order" and "motions" of nature would not "continue" or "unfold" without "one remaining who would himself arrange these varieties of changes."[15] God is like an artificer who conceives in His mind the form of what He wishes to make and then effects His work over time ("through temporal orders"), administering His plan by the God-ordained dispositions of created things in the world.[16] Significantly, in his work *De Trinitate*, Boethius characterizes eternity as an attribute rooted not in any feature of God in Himself but in His relationship toward external things. Just as ubiquity is not predicated of God because it references a "thing" in God but because every place is present to God, so eternity is predicated of God because He is present in every time (past, present, future).[17] For Boethius, the key point is not that God is strictly speaking "outside" time—indeed, He

---

[10] Augustine, *Confessionum Libri XIII*, 2nd ed., ed. L. Verheijen, CCSL 27 (Turnhout: Brepols, 1981), XI.1.1, 194; XII.11.13, 222; XII.15.18, 224–25; XIII.29.44, 268; XIII.37.52, 272.

[11] Augustine, *Conf.*, I.12.19, 10–11.

[12] Augustine, *Conf.*, XIII.15.16, 250–51.

[13] Augustine, *Conf.*, XI.6.8–8.10, 198–99.

[14] Augustine, *Conf.*, I.4.4, 2.

[15] Boethius, *Phil. Consol.*, I.6, 166–67; III.12, 298–301. The English translations of Boethius are the author's but reflect to some extent those given in the Loeb edition.

[16] Boethius, *Phil. Consol.*, IV.6, 358–61.

[17] Boethius, *De Trinitate*, in *Theological Tractates, Consolation of Philosophy*, IV, 20–23.

quite evidently works within it—but rather that God's perfect life is neither lost nor acquired by Him through temporal change.[18]

In the *Monologion*, Anselm declares that it is "repugnant" that the highest, creative essence should exist "nowhere and never." For this nature exists most truly and supremely, and, indeed, anything that exists anywhere or at any time would not exist without its sustaining presence.[19] God is genuinely present in time, albeit in a unique manner. The highest essence is said to be "in time," but when such language is applied to both God and "local and temporal natures," the meaning is diverse. To say something is "in time" normally signifies that it is (1) present in those times in which it is said to be and (2) contained by those times. Both aspects of the meaning are applicable to the existence of creatures, but only the first is applicable in God's case. In this connection, according to Anselm, it may be helpful to say that God is "with time" more than "in time." However, God is still certainly in time "in his own way," namely, in sustaining all finite, mutable, temporal things so that they do not come to nothing. Thus, in Anselm's view, God is "absent to none."[20] To say that God is eternal is therefore not to try to remove Him or His activity from the temporal world; it is, rather, to underscore God's infinite, perfect, unchanging life. Given the simplicity of God, His eternity is just His essence considered with respect to the temporal mode of fleeting creaturely existence.[21]

The coherence of these authors' claims that God both transcends temporal succession and is present and active in time can be illumined by Thomas' discussion of eternity in conjunction with the concept of motion. For Thomas, God transcends temporal succession precisely because He does not undergo motion, which is what is measured by time.[22] God is eternal in that He enjoys "wholeness" of life in contrast to creatures, whose existence

---

[18] Cf. *Phil. Consol.*, V.6, 422–25.

[19] Anselm, *Monologion*, in vol. 1 of *S. Anselmi Cantuariensis Archiepiscopi Opera Omnia*, ed. F.S. Schmitt (Edinburgh: Thomas Nelson and Sons, 1946), XX, 35.

[20] Anselm, *Monologion*, XXII, 40–41.

[21] Anselm, *Monologion*, XXIV, 42.

[22] Thomas Aquinas, *Commentaria in Octo Libros Physicorum Aristotelis*, in vol. 2 of *Opera Omnia* (Rome: ex Typographia Polyglotta, 1884), III.3.5.15, 114 (hereafter *In Phys.*); *Summa contra Gentiles*, in vol. 13 of *Opera Omnia* (Rome: Typis Riccardi Garroni, 1918), I.15, 41–42 (hereafter *SCG*).

is marked by motion and succession.[23] What is meant by "motion" when Thomas says that God does not experience it as creatures do? It should be noted, first, that there is a qualified sense in which motion can be predicated of God, namely, in that God knows and wills and operates toward creatures to bring them into being, to conserve their being and to give them diverse gifts.[24] Yet, following Aristotle, Thomas understands motion more strictly to be the "act of one existing in potency." In other words, for Thomas as for Aristotle, motion is not the actuality of something that is perfectly in act but rather the "imperfect act" of something that is no longer wholly idle and is increasing in actuality (like a physical object heating up to a higher temperature).[25] In addition, in a broader sense motion can be predicated of an acting subject whose operation (knowing, willing, causing something to happen outwardly in the world) involves a transition from inactive potency or idleness to act.[26] Because Thomas believes that God is pure act with no potency yet to be fulfilled, he rejects the notion that God's operation would be characterized by such reduction of potency to act and would deny that God "moves" in this sense, which entails, in his theological framework, that God's life and actuality are eternal rather than temporal.[27] Yet, God is still

[23] Thomas Aquinas, *Summa Theologiae, Pars Prima*, in vol. 4 of *Opera Omnia* (Rome: ex Typographia Polyglotta, 1888), Ia.10.2 corp. and ad 3, 96; 10.3 corp., 97–98 (hereafter *ST*).

[24] Thomas Aquinas, *Scriptum super Libros Sententiarum*, 2 vols., ed. R.P. Mandonnet (Paris, 1929), I.8.3.1 ad 1 and 2, 211–12 (hereafter *Sent.*); *De Div. Nom.*, IX.4.840–41, 316; *ST*, Ia.9.1 ad 1 and 2, 90; 18.3 ad 1, 228.

[25] Thomas, *In Phys.*, III.1.2.3, 6–7, 105, 106; 1.3.2, 107–108; III.2.4.1, 109; cf. 1.3.6, 108; 3.5.17, 115; *Sent.*, I.8.3.1 sol., 211; *SCG*, I.13, 31.

[26] Thomas, *Sent.*, I.8.3.1 ad 4, 212; II.1.1.5 ad 11, 37; *Sentencia Libri De Anima*, in vol. 45/1 of *Opera Omnia* (Rome: Commissio Leonina; Paris: J. Vrin, 1984), III.6, 229; *De Div. Nom.*, IV.7.369, 121; *SCG*, I.13, 30–34; 68, 198–99; II.33, 348; *ST*, Ia.18.3 corp., 228; *ST, Pars Secunda*, in vol. 6 of *Opera Omnia* (Rome: ex Typographia Polyglotta, 1891), IaIIae.9.1 and 3, 74–75, 77–78.

[27] Thomas identifies God's action as God's own essence, with a relation to the creature (*Sent.*, I.2.1.2 ad 2, 63; *De Potentia*, in vol. 2 of *Quaestiones Disputatae*, ed. P. Bazzi et al. (Rome-Turin: Marietti, 1965), I.1 ad 1, 9; III.3 corp., 43; *SCG*, II.8–9, 283–84; 35, 348; *ST*, Ia.25.1 ad 2, 290; 45.3 ad 1, 467). This distinguishes God's action from even that of "aeviternal" creatures like angels, who, though unchanging in their being, can change with regard to understanding, affections, and place and whose operation is not identical with essence (so *De Spiritualibus Creaturis*, in vol. 24/2 of *Opera Omnia* (Rome: Commissio Leonina; Paris: Éditions Du Cerf, 2000), 11 corp.; *ST*, Ia.10.5, 100–1).

present and active in the field of temporal reality. Thomas insists that God acts in all things—indeed, "immediately" in all things—in conserving their existence. God is actively present "as long as a thing has being."[28] Divine eternity, then, does not exclude time but rather in this sense "includes all times."[29]

But if God's actuality never changes or increases when He chooses to effect something new in the world, what would explain the fact that God's effects occur at different times and places? While I think it is unwise to assume that finite creatures can fully understand this matter, I would suggest that some statements from Reformed orthodox theologians can shed light here. In particular, their talk of the "egression" (breaking forth) or "termination" of God's actuality is helpful.[30] On the one hand, there is the actuality of God itself, which is just God's own essence in its pure activity (with no unrealized potential yet to be brought forth). On the other hand, there is the "egression" or breaking forth of that actuality to bring about different effects at different times.[31] In that egression God is not transitioning from idleness to activity but is rather just applying or directing His essential actuality to the accomplishment of some outward work (e.g., creation, blessing, judgment, regeneration). On the one hand, then, God transcends time and is not determined or measured by it in that His actuality does not fluctuate. Indeed, the actuality by which He accomplishes His outward works is the same as that of His own essence, whereas in creatures outward actions require a newly prompted actuality added to the activity of our mere act of existing. On the other hand, God is present and active with and in time in

---

[28] Thomas, *ST*, Ia.8.1 corp. and ad 1, 82; cf. 8.3 ad 1, 87. Thomas comments that things are never distant from God spatially (or, we might add, temporally), but only by "dissimilitude of nature and grace, as he himself is above all things by the excellence of his own nature" (8.1 ad 3, 82).

[29] Thomas, *ST*, Ia.10.2 ad 4, 96. Put differently, God's eternity is indivisibly "outside" the continuum of temporal duration and yet precisely by virtue of this also "coexists" with each point on the continuum (*SCG*, I.67, 185).

[30] For more on this, see Steven J. Duby, "Divine Immutability, Divine Action and the God-world Relation," *International Journal of Systematic Theology* 19 (2017), 144–62.

[31] See Johann Alsted, *Theologia Naturalis* (Antonius Hummius, 1615), I.16, 140, 147–51; Gisbertus Voetius, *Selectarum Disputationum Theologicarum* (Utrecht, 1648), I.13, 233; Francis Turretin, *Institutio Theologiae Elencticae*, vol. 1 (Geneva, 1688), III.10.15, 225.; V.3.16, 484–85; John Owen, *A Dissertation on Divine Justice*, in vol. 10 of *The Works of John Owen*, ed. William H. Goold (Edinburgh: Banner of Truth, 1967), I.1, 498–500.

that He operates toward creatures (by the actuality or efficacy of His own essence) to sustain their life and to bring about various effects in the world. The actuality of God itself never changes, but God is still at work in diverse ways and at diverse times in history. God's action taken with respect to its actuality or force and efficacy is identical with His essence and never requires a reduction of potency to act. God is thus eternal (without succession in His life and actuality) and can be present in time without being determined by or contained in it.

At this point it may be worthwhile to clarify two things. First, in drawing this distinction between the actuality of God's essence and the "egression" of God's actuality, I am in light of Scripture taking it as a given (1) that God is constant in His actuality and thus "eternal" and (2) that God produces diverse effects at diverse times. In other words, we do not begin with the question of whether God's constant actuality is an obstacle to His presence and activity in time. We know that the world simply would not continue in existence in the first place without God internally sustaining its being moment by moment. It is not a self-sustaining system which God must enter from the outside but rather a system held together by its living and moving "in God" (i.e., by God's presence in providential action) (Acts 17:28; Col. 1:17; Heb. 1:3). Thus, rather than trying to solve a problem, we are simply exploring how we might best describe and hold together two facts (God's eternity, God's historical presence and action) that we are already bound to affirm. Divine presence with creatures in time is, accordingly, not a conclusion toward which we are working but rather a principle with which we are beginning the inquiry about God's eternity.

Second, it may also be asked whether talk of God's "application" or "direction" of His actuality still implies a transition from potency to act that would end up meaning God does still undergo motion and cannot be eternal in the sense intended by the traditional authors we have considered. In response, I would emphasize that if it is true that God is already complete and active in Himself and yet also produces effects at different times, something like the affirmation of an essential actuality never augmented by a secondary actuality but nevertheless applied at different times will follow, even if the precise manner in which God applies and terminates His essential actuality is mysterious to us. Furthermore, it seems that an actuality that is applied without a transition from a prior potency to actuality ultimately underlies any series of transitions from potency to actuality, since potency cannot have ultimate priority (insofar as inactive potency itself would never initially actuate anything). In the analysis of divine action here, it might be said that we are simply locating this ultimate actuality that is applied without a potency-act transition not in a divine essential actuality that is really distinct from a secondary actuality but rather in God's essential actuality as inclusive of the efficacy of His action toward us (which, in classical metaphysics, would normally be termed a secondary actuality). If we return to address specifically some of the questions raised at the beginning of this essay about whether creation *ex nihilo* and divine providence require us to affirm that God experiences succession or is "temporal," we might say the following.

V. DIVINE ETERNITY AND GOD'S WORKS OF CREATION AND PROVIDENCE

(1) In His perfect actuality, the triune God freely creates a contingent world. The concern that we noted earlier in theologians like Moltmann and Torrance about preserving the contingency of the world should not be brushed aside. At the same time, that contingency is grounded, not in a divine temporal succession in which God might exist in temporal priority to creation, but rather in God's fullness and completeness that entails, in scholastic terms, His "liberty of indifference" (freedom to create or not to create the world without any fulfillment or declension of His being hanging in the balance). Given that God is already actively fulfilled in Himself in trinitarian fellowship, He needs no external counterpart or external object of love. In choosing to create the world and in performing the act of creation itself, He does not fulfill a potency in His being but instead generously directs or turns His essential actuality toward the world. It may be asked whether God accomplishing His outward action by His essential actuality would mean that the outward action is just as necessary as God's own act of being. Why should God's outward action still be taken as ontologically subsequent to His (necessary) act of being? My response is simply to clarify that the argument here does not posit a total identity of essential actuality and outward action. The former is complete in itself and absolutely necessary in God, while the latter is a matter of the application of the former toward creatures. Since the former is perfect in God's triune life, God is by nature "indifferent" toward creatures in a technical sense (unable to be improved or attenuated by willing

to create or not to create).[32] His outward action is thus located under an externally directed, free application of His essential actuality, which then entails a distinction between the (contingent) action or egression and the necessary essential act of God.

(2) In His non-successive life, God creates *ex nihilo* a world whose age is finite. As we saw above, some authors have raised the question of whether the finite age of the world must be grounded in a succession in God's life by virtue of which, to put it crudely, He could create "later" than He otherwise might have. However, the approach advocated here reframes the discussion and supplies a different rationale for the temporal finitude of the world. In the first place, the perfect life and actuality of God, with the consequent absence of motion on God's part, entail that God decrees and creates with no timeline prior to the existence of the world on which to position the world's beginning. He is ontologically prior to the world and its temporality but not, strictly speaking, chronologically prior to it. And, if there is no temporal succession in God's ontological priority to the world, there simply is no infinite succession of past moments in which the universe might have been infinitely old over against the doctrine of *creatio ex nihilo*.[33] In His pure actuality, God was not required to create "earlier" than the Bible teaches, for in that actuality there was no "earlier" or "later" at all. God did not create the world *in time* but rather in creating the world concreated time itself also. We must speak of a "beginning" of the world here not to situate the foundation of creation between earlier and later moments in a pre-existing time but, instead, to acknowledge that the present course of time traces back to a point of absolute origin.

Though we can speak strictly of only an ontological priority of God to the temporal world, we can still say something about world's origination or, in Turretin's words, its "novelty of being."[34] God creates by an application,

---

[32] So Turretin, *Inst.*, IV.2.13, 346; Peter van Mastricht, *Theoretico-Practica Theologia*, 2nd ed. (Utrecht, 1724), III.1.21, 276. The terminology of "indifference" does not mean that God does not care for creation; in granting creatures finite participation in his life, God delights in them as his good works (so, e.g., Gen. 1:31; Ps. 149:4).

[33] Augustine expresses this well when he observes that time did not pass before God made time: "For there was no 'then' where there was no time" (*Conf.*, XI.13.15, 202).

[34] Turretin, *Inst.*, V.3.3, 9, 583. As Turretin notes, God could not have created the world "sooner" or "later" than He did with respect to His own successionless eternity (V.3.17, 485). Yet, given that He did create the world and that the world has a finite duration, it is fitting to speak of the world's "newness."

egression, or outward termination of His own essential actuality. Unlike creatures, who, in their actions, pass from idleness to activity and add secondary actuality to primary actuality, God does undertake actions but not by adding to His already active triune being. To elaborate on the Bible's emphasis on God creating by sheer command, God just directs His essential, prevenient actuality toward His outward works. The distinction between God's application of His essential actuality and that essential actuality in itself accounts for the contingency and "newness" of the world, while still retaining the pure actuality of God in which He does not transition from idleness to activity. In other words, God in Himself is eternally sufficient in His actuality to create the world but still not creating an eternal world.[35] Thus, while it is appropriate, given God's aseity and pure actuality, to affirm that in creation the change lies on the side of the creature,[36] this need not mean that God does not truly perform an action to bring creation into being. The point of affirming that God is pure act is just that God is complete and sufficiently in act in Himself and does not shift from idleness to activity, and it leaves room to discern a specific application of God's actuality to a particular work like creation.

(3) Finally, as complete in Himself and needing no supplementary actuality to meet us in history, the triune God lives in the closest intimacy with His creatures, without altering Himself to be present and active with them in time. He does not change or grow in actuality to perform His providential works; rather, unlike creatures, He simply acts by His own essence in blessing and sustaining, judging and saving us. As God acts toward us in the fullness that He originally is in Himself, God "for us" and God "in himself" are not different two versions of God; the former is the latter (contingently) turned outward to generate fellowship with human image-bearers. Because it is God who creates and sustains, because creatures would not exist without His preserving activity, God's life does not exclude creaturely time but rather includes it in that He applies His essential actuality

[35] Turretin expresses this in a distinction between an active sufficient cause (*causa sufficiens actu*) and an active sufficient cause undertaking this specific action (*causa sufficiens in actu*) (see *Inst.*, V.3.12, 484).

[36] Borrowing Turretin's language again, a "hyperphysical" change—one that transcends the ordinary dynamics of change in the created order—for there was no initial *terminus a quo* for the origin of universe (*Inst.*, III.11.5, 226). Compare Mastricht, *Theoretico-Practica Theologia*, II.20.10, 210.

to preserve the life of creatures and bring about various effects in the world. In this way His work of providence includes the past, present, and future of creatures. It is not that God undergoes succession through past, present, and future as though His life and actuality in itself might be determined by succession and time; instead, God possesses all that He is indivisibly and remains the same even as He engages the world's succession of moments in His outward activity.[37] Because God need not change Himself to relate to and act toward creatures, His fullness of life is not in competition with creatures' time. In His eternity He co-exists with each passing moment of creation. Yet, because creatures are really distinct from Him, this does not compromise the genuine passing of time, nor does it entail that all times must be co-existent with one another.[38] As God providentially acts in the world, He undergoes no succession because He undergoes no motion (reduction of inactive potency to act), and He undergoes no motion because He is perfectly in act in His prevenient triune life. Yet, He can and does apply or direct that perfect, immanent actuality to accomplish His providential works at various times. While the force and efficacy of God's providential actions are unchanging since they are the same as God's own essence, the egression and termination of God's providential actions are wrought by God in time and at specific times. In light of all this, there is no tension between an eternal cause and a temporal effect when it is clear that (1) God's constant actuality does not disconnect Him from time even as He is not measured by time and (2) God's essential actuality is not applied or terminated in a uniform manner. Likewise, there is no tension between an immutable cause and a novel effect when we clarify that God is an immutable cause in the sense that He can

[37] To distill the point in Turretin's concise words once more, God's life includes time not "divisibly" or "formally" as though He Himself should undergo succession but rather "indivisibly" and "eminently" in that He is always present with creatures without division or fluctuation in His actuality and comprehends all of time by applying His actuality in providential oversight of history (*Inst.*, III.10.11, 224). This circumvents the awkward question of whether God knows what time it is right now. The question presupposes that the mind of God itself undergoes a sequence of thoughts that ought to keep pace with the passing of creatures' time. But that is not the case. As God Himself is present in time but without succession, He knows the temporal location of his creatures without continually "updating" his own awareness of the time.

[38] Turretin, *Inst.*, III.10.7–12, 223–24.

produce a new effect by applying His essential, constant actuality to a created object, without having to transition from idleness to activity.

VI. CONCLUSION

At the beginning of this essay, we noted that there are ongoing debates about the meaning of divine eternity today and observed that some writers argue that the biblical teaching on creation *ex nihilo* and divine action in time should compel us to hold that God undergoes succession in His life and is "temporal." After this, we examined scriptural teaching about the fullness of God's triune life that has driven various authors in the Christian tradition to conclude that God does not undergo motion or succession and should therefore be called "eternal." We then explored the coherence of God's eternity and God's production of diverse effects at diverse times by making use of a distinction between God's essential actuality and the "egression" or breaking forth of that actuality at different points in time. The final section of the essay then returned to the matters of creation and divine providence to offer some summary statements about how someone holding that God is eternal and without succession can genuinely affirm and make sense of biblical teaching on creation *ex nihilo* and divine providence.

With this essay, I hope to encourage further reflection on not only God's relationship to time in historical theology and biblical exegesis but also the implications of catholic theology proper for the God-world relation in general. I would contend that, far from driving a wedge between God and the world, the work of theologians like Augustine, Thomas, and the early Protestant dogmaticians actually helps us to elucidate what is said in the Bible about the striking nearness of God to His creatures. Retrieving these insights need not be a matter of simply repeating what others have already said but can be freshly utilized today to help strengthen the church's understanding of (and gratitude for) both God's transcendence and His immanence.

BIBLIOGRAPHY

Alsted, Johann. *Theologia Naturalis*. Antonius Hummius, 1615.

Anselm. *Monologion*. In Vol. 1 of *S. Anselmi Cantuariensis Archiepiscopi Opera Omnia*. Edited by F.S. Schmitt. Edinburgh: Thomas Nelson and Sons, 1946.

Aquinas, Thomas. *Commentaria in Octo Libros Physicorum Aristotelis*. In Vol. 2 of *Opera Omnia*. Rome: ex Typographia Polyglotta, 1884.

Summa Theologiae, Pars Prima. In Vol. 4 of *Opera Omnia*. Rome: ex Typographia Polyglotta, 1888.

——. *ST, Pars Secunda*. In Vol. 6 of *Opera Omnia*. Rome: ex Typographia Polyglotta, 1891.

——. *Summa contra Gentiles*. In Vol. 13 of *Opera Omnia*. Rome: Typis Riccardi Garroni, 1918.

——. *Scriptum super Libros Sententiarum*. 2 vols. Edited by R.P. Mandonnet. Paris, 1929.

——. *In Librum Beati Dionysii De Divinis Nominibus Expositio*. Edited by Ceslai Pera. Rome-Turin: Marietti, 1950.

——. *De Potentia*. In Vol. 2 of *Quaestiones Disputatae*. Edited by P. Bazzi and M. Calcaterra. Rome-Turin: Marietti, 1965.

——. *Sentencia Libri De Anima*. In Vol. 45/1 of *Opera Omnia*. Rome: Commissio Leonina; Paris: J. Vrin, 1984.

——. *De Spiritualibus Creaturis*. In Vol. 24/2 of *Opera Omnia*. Rome: Commissio Leonina; Paris: Éditions Du Cerf, 2000.

Augustine. *Confessionum Libri XIII*. 2nd ed. Edited by L. Verheijen. CCSL 27. Turnhout: Brepols, 1981.

Boethius. *The Theological Tractates, The Consolation of Philosophy*. Translated by S.J. Tester. Cambridge: Harvard University Press, 1973.

Craig, William Lane. *Time and Eternity: Exploring God's Relationship to Time*. Wheaton: Crossway, 2001.

DeWeese, Garrett J. *God and the Nature of Time*. Aldershot: Ashgate, 2004.

Duby, Steven J. "Divine Immutability, Divine Action and the God-world Relation." *International Journal of Systematic Theology* 19 (2017): 144–62.

Goldingay, John. *Old Testament Theology, Volume Two: Israel's Faith*. Downers Grove: InterVarsity Press, 2006.

Van Mastricht, Peter. *Theoretico-Practica Theologia*. 2nd ed. Utrecht, 1724.

Moltmann, Jürgen. *God and Creation: A New Theology of Creation and the Spirit of God.* Translated by Margaret Kohl. Minneapolis: Fortress Press, 1993.

Mullins, R. T. *The End of the Timeless God.* Oxford: Oxford University Press, 2016.

Owen, John. *A Dissertation on Divine Justice*. In Vol. 10 of *The Works of John Owen*, edited by William H. Goold, 481-624. Edinburgh: Banner of Truth, 1967.

Padgett, Alan G. *God, Eternity and the Nature of Time*. New York: St. Martin's Press, 1992.

Torrance, T.F. *The Christian Doctrine of God: One Being, Three Persons*. London: T&T Clark, 1996.

Turretin, Francis. *Institutio Theologiae Elencticae*. Vol. 1. Geneva: 1688.

Voetius, Gisbertus. *Selectarum Disputationum Theologicarum*. Utrecht, 1648.

Wolterstorff, Nicholas. "God Everlasting" and "Unqualified Divine Temporality." In *Inquiring about God: Selected Essays, Volume I*, edited by Terence Cuneo, 133-56. Cambridge: Cambridge University Press, 2010.

IV:
"ARID SCHOLARS" VS. THE BIBLE?
A THEOLOGICAL AND EXEGETICAL CRITIQUE OF THE ETERNAL SUBORDINATION OF THE SON

Alastair Roberts, The Davenant Institute

TRINITY, GENDER, AND CONTROVERSY

THE DOCTRINE of the eternal subordination of the Son has been a cause of considerable controversy in evangelical circles in recent years. Snarled up in the gender debates and fractious evangelical politics, it has excited a complicated sort of outrage, driven both by the high stakes theological concerns of the Church's historic doctrine of God and by the personal, institutional, and factional antagonisms of the American evangelical subculture. The conjoining of these motivations in disputes regarding the position have regrettably made discerning the difference between doctrinal principle and opportunistic theological recriminations or reactive partisanship difficult for many. This essay is, in part, an attempt to bring some clarity to the issues that are at stake.

Beyond the theological matters directly involved within them, however, controversies surrounding the eternal subordination of the Son have revealed fault lines and tensions between theological disciplines, along with the challenge of practically reconciling a Protestant emphasis upon the authority of Scripture with a commitment to historic Christian orthodoxy. Within this essay, I take disputes surrounding the eternal subordination of the Son as an occasion for considering the proper relationship between dogmatic or systematic theology and biblical theology more broadly and consider a possible means for addressing the tensions between them.

The doctrine of the eternal subordination of the Son, also known as "eternal relational authority-submission," upholds the claim that, in all eternity, the Son submits to the authority of the Father, that the life of the Trinity is characterized by relations of authority and submission.[1] In recent years, the position has perhaps been most prominently represented by Wayne Grudem and Bruce Ware. Writing in a book defending the doctrine, Bruce Ware describes it as follows:

> This view holds that God reveals himself in Scripture as one God in three persons, such that the Father, Son, and Holy Spirit are fully equal in their deity as each possesses fully and eternally the one and undivided divine nature; yet the Father is revealed as having the highest authority among the Trinitarian persons, such that the Son, as agent of the Father, eternally implements the will of the Father and is under the Father's authority, and the Holy Spirit likewise serves to advance the Father's purposes fulfilled through the Son, under the authority of the Father and also of the Son.[2]

While such claims have provoked considerable criticism among theologians concerned with the doctrine of the Trinity, the ferocity of recent controversies probably owes much more to the way in which the doctrine of the Trinity has become a field upon which arguments about gender have played out. In an argument that rests in part upon an analogy between the submission of the Son to the Father in the natural equality of the Godhead and the submission of wives to husbands in the natural equality of their common humanity and in part upon the exegesis of verses such as 1 Corinthians 11:3, the eternal subordination of the Son supposedly provides support or even a foundation for the submission of women to men in marriage. Philip Gons and Andrew Naselli observe:

> Behind the Trinity debate, complementarians and egalitarians clash about the roles of men and women in the

---

[1] Bruce Ware, "Does Affirming an Eternal Authority-Submission Relationship in the Trinity Entail a Denial of *Homoousios*?" in One *God in Three Persons: Unity of Essence, Distinction of Persons, Implications for Life*, ed. Bruce A. Ware and John Starke (Wheaton, IL: Crossway, 2015), 237.

[2] Bruce Ware, "Does Affirming an Eternal Authority-Submission Relationship in the Trinity Entail a Denial of *Homoousios*?," 237–38.

> church and the home. What started as an exegetical debate over biblical texts about the relationship between men and women has turned into a theological and philosophical debate about the inner life of the eternal Trinity.[3]

The theological doctrine of the eternal subordination of the Son has thereby come to represent a brand of complementarianism, and to function as a lightning rod for all the opposition to it.[4]

A MENAGERIE OF SOCIAL TRINITARIANISMS

It should be recognized that, in using the doctrine of the Trinity as the foundation for a theory of society or the Church, complementarian supporters of the eternal submission of the Son are in large company; debates often revolve around *which* vision of society the Trinity underwrites, not *whether* it ought to function in such a manner. Through the influence of social Trinitarians such as Jürgen Moltmann, Miroslav Volf, John Zizioulas, and Leonardo Boff the doctrine of the Trinity has come to be seen by many as paradigmatic for human society.[5]

As the doctrine of the Trinity has been used to underwrite every ecclesiology or form of society or polity from the primacy of the episcopal office (John Zizioulas), to a feminist vision of openness, equality, and mutuality in relationship,[6] to a free church ecclesiology (Volf), to the submission of women to their husbands in marriage, a certain scepticism concerning the actual usefulness of the doctrine of the Trinity for illumining social theory would seem to be in order. Stephen Holmes wryly remarks:

---

[3] Philip Gons and Andrew Naselli, "An Examination of Three Recent Philosophical Arguments against Hierarchy in the Immanent Trinity," in *One God in Three Person*, 196.

[4] Perhaps not entirely fairly, as it is neither the official position of the organization nor a matter on which there exists a consensus among its members, the eternal subordination of the Son is widely associated with the Council on Biblical Manhood and Womanhood (CBMW).

[5] See, for instance, Miroslav Volf, "'The Trinity Is Our Social Program': The Doctrine of the Trinity and the Shape of Social Engagement," *Modern Theology* 14 (1998): 405.

[6] Patricia Wilson-Kastner, *Faith, Feminism and the Christ* (Philadelphia: Fortress Press, 1983), 127; Shirley C. Guthrie, *Christian Doctrine*, rev. ed. (Louisville, KY: Westminster John Knox, 1994), 93.

> Volf proclaims his loyalty to Zizioulas's Trinitarian programme, yet by a seemingly minor technical variation, he effectively completely inverts all the ecclesiological implications of it, generating a radically different vision of the life of the church. It might be that this is the reality, that the difference (transposing the argument into the political realm) between democracy and fascism (say) is determined by the most abstruse of theological differences, but this feels to me uncomfortable; I would rather believe that the error of fascism is demonstrable on the basis of fundamental positions in anthropology, and does not rely on subtle distinctions in theology proper.[7]

Attempts to ground our vision of society upon our doctrine of the Trinity depend upon the analogy between the personhood of the Triune persons and human personhood, upon the assumption that "the triune persons are very like us, in their personhood at least, so their perfect relations might be a model for our attempts to imagine what well-lived relationships might look like."[8] More troubling, this analogy allows for traffic in both directions. As Holmes observes, both Volf and Boff airbrush the inconvenient asymmetry of divine *taxis*—something which Zizioulas accents—in their doctrine of the Trinity, as it disrupts the egalitarian picture that they desire.[9]

A DOCTRINE OF QUESTIONABLE PEDIGREE

Although theological discourse in the context of contemporary social media is far more flammable and explosive than that which occurs in more traditional media, recent controversies about this doctrine are merely the latest iteration of controversies surrounding the doctrine of the eternal

---

[7] Stephen R. Holmes, *The Quest for the Trinity: The Doctrine of God in Scripture, History and Modernity* (Downers Grove, IL: IVP Academic, 2012), 28.

[8] Holmes, *The Quest for the Trinity*, 29.

[9] Holmes, *The Quest for the Trinity*, 28. The same concern has led Millard Erickson to resist eternal generation and historic understandings of divine *taxis*, in order to emphasize a radical symmetry in the divine life. *Who's Tampering with the Trinity?: An Assessment of the Subordination Debate* (Grand Rapids, MI: Kregel Publications, 2009), 251; *God In Three Persons: A Contemporary Interpretation of the Trinity* (Grand Rapids, MI: Baker Academic, 1995), 310.

generation of the Son that have been constantly rumbling away and intermittently erupting for several years now. Several books have been written on various sides of these debates, defending, attacking, theologically articulating, and qualifying the doctrine of the eternal subordination of the Son.

The egalitarian theologian, Kevin Giles, one of the loudest critics of the doctrine, recently published his fourth book in which he addresses this matter in detail.[10] In 2009, Millard J. Erickson wrote *Who's Tampering With the Trinity? An Assessment of the Subordination Debate.* In defence of the doctrine, Bruce Ware and John Starke edited *One God in Three Person, Implications for Life* (2015), within which a variety of species of eternal subordination arguments are articulated and defended. More recently, the late Mike Ovey's book *Your Will Be Done: Exploring Eternal Subordination, Divine Monarchy and Divine Humility* also defended the eternal subordination position.[11]

Grudem has insisted upon the historical pedigree of the doctrine, appealing to figures such as Augustine, John Calvin, B.B. Warfield, Augustus Strong, and Louis Berkhof.[12] In what might be one of the most important pieces of evidence for Grudem's claims, Strong uses the relation between man and woman to illustrate the more general point that order doesn't require inequality in the context of his treatment of the Trinity:

> The subordination of the person of the Son to the person of the Father to be officially first, the Son second, and the Spirit third, is perfectly consistent with equality. Priority is not necessarily superiority. The possibility of an order, which yet involves no inequality, may be illustrated by the relation between man and woman. In office man is first and woman is second, but woman's soul is worth as much as man's; see *1 Cor 11:3*—"the head of every man is Christ; and

---

[10] Kevin Giles, *The Trinity & Subordinationism: The Doctrine of God & the Contemporary Gender Debate* (Downers Grove, IL: Intervarsity Press, 2002) *Jesus and the Father: Modern Evangelicals Reinvent the Doctrine of the Trinity* (Grand Rapids, MI: Zondervan, 2006), *The Eternal Generation of the Son: Maintaining Orthodoxy in Trinitarian Theology* (Downers Grove, IL: IVP Academic, 2012), *The Rise and Fall of the Complementarian Doctrine of the Trinity* (Eugene, OR: Wipf and Stock, 2017).

[11] Mike Ovey, *Your Will Be Done: Exploring Eternal Subordination, Divine Monarchy and Divine Humility* (Oxford: Latimer Trust, 2016).

[12] Wayne Grudem, *Evangelical Feminism and Biblical Truth: An Analysis of More Than 100 Disputed Questions* (Wheaton, IL: Crossway, 2012), 415ff.

> the head of the woman is the man: and the head of Christ is God."[13]

It is noteworthy that the passages of various theologians that Grudem appeals to are almost without exception speaking either of the Son's being begotten of the Father or of "subordination" in reference to divine *taxis*, both truths concerning the order of the persons of the Trinity and their relations. The Father is the first, the Son the second, and the Spirit the third person of the Trinity, the Son is begotten of the Father and the Spirit proceeds from the Father and the Son, and divine action is from the Father, through the Son, and in the Spirit. Although theologians may increasingly recognize the infelicity of the term "subordination" and seek to avoid it, precisely on account of its vulnerability to misreadings such as Grudem's, some form of "subordination" has always been a feature of Trinitarian theology. The problems arise when an orthodox "subordination" of divine *taxis* is reimagined as relations of authority and submission between the persons of the Trinity, considered as highly analogous with the relation between husband and wife. With reference to the Trinity, "subordination," in the orthodox sense of the term, is most definitely not a relation of authority and submission, a relation in which the persons are considered as if distinct centers of consciousness.[14]

Not only has its content mutated, the place that the doctrine of the eternal subordination of the Son now occupies in the theologies of its advocates is also largely a new development. The doctrine has become a particularly load-bearing one, with the result that a poorly formed understanding of the Trinity has become the cause of considerable mischief. Whereas someone like Strong might have referenced relations between the sexes in the context of his doctrine of the Trinity to prove a point about the possibility of order without inequality, modern defenders of the doctrine are

---

[13] Augustus H. Strong, *Systematic Theology* (Valley Forge, PA: Judson Press, 1907), 342.

[14] It is my suspicion that no small part of the problem here—a problem that also afflicts understandings of relations between the sexes—lies in the flattening out of the subtle order of historic treatments of divine *taxis* into something more like a chain of command ordered into terms of ranked degrees of authority. Grudem and others press the ordinal designations of the persons of the Trinity (first, second, third person) into the service of a hierarchical ranking, downplaying the designations of Triune relations in terms of "qualitative" processions (begotten or spirated) in favour of claims about relative degrees of authority.

more likely to regard the eternal relations of authority and submission that they perceive within the life of the Trinity as a foundation and rationale for relations of authority and submission between the sexes.

The notion of eternal relations of authority and submission is architectonic for Ware's understanding of the Trinity, for instance, in a way that has deeply troubling repercussions on various aspects of his theology. It completely undermines any doctrine of inseparable operations. Ware writes: "For, though the Father is supreme, though he has in the trinitarian order the place of highest authority, the place of highest honor, yet he chooses to do his work in many cases through the Son and through the Spirit rather than unilaterally."[15] He also speaks of the Father "delegating" his work to other persons of the Trinity.[16] Grudem questions inseparable operations too.[17]

A widely-held doctrine that was once appealed to within discussions about the relationship between men and women chiefly to illustrate the fact and to support the general claim that functional submission need not entail ontological subordination has since become the foundation for a very specific vision of gender relations.[18] In the process, the doctrine itself has, as I have observed, become considerably more fraught by the polarizing tensions that exist between people on various sides of the gender debates.

UNDERSTANDING THE ANTAGONISTS

In tracing the threads of the debate, one also soon notices that they can be deeply knotted together: positions don't neatly divide into two or more distinct sides. Some of the strongest egalitarian critics of the eternal subordination of the Son also fall foul of many of the same arguments that are brought forward against the doctrine from the historic orthodox position. Erickson, for example, rejects the doctrine of the eternal generation of the

---

[15] Note the words "in many cases." Bruce A. Ware, *Father, Son, and Holy Spirit: Relationships, Roles, and Relevance* (Wheaton, IL: Crossway, 2005), 55.

[16] Ware, *Father, Son, and Holy Spirit*, 65.

[17] Wayne Grudem, "Doctrinal Deviations in Evangelical-Feminist Arguments about the Trinity," in *One God in Three Persons*, 19.

[18] Stephen Kovach and Peter Schemm argue, not uncontroversially, that it was the majority position among evangelical theologians in the twentieth century. "A Defence of the Doctrine of the Eternal Subordination of the Son," *JETS* 42/3 (1999): 473.

Son, in part on the basis of its association with the eternal subordination of the Son.[19] On the other side, however, Grudem and Ware have both questioned the doctrine of the eternal generation of the Son, suggesting that the differentiation of the divine persons should be articulated in terms of relations of authority and submission.[20] The casual observer could be forgiven for being rather confused.

The resistance to subordination in the Trinity on the part of theologians such as Erickson and Giles has also been accompanied by a manifest attraction to a social or communal vision of the Trinity as a quasi-egalitarian community. Erickson has argued and was formerly favourably quoted by Giles in claiming that "The Trinity is a communion of three persons, three centers of consciousness, who exist and always have existed in union with one another and in dependence on one another."[21]

Like a number of social Trinitarians, the specter of subordination has also rendered Erickson suspicious of Trinitarian *taxis* and of a relationship between the economic missions and the eternal processions of the Trinity. Erickson insists:

> There is no permanent distinction of one from the other in terms of origination. While the Father may be the cause of

---

[19] Millard Erickson, *Who's Tampering with the Trinity?: An Assessment of the Subordination Debate* (Grand Rapids, MI: Kregel Publications, 2009), 251.

[20] Ware questions the eternal generation of the Son in *Father, Son, and Holy Spirit*, 162. Kyle Claunch remarks of Grudem's position that he "indicates that the eternal functional subordination in role is the only means by which Father, Son, and Spirit are distinguished eternally" (Kyle Claunch, "God is the Head of Christ: Does 1 Corinthians 11:3 Ground Gender Complimentarity in the Immanent Trinity?" in *One God in Three Persons*, 89n52).

[21] Millard Erickson, *God In Three Persons*, 331. Cited by Kevin N. Giles, 'The Doctrine of the Trinity and Subordination,' https://godswordtowomen.org/trinity.htm, accessed November 10, 2017. Giles has since explicitly repudiated such uses of the doctrine of the Trinity: "I must admit … that in my big book, *The Trinity and Subordinationism*, published in 2002, I speak warmly of Millard Erickson's social doctrine of the Trinity and of his argument that this has social implications, and I commend others of this opinion as well. This was my first work on the Trinity and when I wrote social trinitarianism was very much in favor. It is to be noted, nevertheless, that even in this book I do not ground male-female equality in the Trinity... In the last ten years or more I have openly and unambiguously argued that the Trinity should not be appealed to by either side in this debate" (Giles, *The Rise and Fall*, 6n20).

> the existence of the Son and the Spirit, they are also mutually the cause of his existence and the existence of one another. There is an eternal symmetry of all three persons.[22]

Perhaps one of the more significant tensions that one observes in tracing the threads of the debate, however, and a subject that I particularly wish to focus upon, is the tension that exists between more systematic theological and biblical theological approaches to the question of the Trinity. Support for the doctrine of the eternal subordination of the Son has tended to be associated with a certain Biblicist impulse, an impulse that is not exclusive to complementarians. Craig Keener is an example of an egalitarian biblical scholar who has formerly come out in favour of the doctrine of the subordination of the Son.[23] However, Keener's position seems to be characterized by the absence of a robust account of God's eternity, of the existence of God beyond and above all created time. He articulates his stance in terms of a sort of aeviternity, of an enduring divine existence in a sort of heavenly time, that nonetheless exists within the confines of the created order.

It is here that we encounter a characteristic danger of an approach that focuses so firmly upon the biblical narrative: our doctrine of God is in danger of collapsing into the created realm of His work. Although it is in the context of His work in creation and redemption that we come to know the Triune God, without upholding the existence of God in Himself beyond and above all of His works, our account of God's works will lose its proper integrity. The immanent Trinity may not be the immediate subject matter of the biblical narrative, yet it is the necessary presupposition for its theological intelligibility throughout.

However, when many biblical theologians encounter the doctrine of the Trinity as it is presented in the work of certain systematic theologians, they can see an abstruse and abstract doctrine that is constantly in jeopardy of eclipsing and effacing the scriptural witness, rather than serving as the foundation and precondition for its meaning. As in the case of the foundations of a building, the architectonic priority that the doctrine of the Trinity possesses in the structure of our theology need not entail a

---

[22] Erickson, *God In Three Persons*, 310.

[23] Craig S. Keener, "Is Subordination Within the Trinity Really Heresy? A Study of John 5:18 in Context," *Trinity Journal* 20, no. 1 (1999): 39–51.

corresponding prominence in the immediate visual aspect of the completed edifice.

The biblical theological attention to the aspects of the edifice of divine revelation as they are displayed for us in Scripture contrasts with the systematic theological attention to the distribution of forces and the architectonic structure of that same edifice. If biblical theologians are at risk of neglecting or even jeopardizing the architectural logic of Christian truth, systematic theologians are at risk of ignoring the revelatory form in which that truth is disclosed. If biblical theologians are chiefly concerned with exploring and understanding the beauty of the lavishly decorated interiors of the house of scriptural revelation, systematic theologians are more concerned with appreciating and maintaining its structural integrity. Both concerns are extremely important, yet sadly they often misunderstand and exist at odds with each other.

SCHOLASTICS VERSUS BIBLICISTS?

A recent dispute about the doctrine of the eternal subordination of the Son powerfully illustrated this antagonism between biblical and systematic theology. Owen Strachan argued that the opponents of the eternal subordination of the Son were in danger of a "New Scholasticism," by which the clarity of the biblical witness was obscured for lay—and apparently also many theologically trained—Christians, leaving theology as the preserve of "arid scholars."[24] Philosophical and historical Trinitarianism must, he insisted, "ultimately kneel before exegesis-and-theology." Speaking on behalf of the "arid New Scholasticism," Mark Jones castigated Strachan for his "anti-metaphysical Biblicism," which displays, Jones maintained, the characteristic failures of the Socinians.[25] Indeed, quite apart from the problems of squaring the position of Strachan and other advocates of the eternal subordination of the Son with historic orthodoxy, Jones maintained,

---

[24] Owen Strachan, "The Glorious Godhead and Proto-Arian Bulls," *Thought Life*, June 13, 2016. http://www.patheos.com/blogs/thoughtlife/2016/06/the-glorious-godhead-and-proto-arian-bulls/, accessed November 10, 2017.

[25] Mark Jones, "Biblicism, Socianism, and 'Arid' Scholasticism," *New City Times*, June 14, 2016, https://www.newcitytimes.com/news/story/biblicism-socinianism-and-arid-scholasticism, accessed November 10, 2017.

close examination of their exegesis also often reveals lazy readings that depart from the historical mainstream of scriptural interpretation.

On various sides of such debates, one discovers an intense mutual frustration between dogmatic and biblical theology and a fraught relation between the tasks of systematic theology and scriptural exegesis. That these antagonisms should be especially pronounced in the context of the doctrine of the Trinity is not entirely surprising when one considers that, although the doctrine has an appropriate dogmatic centrality for systematic theologians, it seemingly does not enjoy a corresponding prominence in the immediate aspect of the biblical text. Both sides can be suspicious of the very different place that the doctrine of the Trinity occupies within their respective systems of thought. Furthermore, the dogmatic authority of the doctrine of the Trinity makes demands upon and constrains the work of exegetes, even while often seeming to resist exegetical correction itself.

The suspicions on both sides are not entirely without justification. On the one hand, it can often appear as if the dogmatic doctrine of the Trinity has left the orbit of the biblical text, spinning out into the deep space of speculative philosophical theology. A preoccupation with God as He is in Himself, when proceeding in detachment from the revelation and action of God in history, is always in danger of distorting the character of Christian faith, replacing the intensely historical and relational realities of the scriptural text with doctrinal abstractions. On the other hand, the vigorously anti-speculative impulse of those who appeal to the plain meaning of the biblical text can harbour a culpable inattention to the greater reality that is revealed through and in and is presupposed by that text.

Sadly, such tensions have often been intensified, rather than addressed and relieved, within debates about the eternal subordination of the Son. The historic orthodox doctrine of the Trinity has often sought vindication against the challenges of those appealing to the plain sense of Scripture, not in the demonstration of its power to explicate the fundamental divine truths that serve as the precondition for the integrity of the biblical narrative, but solely in its appeal to the claims of the tradition and the more abstract theological logic of Trinitarian doctrine. Although these are valid lines of support for the orthodox doctrine, they leave unaddressed, and thereby exacerbate, the tension that many feel between Scripture and dogma. In such a manner, biblical theologians can come to regard dogmatic theologians as frustrating rather than serving their work, like the sound of wailing sirens behind them as they drive down the road of exegesis.

Dogmatic theologians are engaged in an enterprise that is apparently removed from, in tension with, and yet ecclesiastically privileged over the work of biblical theologians in such a way that interactions between the two will almost always represent a source of Kafkaesque frustrations, burdens, and obstructions to the work of the biblical theologian. This is quite unfortunate, as there is no reason why dogmatic theology could not rather function as an empowering and deepening of biblical theology's conceptual traction upon the theological realities presupposed by the texts that are the objects of its study.

At its best, dogmatic theology manifests its importance and legitimacy through the frequent demonstration of its capacity to uphold and actualize the authority that belongs to Scripture itself. Such an authority has a promissory character, assuring us that, as we submit to the historic wisdom of the Church, we will be equipped to read the Bible far better than we would otherwise.[26] Yet it faces the insistent temptation to reduce the Scripture to the handmaiden of its own authority, or as the raw material for its own conceptual edifices. The dogmatician is in danger of approaching Scripture as if it were a mirror for his theological self-regard, within which to seek the confirming reflection of his doctrine (a posture most commonly seen in proof-texting approaches), rather than recognizing his proper mission to establish a coordinating and integrating vantage point upon the terrain of scriptural truth from which those who travel upon scriptural itineraries can be gainfully and powerfully directed. Still worse, dogmatic theologians can occasionally regard the Scripture as if an unwelcome threat to their own tight philosophical systems.

There is no reason, however, why dogmatic theologians must act as the fussy grammarians of the Church, as those who constantly present obstacles to our attempts to express scriptural truths, rather than as those who enhance our expression by clarifying and sharpening it. The theological grammar which the systematic theologian seeks to explicate and uphold is that which makes possible the fluid, forceful, and cogent expression of scriptural truth. Its laws need not be experienced as restrictive, as properly approached they can be empowering. However, such an experience of

---

[26] For a helpful discussion of the character of authority, see Oliver O'Donovan, *The Ways of Judgment* (Grand Rapids, MI: Eerdmans, 2005), 130–132.

dogmatic theology is considerably less likely to emerge where theologians lack a healthy relation to exegetes.

An unhealthy relationship between exegetes and systematicians or dogmaticians is sadly a marked feature of debates about the eternal subordination of the Son, as biblical texts that function as essential planks of the arguments of those advocating for the eternal subordination of the Son can be widely ignored by their critics. Where such texts are addressed, the text can be handled as if it were an awkward problem to be warded off. Dogmaticians can approach the text as if they were a bomb disposal unit, rather than as mechanics tuning up and servicing our language about God, so that it is maximally responsive to, concordant with, and expressive of God's truth. In an ideal world, the biblical exegete who has engaged with dogmatic theology should feel like the person driving their car after it has received a thorough service: the once mysterious shudders, clunks, creaks, and groans have vanished and now the vehicle beautifully answers to its driver and operates in a manner that manifests that its internal processes are all in optimal order.

DOGMATICS FOR EXEGETES

What, then, might exegetes gain from dogmaticians in treating a text such as 1 Corinthians 11, a text which has been one of the principal supports of the eternal subordination of the Son position?

Perhaps the first thing that the systematic theologian can offer to the exegete at this point are some illuminating and exceedingly important distinctions. To the extent that the eternal subordination of the Son appears to be substantiated from 1 Corinthians 11:3, the crucial moves in the argument might involve a certain sleight of hand, as the loss or absence of a clear distinction between the immanent Trinity and the economic Trinity and between the divine and human natures of Christ allow for the collapsing of statements made about the incarnate Christ into statements about the eternal relation between the first and second Persons of the Trinity. Without such distinctions, we court all sorts of confusion. Calvin writes:

> God, then, occupies the first place: Christ holds the second place. How so? Inasmuch as he has in our flesh made himself subject to the Father, for, apart from this, being of one essence with the Father, he is his equal. Let us,

> therefore, bear it in mind, that this is spoken of Christ as mediator. He is, I say, inferior to the Father, inasmuch as he assumed our nature, that he might be the first-born among many brethren.[27]

The distinctions Calvin emphasizes here may not generally be foregrounded within the biblical narrative. However, although some might deem them abstruse and speculative on that account, the drawing of such distinctions could not be of more importance for preserving the sense and integrity of the biblical narrative. Without something resembling classical Trinitarian theology and a Chalcedonian understanding of Christ, the entire gospel narrative will assume a different character. The Creator will not be allowed to exceed His works and the deity of Christ, a truth revealed through the gospel narrative, will be radically constrained by His human nature. The economic and immanent distinction and the distinction between Christ's human and divine natures exist to protect the integrity of creation and salvation as realms of God's free self-revelation, rather than His necessary being.

If we abandon these distinctions on account of an anti-speculative Biblicism, the very gospel narrative that we seek to uphold may begin to unravel. If Jesus of Nazareth is truly divine, then his human nature, and the obedience that is proper to it, would seem to be freely assumed, rather than definitive of His divine nature. The biblical revelation of the deity of Christ compels us to engage in the sort of theological reflection that the creedal tradition has pursued.

By itself, the distinction between Christ's divine and human nature may not settle the eternal subordination of the Son question: perhaps the submission of Christ to God spoken of in 1 Corinthians 11 reflects the eternal relation between Father and Son. However, the presence of the distinction is itself important, as it unsettles the assumption that the eternal relations of the Trinity self-evidently have such a character. Any argument that would seek to maintain such a claim still finds itself considerably short of its designed destination.

A further important passage for the eternal subordination of the Son position is found in 1 Corinthians 15:24-28, which speaks of the Son

---

[27] John Calvin, *Commentary on the Epistles of Paul the Apostle to the Corinthians, Volume 1*, trans. John Pringle (Grand Rapids, MI: Eerdmans, 1948), 353.

delivering up the kingdom to the Father in the end, and being subject to Him. Once again, it is important to bear in mind that this reveals Triune relations in terms of the Creator-creature framework. This passage refers, not to the eternal relation between Father and Son, but to the culminating moment in the great drama of redemption, the moment when the submission of the Son arrives at its perfect completion. The submission of the Son in these verses is not a reference to the eternal unbroken relation between Father and Son in the Godhead, but to the climax of the work of the incarnate Son, when His mission arrives at its final *telos*, the reality of His authoritative obedience has been utterly fulfilled, and the complete divine authority He has effected is exhaustively related back to the Father as its source.

TRINITY AND DIVINE AUTHORITY

A closer look at this passage reveals the mutually defining relation between Father and Son. All divine authority in the world is effected through the Son and without Him no divine authority is effected—all things are put under Him. Indeed, the Son's effecting of the divine authority is the precondition for the Father's being all in all. On the other hand, it is the Father who exhaustively authorizes the Son. The Father places all things under His Son; the Son renders all things up to the Father. The differentiation between the persons here is, as we shall see, a modal or prepositional differentiation of a single divine property: the one and undivided divine authority and will.

As a clearer grasp of Trinitarian theology and orthodox Christology enables us to draw distinctions that support the integrity of the biblical narrative, it also gives the biblical narrative itself greater force. Without an orthodox Trinitarianism and Christology, for instance, we will likely struggle to express Christ's incarnation in a manner that gives Him full divine agency. We will be in danger of conceiving of Christ chiefly as a faithful functionary of the divine will and authority. However, both the divine will and authority will be associated primarily with the Father. It will be difficult to perceive in Christ the authoritative God who wills to save.

Here arid scholasticism can come to the rescue in the form of doctrine of inseparable operations and a doctrine of appropriation. John Webster writes:

> Indivisibility does not disqualify personal differentiation or restrict it simply to the *opera internae*. But it does indicate that

> economic differentiation is modal, not real, and reinforces the importance of prepositional rather than substantive differentiation ("from" the Father, "through" the Son, "in" the Spirit). Modal differentiation does not deny personal agency, however; it simply specifies *how* the divine persons act. Owen notes that "the several persons are undivided in their operations, acting all by the same will, the same wisdom, the same power. Every person, therefore, is the author of every work of God, because each person is God, and the divine nature is the same undivided principle of all divine operations; and this ariseth from the unity of the person in the same essence."[28]

Relating this to the divine authority seen in God's saving work, we could speak of the Father as the source of authority and the authorizing One—authority comes *from* him. The Son is the entirely authorized One and the One *through* whom God's authority is exhaustively effected. The Spirit is the One *in* whom authority is given, enjoyed, and perfected. Authority thus understood is singular, eminently assigned to the Father, yet the inseparable possession and work of the undivided Godhead.

This in turn can serve to clarify our understanding of the incarnate Christ's mission. Rather than understanding the Son's relation to the Father in terms of a framework of authority and submission, this suggests that we should think in terms of different modes of a single, undivided divine authority. It is through the incarnate Son that the one authority of God is effected.

The manner in which the Son brings about the authority of God in history is through the path of human obedience. As a man with a human nature and will Christ submits to and is obedient to the will of God. However, this obedience can only truly be perceived for what it is when it is seen against the background of the fact that He is the authoritative divine Son. Herman Bavinck writes:

> And although as mediator Christ is represented as being dependent on, and subject to, the Father, these expressions are never meant to detract from his essential unity with the Father. In John 14:28 Jesus asserts that for his disciples his

[28] John Webster, "Trinity and Creation," *International Journal of Systematic Theology*, 12, no. 1 (2010): 16.

> going to the Father is an occasion for rejoicing, "because the Father is greater than I." Jesus is not saying that the Father is greater than he in power, something specifically denied in John 10:28-30, but refers to his relation to the Father in the state of humiliation. *Now* the Father is greater. But this lesser greatness of Jesus will end precisely when he goes to the Father, and so his disciples can rejoice over his going away. The case is this: in his essence and nature he is equal to the Father, though in his position and office he is presently less than the Father. He is not a creature, but is and was and remains God, who is over all, blessed forever…[29]

CONCLUSION

It is this truth of Christ's authoritative divinity that discloses the true character of his mission. Orthodox Trinitarian theology and Christology are the precondition for the gospel's true intelligibility. Christ is the one who can forgive sins. He is the one who can command the elements, cast out demons, and heal the sick, exercising the authority of God as his own. He is the one who receives the Spirit without measure and is the radiant and glorious theophanic revelation of God on the Mount of Transfiguration. We are left in no doubt of the divine authority of Christ. The obedience and humiliation of Christ is the (paradoxically) *authoritative* work by which He overcomes human rebellion, reconciles humanity to God, and defeats Satan.

As we recognize this, it is possible to appreciate the work of Christ as revelatory of and congruent with the eternal relation between the Father and Son, without collapsing the necessary distinctions between the two and reading back Christ's human obedience and submission into the being of God. This obedience and submission exists on account of the revelation of the Father-Son relation within the framework of the Creator-creature divide. However, when we look closer, what is seen is not just the Son's self-rendering in obedience to the Father, but also the Father's exhaustive donation of authority to His Son.

This undoes any simplistic authority-submission polarity. God cannot be alienated from His authority nor give His glory to another. Yet God's

---

[29] Herman Bavinck, *Reformed Dogmatics: God and Creation (Volume 2)*, trans. John Vriend (Grand Rapids, MI: Baker Academic, 2004), 276.

authority and glory are found precisely in Christ, the Son who bears the divine name (cf. John 8:58; Philippians 2:9). The Father and the Son are mutually defining (as the names "Father" and "Son" suggest). The Father is glorified as the authority of His Son is confessed, as the Father is who He is only in relation to His Son (Philippians 2:11). The Son is the one through whom the Father's authority is effected; the Father is the one from whom the Son's authority comes: the authority of Father and Son is the one indivisible divine authority.

Getting these points correct is imperative, not simply for orthodox conformity to Trinitarian creeds, but for a clear understanding of the shape of the biblical narrative, and of the authoritative Saviour that we have in Jesus Christ. The creeds exist to serve and advance a clear apprehension of the scriptural testimony. In contrast to the extreme position advanced by Ware, the Son is not performing a mission graciously "delegated" to Him by a higher authority, but is the authoritative God Himself come in the flesh. The Son's being sent and His coming are of one piece; the authority of the Father and the authority of the Son are the same single, undivided divine authority. In recognizing this, the true wonder of the incarnation is discovered.

BIBLIOGRAPHY

Bavinck, Herman. *Reformed Dogmatics: God and Creation (Volume 2)*. Translated by John Vriend. Grand Rapids, MI: Baker Academic, 2004.

Calvin, John. *Commentary on the Epistles of Paul the Apostle to the Corinthians, Volume 1*. Translated by John Pringle. Grand Rapids, MI: Eerdmans, 1948.

Erickson, Millard. *God In Three Persons: A Contemporary Interpretation of the Trinity*. Grand Rapids, MI: Baker Academic, 1995.

——. *Who's Tampering with the Trinity?: An Assessment of the Subordination Debate*. Grand Rapids, MI: Kregel Publications, 2009.

Giles, Kevin. *The Trinity & Subordinationism: The Doctrine of God & the Contemporary Gender Debate*. Downers Grove, IL: Intervarsity Press, 2002.

——. *Jesus and the Father: Modern Evangelicals Reinvent the Doctrine of the Trinity*. Grand Rapids, MI: Zondervan, 2006.

——. *The Eternal Generation of the Son: Maintaining Orthodoxy in Trinitarian Theology*. Downers Grove, IL: IVP Academic, 2012.

——. *The Rise and Fall of the Complementarian Doctrine of the Trinity*. Eugene, OR: Wipf and Stock, 2017.

Giles, Kevin N. "The Doctrine of the Trinity and Subordination." https://godswordtowomen.org/trinity.htm. Accessed November 10, 2017.

Grudem, Wayne. *Evangelical Feminism and Biblical Truth: An Analysis of More Than 100 Disputed Questions*. Wheaton, IL: Crossway, 2012.

Guthrie, Shirley C. *Christian Doctrine*. Revised edition. Louisville, KY: Westminster John Knox, 1994.

Holmes, Stephen R. *The Quest for the Trinity: The Doctrine of God in Scripture, History and Modernity*. Downers Grove, IL: IVP Academic, 2012.

Jones, Mark. "Biblicism, Socianism, and 'Arid' Scholasticism." *New City Times*, June 14, 2016. https://www.newcitytimes.com/news/story/biblicism-socinianism-and-arid-scholasticism. Accessed November 10, 2017.

Keener, Craig S. "Is Subordination Within the Trinity Really Heresy? A Study of John 5:18 in Context." *Trinity Journal* 20, no. 1 (1999): 39-51.

Kovach, Stephen and Peter Schemm. "A Defence of the Doctrine of the Eternal Subordination of the Son." *JETS* 42, no. 3 (1999): 461-476.

O'Donovan, Oliver. *The Ways of Judgment*. Grand Rapids, MI: Eerdmans, 2005.

Ovey, Mike. *Your Will Be Done: Exploring Eternal Subordination, Divine Monarchy and Divine Humility*. Oxford: Latimer Trust, 2016.

Strachan, Owen. "The Glorious Godhead and Proto-Arian Bulls." *Thought Life*, June 13, 2016. http://www.patheos.com/blogs/thoughtlife/2016/06/the-glorious-godhead-and-proto-arian-bulls/. Accessed November 10, 2017.

Strong, Augustus H. *Systematic Theology*. Valley Forge, PA: Judson Press, 1907.

Volf, Miroslav. "'The Trinity Is Our Social Program': The Doctrine of the Trinity and the Shape of Social Engagement." *Modern Theology* 14 (1998): 403-423.

Ware, Bruce A. *Father, Son, and Holy Spirit: Relationships, Roles, and Relevance*. Wheaton, IL: Crossway, 2005.

Ware, Bruce A. and John Starke ed. *One God in Three Persons: Unity of Essence, Distinction of Persons, Implications for Life*. Wheaton, IL: Crossway, 2015.

Webster, John. "Trinity and Creation." *International Journal of Systematic Theology* 12, no. 1 (2010): 4-19.

Wilson-Kastner, Patricia. *Faith, Feminism and the Christ*. Philadelphia: Fortress Press, 198.

V:
CAN THE TRINITY SAVE EVERYTHING? HERMAN BAVINCK, MISSIONAL THEOLOGY, AND THE DOGMATIC IMPORTANCE OF THE DOCTRINE OF THE TRINITY

Gayle Doornbos, Wycliffe College, University of Toronto

I. INTRODUCTION

THE DOCTRINE of the Trinity is undoubtedly a trendy topic in theology today. The subject of countless academic tomes and popular theological literature, its current popularity is traceable to the so-called Trinitarian revival of the mid-twentieth century. Yet, like all doctrines that enter into theological vogue, it is being treated as the dogmatic panacea for every theological conundrum, social evil, ethical wrongdoing, or ecclesiastical error.[1] On the surface, the contemporary impetus to place the Trinity at the center of theological reflection and to refer every aspect of life to the Triune God is commendable rather than reprehensible. The Christian faith is uniquely and irreducibly Trinitarian, and theologians must do justice to the theological realities that uphold Christian life and worship.

Nevertheless, simply claiming the centrality of the doctrine of the Trinity does not automatically guarantee well-formulated or beneficial

---

[1] See, for example, the contemporary debate concerning gender relationships and the Trinity, wherein both egalitarian and complementation theologians seek to ground gender relationships and roles in the Trinity. A summary of which can be found in Mildred Erikson, *Who's Tampering with the Trinity? An Assessment of the Subordination Debate* (Grand Rapids: Kregel Academic, 2009), esp. introduction, chapters 1–2.

theology. Furthermore, no single doctrine (no matter how central) can bear the weight of curing every doctrinal, ethical, social, or ecclesiastical ill. At best, renewed interest in a core doctrine and its relationship to Christian life and praxis leads to genuine theological development and insight. At worst, it produces a doctrinal myopathy that confuses doctrinal centrality with the necessity of subsuming, deducing, and generating all other doctrines from one dogma, thereby creating a method of doctrinal formulation that collapses carefully constructed distinctions between theological loci in order to identify the immediate relevance of the core or central doctrine for the topic at hand.[2] While the Trinitarian revival in contemporary theology contains much to celebrate, it has also lead to many theological proposals that exhibit the latter rather than the former.[3] As such, we neglect serious and sustained engagement with these proposals to our peril. Have they really produced new, paradigm-shifting theological insights that can solve our doctrinal and practical ills? Or, have they rushed too quickly into new doctrinal formulations and left us with new and even more precarious doctrinal conundrums?

What, then, does serious engagement with contemporary Trinitarian theologies look like? Certainly, it must engage in multifaceted and complex ways with broad trends as well as specific theological proposals, and it must

---

[2] The author is aware that the so-called modern Trinitarian revival is often predicated on the idea that the traditional categories and distinctions utilized to articulate the doctrine of God as well as its systematic placement are the reason for the doctrine's demise and neglect. It will become apparent that the author does not agree that traditional categories, distinctions, and systematic placement of the Doctrine of the Trinity necessarily create a speculative, remote, and marginalized doctrine of God. Instead, it will be argued that these distinctions *can* serve a vital role in theological formulation. See for example Karl Barth, *Church Dogmatics,* 2nd edition, ed. T.F Torrance and G.W. Bromiley, trans. by G.W. Bromiley, 14 vols (Peabody: Hendrickson Publishers, 2010); Robert Jenson, *Systematic Theology, Volume 1: The Triune God* (New York: Oxford University Press, 1997); Catherine Mowry LaCunga, *God for Us: The Trinity and Christian Life* (New York: HarperCollins, 1991); Jürgen Moltmann, *The Crucified God,* trans. R.A. Wilson and John Bowden (New York: Harper and Row, 1974); Karl Rahner, *The Trinity,* trans. Joseph Donceel (New York: Herder and Herder, 1970); Miroslav Volf, *After Our Likeness: The Church as the Image of the Trinity* (Grand Rapids: Eerdmans, 1997); and John D. Zizioulas, *Being as Communion: Studies in Personhood and the Chruch* (London: Darton, Longman, and Todd, 1985).

[3] See Stephen R. Holmes, *Quest for the Doctrine of the Trinity: The Doctrine of God in Scripture, History, and Modernity* (Downers Grove: IVP Academic, 2012), 2–3, 198.

be carried out in careful conversation with the larger Christian theological tradition. In this paper, I offer an example of this type of engagement by putting the Trinitarian theology of Dutch theologian Herman Bavinck (1854-1921) in conversation with a set of Trinitarian proposals arising from contemporary missiology, broadly classified as Missional Theology, in order to show how inattentiveness to careful systematic construction of categories and distinctions can result in unintended consequences. Specifically with regard to many (but not all) missional theologies, such disregard or intentional blurring of boundaries results in an inability to maintain the non-necessity and integrity of creation.

I have chosen Bavinck and Missional Theology intentionally. First, Bavinck, although not above reproach, represents a theologian who identifies the centrality of the doctrine of the Trinity for doctrinal formulation but rejects the Trinitarian schematization of theology. His refusal to subsume every doctrine under the doctrine of God proper while maintaining that the theological task is to consider all things in light of God makes him an ideal dialogue partner.[4] Furthermore, Bavinck critically appropriates the Reformed Orthodox tradition in order to articulate a truly Reformed, thoroughly Trinitarian theology in and for modernity; thereby, he offers a model of theological retrieval and development that contrasts many (but not all) of the modern Trinitarian revivalists, shown in this paper with specific reference to Missional Theology.[5]

---

[4] Bavinck claims that the task of theology is to describe God and God alone: "All the doctrines treated in dogmatics—whether they concern the universe, humanity, Christ, and so forth—are but the explication of the one central dogma of the knowledge of God. All things are considered in light of God, subsumed under him, traced back to him as the starting point. Dogmatics is always called upon to ponder and describe God and God alone, whose glory is in creation and re-creation, in nature and grace, in the world and in the church. It is the knowledge of him alone that dogmatics must put on display" (*Reformed Dogmatics [henceforward RD]*, 4 vols., ed. John Bolt, trans. John Vriend [Grand Rapids: Baker Academic, 2003–08], II.29). While this may sound strikingly similar to the critical issues in contemporary Trinitarian theology, there is a significant difference between systematically subsuming all doctrine under one dogma and claiming the central task of theology is to unpack the knowledge of God.

[5] John G. Flett, *The Witness of God: The Trinity, Missio Dei, Karl Barth, and the Nature of Christian Community* (Grand Rapids: Eerdmans, 2010), 35; David J. Bosch, *Transforming Mission: Paradigm Shifts in the Theology of Mission* (New York: Orbis Books, 1991), 389–93; Francis Anekwe Oborji, *Concepts of Mission: The Evaluation of Contemporary Missiology* (New York: Orbis Books, 2006), 134–49; Stephen B. Bevans, and Roger P.

Second, Missional Theology, although diverse and notoriously difficult to define, is a set of academic and popular theological projects that to some degree adhere to the idea that "as God is missional so the church is missional," utilize the term *missio Dei* to refer to God's missional nature, and generate missional praxis from the nature of the Triune God.[6] Thus, Missional Theology serves as an excellent exemplar of the methods, commitments, and assumptions that many (but not all) theologians within the broader landscape of contemporary Trinitarian theology presume and utilize. Especially in its academic development, many (but not all) academic missional theologians self-consciously move mission from soteriology and ecclesiology into the doctrine of God.[7] Subsequently, this methodological movement is used to generate theological accounts of the church's missional nature and necessary praxis. Furthermore, Missional Theology bridges the gap between academic theology and popular theology surprisingly well.[8] Particularly within evangelical circles, appeals to God as a "missional God" are common. As a set of academic and popular theological projects, then,

---

Schroeder, *Constants in Context: A Theology of Mission for Today* (New York: Orbis Books, 2004), 286–304; Seven B. Bevans, "Wisdom from the Margins: Systematic Theology and the Missiological Imagination," *Australian eJournal of Theology* 5 (August 2005): 1–17; Ross Hastings, *Missional God, Missional Church: Hope for Re-Evangelizing the West* (Downers Grove: IVP Academic, 2012), 86–7; Timothy C. Tennent, *Invitation to World Missions: A Trinitarian Missiology for the Twenty-First Century* (Grand Rapids: Kregel Publications, 2010), 54–5; Charles Fensham, *Emerging from the Dark Age Ahead: The Future of the North American Church* (Toronto: Clements Academic, 2011), introduction; and Georg Vicedom, *Mission of God: An Introduction to the Theology of Mission*, trans. Gilbert A. Thiele and Dennis Hilgendorf (Saint Louis: Concordia, 1965), 5.

[6] As John Flett writes: "*Missio* Dei [is] an elastic concept capable of accommodating an ever-expanding range of meanings" (Flett, *The Witness of God*, 5).

[7] David Bosch describes this systematic shift: "Mission was understood as being derived from the very nature of God. It was thus put in the context of the doctrine of the Trinity, not of ecclesiology or soteriology" (Bosch, *Transforming Mission*, 390).

[8] For examples of popular missional literature see Alan J. Roxburgh and M. Scott Boren, *Introducing the Missional Church: What it is, Why it Matters, and How to Become One* (Grand Rapids: Baker Books, 2009); Craig Van Gelder, *The Ministry of the Missional Church: Community Led by the Spirit* (Grand Rapids: Baker, 2007); Craig Van Gelder and Dwight J Zscheile, *The Missional Church in Perspective: Mapping Trends and Shaping the Conversation* (Grand Rapids: Baker Academic, 2011); Ed Stetzer and David Putnum, *Breaking the Missional Code: Your Church Can Become a Missionary in Your Community* (Nashville: B &H, 2006); and Alan Hirsch, *The Forgotten Ways: Reactivating the Missional Church* (Grand Rapids: Brazos, 2007).

Missional Theology exemplifies broad trends within contemporary Trinitarian theology as well as its pitfalls. And, its prevalence within the life of the church makes it an important trend with which to engage.[9]

The discussion proceeds in two parts. Part One focuses on Bavinck's Trinitarian theology and offers a constructive reading of Bavinck's theology based on a seemingly offhand statement made by Bavinck in his *Reformed Dogmatics* concerning the ontological, cosmological, and soteriological dimensions of the Doctrine of the Trinity. [10] Using these dimensions as a window into Bavinck's development of a truly Trinitarian theology that does

[9] It is imperative to note that I affirm the evangelistic aim and theocentric orientation of contemporary missiological literature—particularly in missiological literature committed to the *missio Dei.* These are wonderful intentions and should be applauded. However, affirming the goal does not eliminate the need to question the means by which this goal is attained.

[10] Reference needs to be made here to the so-called "Two Bavincks Hypothesis," which in its various iterations presents Bavinck as a dichotomous thinker who vacillates between the arid, dry, intellectualism of scholasticism and the relational, kerygmatic, Christocentrism of a biblical theological approach. It will become clear throughout the essay that the author does not agree with this reading of Bavinck. For various iterations of this "Two Bavincks Hypothesis" see David VanDrunen, "The Kingship of Christ is Twofold: Natural Law and the Two Kingdoms in the Thought of Herman Bavinck," *Calvin Theological Journal* 45, no. 1 (April 2010): 147–64; Scott Oliphint, "Bavinck's Realism, The Logos Principle, and *Sola Scriptura*," *Westminster Theological Journal* 72 (2010): 359–90; Cornelius Van Til, "Bavinck the Theologian," *Westminster Theological Journal* 24 (1961): 48–64; E.P. Heideman, *The Relation of Revelation and Reason in E. Brunner and H. Bavinck*, Part II (Assen, Netherlands: Van Gorcum, 1959); Syd Heilema, "Eschatological Understanding of Redemption" (ThD diss., Wycliffe College, Toroto, 1998), esp. 103–166; Adam Eitel, "Trinity and History: Bavinck, Hegel, and Nineteenth Century Doctrines of God," in *Five Studies in the Thought of Herman Bavinck, A Creator of Modern Dutch Theology*, ed. John Bolt (Lewiston: Edwin Mellen Press, 2011), 101–128; and Hendrikus Berkhof, *Two Hundred Years of Thelogy: Report of a Personal Journey* (Grand Rapids: Eerdmans, 1989), 113–15. For recent critics of this reading of Bavinck see Eglinton, *Trinity and Organism, Towards a New Reading of Herman Bavinck's Organic Motif* (London: T&T Clark, 2012), esp. chapter 3; George Harinck, "'Something that Must Remain, if the Truth is to be Sweet and Precious to Us': The Reformed Spirituality of Herman Bavinck," *Calvin Theological Journal* 38 (2003): 248–62; Nelson Kloosterman, "A Response to 'The Kingdom of God is Twofold': Natural Law and the Two Kingdoms in the Thought of Herman Bavinck by David VanDrunen," *Calvin Theological Journal* 45 (April 2010): 174–75; Mattson, *Restored to Our Destiny: Eschatology and the Image of God in Herman Bavinck*, Studies in Reformed Theology 21(Leiden: Brill, 2001): 9–18; Henk van den Belt, *Autopistia: The Self-Convincing Authority of Scripture in Reformed Theology* (Leiden, Netherlands: Leiden University Press, 2006), chapter 6.

not subsume all loci into the Doctrine of God proper, Part One concludes with an extended examination of the systematic relationship between Bavinck's doctrines of God and creation (the ontological and cosmological dimensions). The aim of Part One is twofold. First, it is to identify categories and distinctions within Bavinck's systematic theology that can be used to aid us in asking constructive and critical questions of Missional Theology. Second, it is to exemplify how Bavinck seeks to do justice to the Trinitarian, theological realities that undergird creation and salvation through his critical appropriation of Reformed Orthodoxy and the Church Fathers. This section primarily focuses on Bavinck without reference to contemporary questions in order to present the internal logic and method of Bavinck's systematic theology.

Part Two contains the theologically constructive part of the paper wherein I propose Bavinck as a conversation partner to Missional Theology and suggest some of the insights that arise from placing the two in conversation. In order to do so, Part Two not only engages the broad themes of Missional Theology but also categories and classifies different types of Missional Theology in order to offer precision to the conversation.

II. HERMAN BAVINCK'S TRINITARIAN THEOLOGY

A. The Trinitarian Shape of Bavinck's Theology:

Throughout his magnum opus, *Reformed Dogmatics,* Bavinck contends for the irreducible importance of the confession of God's Triunity for the Christian faith and the dogmatic task. Reflecting on the centrality of the Trinity, Bavinck claims: "The entire Christian belief system, all of special revelation, stands or falls with the confession of God's Trinity. It is the core of the Christian faith, the root of all its dogmas, the basic content of the new covenant."[11] Given this assertion alongside of bold claims, such as "every error [in doctrine] results from, or upon deeper reflection is traceable to, a departure in the doctrine of the Trinity" and "the Christian mind remains unsatisfied until all existence is referred back to the triune God, and until the confession of God's Trinity functions at the center of our thought and life," it is clear that Bavinck sought to place the Trinity at the centre of his

[11] *RD*, II.333.

theological reflection.[12] This section suggests a framework for understanding the Trinitarian shape of Bavinck's theology that provides insights that are subsequently useful when offering Bavinck as a conversation partner to contemporary Trinitarian theology, specifically (in this discussion) Missional Theology.

In his section on the historical development of the doctrine of the Trinity in *Reformed Dogmatics*, Bavinck makes a seemingly off-hand statement in his evaluation of Tertullian's contribution to the formulation of Trinitarian dogma. He writes:

> Both formally and materially he has been of incalculable significance for the dogma of the Trinity. Despite his failure always to surmount subordinationism and to adequately *distinguish the ontological, the cosmological, and soteriological dimensions* of the doctrine of the Trinity, it is nevertheless Tertullian who furnished the concepts and terms that the dogma of the Trinity needed to articulate its true meaning.[13]

Within its immediate context, Bavinck's identification of the dimensions serves an evaluative role; however, it also indicates a line of argumentation worth pursing. For Bavinck, it seems, failure to distinguish these dimensions—an inadequate development, an insufficient account of their relationship, or an excessive concentration on one dimension at the expense of the others—leads to an insufficient doctrine of the Trinity. And, given his statements concerning the centrality of the doctrine of the Trinity, an inadequate doctrine of the Trinity undermines the integrity of creation and erodes the foundations of Christian faith.[14] Thus, Bavinck's comment, while brief, offers a window into Bavinck's own theological framework wherein the dimensions can be seen as serving a limiting and positive role in his dogmatic system.[15]

---

[12] *RD*, II.330, 288.

[13] *RD*, II.284 (emphasis added).

[14] I would also argue that these dimensions give shape, structure, and guide the content not only of Bavinck's locus on the doctrine of God but the *Reformed Dogmatics* as a whole, which is particularly evident in his treatment of epistemology, development of a Trinitarian cosmology, and articulation of a holistic understanding of the relationship between nature (creation) and grace (re-creation).

[15] The dimensions might also be a helpful way to interpret Bavinck's claim that the task of theology is to describe God and God alone: "All the doctrines treated in

First, positively, it is possible to frame Bavinck's whole systematic project as the proper development of the dimensions, including an account of their relationship and an articulation of their content. Concluding his treatment of the doctrine of the Trinity, Bavinck sets forth the threefold importance of the doctrine for the dogmatic task, wherein he implicitly appeals to the ontological, cosmological, and soteriological dimensions of the doctrine of the Trinity. First, it "makes God known to us as the truly living God" whose life is full and complete apart from the world.[16] Second, the doctrine of the Trinity alone maintains the possibility but non-necessity of creation, thereby making an account of the God-world relationship that is neither deistic (a world devoid of the divine) nor pantheistic (a world equated with the divine) possible.[17] And, third, according to Bavinck, the work of the triune God is the foundation of Christianity itself: "From God, through God, and in God are all things. Re-creation is one divine work from beginning to end, yet it can be described in terms of three agents."[18] The same triune God who, out of no necessity in His being, created the world is the same God who acts in redemption.[19]

---

dogmatics—whether they concern the universe, humanity, Christ, and so forth—are but the explication of the one central dogma of the knowledge of God. All things are considered in light of God, subsumed under him, traced back to him as the starting point. Dogmatics is always called upon to ponder and describe God and God alone, whose glory is in creation and re-creation, in nature and grace, in the world and in the church. It is the knowledge of him alone that dogmatics must put on display" (*RD*, II.29).

[16] *RD*, II.331: "only by the Trinity do we begin to understand that God as he is in himself—hence also, apart from the world—is the independent, eternal, omniscient, and all-benevolent One, love, holiness, and glory."

[17] *RD*, II.332: "Second, the doctrine of the Trinity is of the greatest importance for the doctrine of creation. The latter alone can be maintained only on the basis of the confession of a Triune God. It alone makes possible—against Deism on the one hand—the connection between God and the world, and—against Pantheism on the other—the difference between God and the world.... The dogma of the Trinity ... tells us that God *can* reveal himself in an absolute sense to the Son and the Spirit, and hence, in a relative sense also to the world."

[18] *RD*, II.334. See also Bavinck, *Our Reasonable Faith: A Survey of Christian Doctrine* (Grand Rapids: Baker, 1977), 158–59.

[19] It is widely held that grace restores nature is the central motif of Bavinck's theology. It is also being increasingly connected to his Trinitarian theology. See John Bolt, *A Theological Analysis of Herman Bavinck's Two Essays on the Imitatio Christi: Between Pietism and Modernism* (Lewiston, NY: Edwin Mellen Press, 2013), 155. Eglinton, *Trinity and Organism*, 96 suggests the Bavinck's motif of 'grace restores nature' is subordinate to

Within his account of the importance of the doctrine of the Trinity, then, Bavinck gives a clear indication of the ontological, cosmological, and soteriological significance of the doctrine as well as how to define each dimension. The ontological dimension of the Trinity affirms the fullness of the divine life apart from the world *ad intra* and grounds divine action *ad extra* in creation and re-creation.[20] The cosmological and soteriological dimensions of the Trinity are grounded in who God is, but they are the outward manifestations of God *ad extra*. The whole of Bavinck's systematic theology is about God and His works from beginning to end, examined in different dimensions in order to produce a truly Trinitarian theology.[21] The dogma of the Trinity is truly the root of all other dogmas from creation to re-creation. As Bavinck himself writes: "The thinking mind situates the doctrine of the Trinity squarely amid the full-orbed life of nature and humanity. A Christian's confession is not an island in the ocean but a high mountaintop from which the whole creation can be surveyed. And it is the task of Christian theologians to present clearly the connectedness of God's revelation with, and its significance for, all of life…."[22]

As the dimensions serve a positive role in Bavinck's dogmatic construction, they also function in a limiting role. Bavinck's identification of the ontological, cosmological, and soteriological dimensions serves as a

---

the doctrine of the Trinity in Bavinck: "The Triune God is the literal centerpiece of Bavinck's theology: he is the one approached in the *Prolegomena* and whose works in creation and providence are the subject of the remainder of *Reformed Dogmatics*. The Trinity is the heart of the Reformed vision and 'grace restores nature' is subordinate to it." Brian Mattson, *Restored to our Destiny*, 4 suggests that the relationship between grace and nature is not only defended on Trinitarian grounds but on the grounds of Reformed covenant theology. One of the benefits of reading 'grace restores nature' through the lens of the dimensions is the capacity to more closely connect the Trinitarian and covenantal grounds of the nature/grace relationship. This, however, is merely suggestive and is not argued in this paper.

[20] An epistemological note must be made to qualify this statement. Bavinck does not think human reflection on the divine being can know the divine essence. For Bavinck, the ontological dimension of the doctrine of the Trinity is a result of *a posteriori* reflection on revelation whereby one rationally reflects on the God who has revealed himself. All knowledge of God for Bavinck is analogical and anthropomorphic. We have no direct access to the divine essence.

[21] *RD*, I.44: "The imperative task of the dogmatician is to think God's thoughts after him and to trace their unity."

[22] *RD*, II.330. This is also important when thinking about Bavinck's neo-Calvinistic task of developing a triniform worldview.

summary statement of what he perceives as *the* key insight of the early church: freeing the doctrine of the Trinity from the philosophical speculation. Contra Arianism and Sabellianism, Bavinck argues, the church Fathers distinguished the ontological Trinity from its cosmological and soteriological dimensions in such a way that God's actions in the economy are not determinative or constitutive of the divine being.[23] This means that for Bavinck the cosmological and soteriological dimensions *cannot* be construed as constitutive of the divine being (ontological dimension) lest one allow philosophical speculation to creep back into theology.[24]

B. Bavinck: The Confession of the Triune God and His Creation

Examining Bavinck's claims concerning the three-fold dimensions of the doctrine of the Trinity would require nothing less than a comprehensive treatment of his entire systematic project. But, specifically turning to Bavinck's doctrines of God and Creation, the role of the ontological and cosmological dimensions of the doctrine of the Trinity and the relationship between them becomes clear; for Bavinck, the confession of the Triune God has cosmological significance.[25] This section examines the cosmological significance of the doctrine of the Trinity in Bavinck's *Reformed Dogmatics* in order to clarify the ontological and cosmological dimensions and clarify the framework used to engage with Missional Theology.

Although treated separately, Bavinck inextricably binds his loci on God and creation together.[26] The Christian confession of the Doctrine of the Trinity, in Bavinck's mind, uniquely maintains the non-necessity of creation for God and the ontological possibility of creation. Both claims together

---

[23] See *RD*, II.284–96.

[24] An underexamined aspect of Bavinck's theological and philosophical project remains his philosophy of history and claim that there are three basic worldviews (humanistic, deistic, and naturalistic) that reoccur in rhythmic waves throughout the history of human thought. See *Philosophy of Revelation* (London: Longmans, Green, and Co, 1909), 21.

[25] This topic builds on a growing consensus concerning the close relationship between Bavinck's doctrines of God and creation. See C.B. Cooke, "World-Formative Rest: Faithful Cultural Discipleship in a Secular Age" (PhD diss., Vrije Universiteit, Amsterdam, 2015), 148–95; Eglinton, *Trinity and Organism,* esp. chapter 4; Mattson, *Restored to our Destiny,* chapter 1.

[26] *RD*, II.332–422.

form the foundation for a truly Christian conception of creation wherein God freely *creates* and *sustains* the world. Furthermore, according to Bavinck, the confession of the doctrine of the Trinity alone provides the epistemological precondition for affirming the doctrine of creation over and against alternate conceptions of the world. And finally, the doctrine of the Trinity grounds the proper relationship between nature and grace, creation and re-creation.

1. The Nature of the Triune God, The Possibility but not Necessity of Creation, & The Divine Decrees

Bavinck's articulation of the cosmological significance of the Doctrine of the Trinity begins with a firm commitment to the non-necessity of creation for God because God is an "infinite fullness of blessed life" whose being from all eternity is full and complete.[27] Certainly, Bavinck states nothing profoundly new in this affirmation. The non-necessity of creation for God is a commonly held position in the theological tradition. Yet, Bavinck's identification of the two religious alternatives to the Christian doctrine of creation (Deism and Pantheism) and sustained engagement with them throughout his Doctrine of God proper (both *de deo uno* and *de deo trino*) is distinctive, especially in his *de deo uno*. Quite surprisingly for modern readers, who are often informed and normed by the current Trinitarian revival, Bavinck consistently argues that the incommunicable divine attributes (independence, immutability, infinity, and unity) are essential for guarding and maintaining God's infinite fullness of life apart from creation.[28] Why? Because they, along with the communicable attributes, describe the divine essence that the persons of the Trinity share apart from creation. For Bavinck, the Christian doctrine of God alone maintains the non-necessity of

---

[27] *RD*, II.308.

[28] Many adherents to the "Two Bavincks Hypothesis" similarly find Bavinck's appeal to independence, immutability, infinity, and unity as inconsistent with his relational, Christocentric theology. Thus, treatments of Bavinck's doctrine of God often jettison elements of his *de deo uno* or *de deo trino*, which are deemed not in line with his "true" theological project. The reading offered in this paper seeks to show the vital relationship between Bavinck's treatments of the divine essence and Trinity, and thus this paper does not agree with the assessment found in the following: Berkhof, *Two Hundred Years*, 114; Heilema, "Eschatological Understanding of Redemption," 104, 442; Heideman, *The Relation of Revelation and Reason*, 171.

creation over-against the alternatives of Pantheism and Deism because it alone can account for the full, complete, and rich life of the one triune God apart from creation.[29]

It is not just the affirmation of divine triunity for Bavinck that guards against Pantheism and Deism, but the *nature* of the Triune Being.[30] Thus, Bavinck starts his doctrine of God with a thorough treatment of the divine essence in order to "know what the divine nature comprises," which is "evident in the locus of the Trinity—in a threefold manner." [31] In other words, the three persons add nothing substantial to the divine Being; the divine nature is always, immediately unfolded tri-personally.[32] The attributes describe the "fullness of life in God" in whom there is no becoming for the Triune God "*is* all that he possesses."[33] This means, according to Bavinck, that the "Trinity reveals God to us as the fullness of being, the true life, eternal beauty," in whom is a perfect unity (nature) in diversity (persons) and diversity in unity[34]—a perfect community of infinite life. The fullness, completeness, and unity-in-diversity of the divine life is what guards against any notion of the necessity of creation. And, it is from this foundational affirmation that Bavinck launches his attacks against the religious alternatives of Deism and Pantheism throughout his *de deo uno*. For Bavinck, each non-

[29] Bavinck's assertion that only the Christian doctrine of the Trinity can maintain a doctrine of creation is not without critique. First, he does not argue why God must be Triune. In other words, Bavinck provides no rationale for why the full life of the divine being is unfolded tripersonally rather than bipersonally, quadpersonally, etc. Furthermore, he does not engage with Jewish or Islamic doctrines of creation. An argument could be extrapolated from his few mentions of Judaism and Islam that Bavinck would have categorized them as a type of Deism, but it would be hard to deduce how Bavinck would have specifically engaged them. These are criticisms also raised by Mattson, *Restored to our Destiny,* 43–44.

[30] The attributes Bavinck predicates of the divine being are rooted in his reflection on scripture, shaped by the Reformed Orthodox tradition, and informed by the Calvinistic emphasis on the anthropomorphic and analogical nature of all human knowledge of God. Affirming divine simplicity, Bavinck argues that the attributes are identical with His essence. And, the essence is immediately unfolded tri-personally.

[31] *RD*, II.150.

[32] *RD*, II.305.

[33] *RD*, II,174.

[34] *RD*, II.331. For an in-depth treatment of Bavinck's organic motif see Eglinton, *Trinity and Organism.*

Trinitarian alternative (Deism or Pantheism) sacrifices either the fullness and the completeness of the divine life shared by the three persons thereby rendering a conception of the divine who needs to create.

For example, divine independence guards against Pantheism because it affirms the independence of God in everything (existence, decrees, perfections, and works). God is who He is from all eternity. Divine immutability guards against Pantheism because it does not allow any conception of divine becoming. Against Deism, divine immutability also disallows a conception of the divine as the efficient cause of His own existence. Instead, God's will is also immutable. God is from all of eternity; he is not the cause of His own existence.[35] Divine infinity guards against Pantheism by positing infinity as God's transcendence over time and space. Time and space are modes of creaturely existence; God does not become through the endless stream of time or in and through the world. Furthermore, it denies Deism's restriction of God's essential presence to a specific location. Finally, divine unity guards against Pantheism by affirming a unity of simplicity and singularity over against pantheistic conceptions of the absolute, which strip the divine of any particularity. Only the Christian doctrine of God, according to Bavinck, can affirm the unity of singularity and simplicity, whereby God is, metaphysically, one being who is everything that he possesses unfolded tri-personally.[36]

In sum, Pantheism and Deism construct alternative doctrines of God whereby the divine is stripped of its fullness apart from creation. Creation is no longer creation in these alternatives; it is the outworking of a mechanistic principle or unconscious emanation. For Bavinck, it is the utter independence of God from creation that can make creation truly *creation*.

Yet, the doctrine of the Trinity not only maintains the non-necessity of creation for God but also grounds the ontological possibility of creation. Turning to Athanasius and Augustine, Bavinck argues that the fecundity of the divine life is what makes creation a metaphysical possibility. With Athanasius, Bavinck writes: "If the divine being were not productive and could not communicate himself inwardly (*ad intra*), then neither could there be any revelation of God *ad extra,* that is, any communication of God in and

---

[35] *RD*, II.157

[36] See *RD*, II, chapter 4.

to his creatures."[37] In other words, creation is ontologically possible because the divine being is communicative *ad intra.* To explain what this means, Bavinck turns to Augustine's account of the relationship between God's self-communication *ad intra* and creation. According to Bavinck, Augustine's key insight was identifying the immanent acts of generation and procession as archetypal for God's work in creation.[38] Agreeing with this, Bavinck argues that the divine act of creation is a weak and pale image of the communication that occurs fully, completely, and from all eternity in the Godhead.[39]

In both his loci on the Trinity and Creation, Bavinck boldly suggests a strong relationship between the immanent relations of the three persons and the manifestation of the divine being *ad extra.* Careful to qualify the relationship by vehemently denying any notion of the necessity of creation, Bavinck follows Augustine in suggesting that the roles attributed to each person in the economy are fitting to the "order of his existence in the divine being."[40] Even as, again following Augustine, all the divine works *ad extra* have one Author (*principium*), they come into being through the cooperation of the three persons, a cooperation which echoes or mirrors the immanent relations.

However, even if divine fecundity makes creation possible, the creation of the world cannot be attributed to mere metaphysical possibility. Thus, Bavinck turns to the Reformed doctrine of decrees to "establish a connection between the immanent works of the divine being and the external works of creation and re-creation."[41]

Most succinctly Bavinck defines the divine decrees as God's work *ad intra* as they relate "to the creatures who will exist outside of his being." These are distinguished from the immanent works of God that are directed towards His own being and are not equated with God's being such that God is obliged to realize them in time. Instead, there is a logical and necessary distinction between God's purely immanent works and those directed towards creatures,

---

[37] *RD,* II.332. Bavinck does not cite Athanasius here, but in his locus on Creation discussing a similar point he cites *Against the Arians,* II.

[38] Bavinck does not provide a citation for Augustine here. However, he does cite the following texts when making a similar point in his locus on Creation: Augustine, *Sermon* 117; *Freedom of the Will,* III.16–17; *On the Trinity,* XI.10; XV.14.

[39] *RD,* II.420.

[40] *RD,* II.319.

[41] *RD,* II.342.

which are further distinguished between the decrees and their execution in time.[42]

The doctrine of Divine decrees serves as the pivot point between the inward and outward actions of God and thus the ontological and cosmological dimensions of the Trinity. The divine decrees still belong to the works of God *ad intra,* but they establish the connection to God's works *ad extra.* The eternal plan of God, which is not "equated with God's being," but is closely connected with it, is that which will be worked out in time by the same God.[43] Given Bavinck's earlier grounding of the metaphysical possibility of creation in divine fecundity and relating the outward operations of the persons to their inner processions, the realization of the divine decree occurs in time through the *ad extra* works of the Triune God. These works remain attached to their metaphysical foundation: they are one divine action accomplished by the three persons of the Triune God. The ontological Trinity is the metaphysical ground for the cosmological work accomplished by the one and same God.

The strong relationship Bavinck asserts between the work of God *ad extra* and its metaphysical foundation is evident in Bavinck's treatment of creation. As the divine decree is God's counsel (*consilium dei*) concerning "all the things that exist or will occur in time," the "realization of the counsel of God begins with creation."[44] As a work of the one, Triune God, Bavinck affirms that God alone is the author of creation. Creation has a single *principium* or Author. As God is one, the outward works of God (*opera ad*

---

[42] Following a classical distinction between God's purely immanent works and the works directed towards creatures, Bavinck still closely relates the decrees—the works directed toward creatures ad intra and the essence of God—without collapsing the two. First, all the decrees are "derived from the fullness of knowledge that is eternally present in God," but they do not exhaust God's wisdom and knowledge. Second, they are the result of His eternal free choice. God's absolute sovereignty and self-sufficiency does not make creation metaphysically necessary for the divine being but makes creation necessary given God's free choice to create from all eternity. "It is his decree that makes the creation and preservation of the world necessary." Thus, while carefully and logically distinguished from the absolute activity that belongs to life of the Triune persons, the decrees cannot be abstracted from God's eternal life, as they are his eternal, full, and complete council of God concerning the whole plan of the whole universe, which is then executed in time (*RD* II.342–43).

[43] *RD*, II.373.

[44] *RD*, II.373, 407.

extra) are also one. God uses no external agents in creating the world.[45] Creation, as noted above, is truly creation. It is the act of creating something out of nothing whereby the product is ontologically distinct from its author.

Yet, drawing on Augustine and Athanasius again and utilizing but augmenting Irenaeus, Bavinck also argues in his locus on creation that each person of the Trinity "performs a task of his own in that one work of creation.... All things originate simultaneously from the Father through the Son in the Spirit."[46] The simultaneity of divine action means that the work of the three persons in creation cannot be diminished to the action of three separate efficient causes or considered in subordination to one another. However, fitting with the processions within the divine being, the Father is "the First cause," the Son is "not an instrument but the personal wisdom, the Logos, by whom everything is created ... and the Holy Spirit is the personal immanent cause by which all things live and move and have their being, receive their own form and configuration, and are led to their destination in God."[47]

God's outward actions (*opera ad extra*) mirror the divine life *ad intra.* In its cosmological dimension, creation proceeds from the Father, through the Son in the Spirit, "in order that, in the Spirit and through the Son, it may return to the Father."[48] As it proceeds from the Father and through the Son, Bavinck establishes the Son as the mediator of creation.[49] While the fecundity of the divine life makes creation possible, the decision to create is rooted in God's eternal decree.[50]

---

[45] *RD*, II.424.

[46] *RD*, II.423. In the course of his argument in this section Bavinck draws from Irenaeus, *Against the Heresies*, IV.20; Augustine, *Enchiridion*, 10; *On the Trinity*, VI.10; *City of God*, XI.24; *Confessions*, XIII.11; Athanasius, *Against the Arians*, II.2; *Ad Serap.*, III.5.

[47] *RD*, II.423.

[48] *RD*, II.426.

[49] *RD*, II.423.

[50] Recognizing the danger of equating the Son with the Greek philosophical conception of the Logos or rational pattern of the universe, Bavinck argues against Logos speculation whereby creation is more a work of the Father than the Son. Instead, Bavinck again draws on the communicability and fecundity of the divine essence from all eternity to defend creation as equally a work of the Father and the Son (and the Spirit) and utilizes a particularly Augustinian account of how the idea of the world is contained in the communication of the divine being from the Father to the Son. As the Father, who is the initiating cause of creation and the first,

The doctrine of the Trinity is cosmologically significant for Bavinck because it alone makes an account of the God-world relationship that is neither deistic nor pantheistic. Returning to the discussion of the dimensions of the doctrine of the Trinity in light of the cosmological significance of the doctrine, one can observe a close relation but necessary distinction between the ontological and cosmological dimensions of the Trinity. The ontological dimension affirms and articulates the divine life in itself apart from creation, and the cosmological dimension describes and defines the works of the one Triune God in relation to the act of creation. They are integrally related but necessarily distinct. Thus, rather than the two dimensions bifurcating the being of God, the cosmological dimension of God's work is always founded on who God is from all eternity. The ontological or immanent Trinity (*ad intra*) is the metaphysical foundation of the work of God *ad extra*. Conversely, the cosmological dimension of the doctrine is the articulation of God's work *ad extra* in creation, its establishment and governance. The Triune God's work is not a phase in God's inner life whereby the divine creates in order to actualize some latent potential.

C. Creation as Revelation: The Epistemological Importance of the Doctrine of the Trinity

Yet, importantly for Bavinck, the outward actions of God do not grant creatures direct access to the divine life *ad intra*. Just as the doctrine of the Trinity maintains the non-necessity yet ontological possibility of creation, so too it maintains the absolute incomprehensibility of God and also His knowability. In other words, as the doctrine of the Trinity assures an

---

unbegotten person of the Trinity, thinks about the idea of the world, He fully and completely communicates that idea to the Son as the divine being is communicated from the Father to the Son. It is not that the idea of the world is constitutive of the communication of the divine being from the Father to the Son, but that it is contained within it. It is not that the Son is the idea of the world, but in the Father's communication to the Son the idea of the world finds its fundamental form. Bavinck writes: "The idea that the Father pronounces in the Son is a seminal word, a fundamental form of the world itself. For that reason the Son is called the beginning (*arche*) and firstborn (*prototokos*), the origin of creation, the firstborn who sustains the creation, for whom it arises as its cause and example, and in whom it rests" (*RD*, II.425).

ontological distinction between God and creation, it also has epistemological importance.

Creation is truly, for Bavinck, an act of divine self-revelation whereby He enacts His decree in time so that His perfections and attributes are made manifest. But, as the Trinity maintains the non-necessity of creation for God, so too it establishes, epistemologically, the doctrine of divine incomprehensibility. So much so that Bavinck opens volume two of the *Reformed Dogmatics* with the statement: "Mystery is the lifeblood of dogmatics."[51] God's being is beyond comprehension. Full and complete in itself, God's knowledge of Himself is full and complete.

However, while incomprehensible, God is knowable. Because God communicates absolutely within Himself, He can communicate Himself in a relative way to creatures.[52] In other words, the doctrine of the Trinity guards against the doctrine of incommunicability of the divine. And, for Bavinck, creation is the first act of divine revelation. Echoing and expanding this point in the *Philosophy of Revelation*, Bavinck writes:

> The world itself rests on revelation; revelation is the presupposition, the foundation, the secret of all that exists in all its forms. The deeper science pushes its investigations, the more clearly will it discover that revelation underlies all created being. In every moment of time beats the pulse of eternity; every point in space is filled with the omnipresence of God; the finite is supported by the infinite, all becoming is rooted in being. Together with all created things, that special revelation which comes to us in the Person of Christ is built on these presuppositions. The foundations of creation and redemption are the same. The Logos who became flesh is the same by whom all things were made.[53]

---

[51] *RD*, II.29.

[52] Bavinck uses the archetype/ectype distinction to describe the relationship between God's self-knowledge and human knowledge of God. Human knowledge of the divine is weak, finite, and limited. It is the ectype of God's archetypal self-knowledge. Bavinck also, alongside the Protestant Orthodox, uses a three-fold distinction to describe the different degrees (not kinds) of human ectypal knowledge: the knowledge of union, the knowledge of vision, and the knowledge of pilgrims. See *RD*, I.212–14.

[53] *Philosophy of Revelation*, 17.

God's revelation in all His works displays who He is in a relative, creaturely way.[54]

Creatures do not possess archetypal knowledge of God, but they can come to true, limited, creaturely knowledge. Furthermore, as creation is the work of a creator God who is known in and through His works in creation, the whole creation is a theater that reveals His glory. Thus, creation does bear the marks or vestiges of the Trinity, not in terms of triads but in and through the unity and diversity of the created order. In sum, the unity-and-diversity of the Godhead is made manifest in a creaturely and relative way as God communicates outside of Himself.[55]

Significantly for Bavinck, the Triune God's actions in creating and sustaining the universe (or the Trinity in its cosmological dimension) not only serve as the epistemological ground for understanding who God is, but also guard against alternative understandings of creation, which he identifies as materialism and Pantheism and are corollary of Deism and Pantheistic conceptions of the divine. Both rooted in non-Trinitarian understandings of the divine, materialism and Pantheism either deny any divine involvement in the world or completely equate divine action in the world. According to

---

[54] As such, in the cosmological dimension of the Triune God's work, God is revealed as the creator and sustainer of the universe in a creaturely way. While God's intra-Trinitarian communication is complete and full, God's relative self-revelation to creation is a condescension to creation. Revealing himself to that which is not God requires that God speak in creaturely ways and through creaturely means. For Bavinck, this means that all knowledge of God anthropomorphic, analogical, ectypal, and mediated through creation.

[55] *RD*, II.333. This affirmation coincides with Bavinck's theology of revelation whereby all revelation is God's self-revelation mediated in and through creation, history, and self-consciousness. Human beings receive this objective, mediated revelation subjectively. In his *Reformed Dogmatics*, Bavinck develops three species of knowledge: Natural Knowledge of the World, which is the foundation of all science; Knowledge of God through General Revelation; and Knowledge of God through Special Revelation. For each, he identifies the *principium essendi* as God, whereas the *principium cogniscendi externum* and *principium cogniscendi internum* are determined based on the species of knowledge. Thus, for natural knowledge of the world, the *principium cogniscendi externum* is the created world, and the *principium cogniscendi internum* is reason as illuminated by the Logos. In general revelation, the *principium cogniscendi externum* is the creation, and the *principium cogniscendi internum* is reason—illuminated by the Logos, aided by the Spirit. In special revelation the *principium cogniscendi externum is* Scripture, and the *principium cogniscendi internum* is the Holy Spirit. See also *RD*, I.Part III: "Foundations of Dogmatic Theology."

Bavinck, both, coincidently, deny the possibility of true revelation just as they deny the possibility of creation.[56]

Epistemologically, then, the cosmological dimension is God's *opera ad extra* in relation to creation (including its preservation) whereby God reveals Himself relatively to His creatures. Through this revelation, one comes to know the one Triune God who is both intimately involved with creation as its creator who maintains, sustains, and draws it to its final end and the one who has a full and complete life in Himself. Only in and through knowing this revelation can one come to a true understanding of the world. The confession of the Trinity is the epistemological precondition for understanding creation amidst the alternatives of materialism and Pantheism.[57]

D. Creation and Re-Creation

In the previous sections, we examined the link between the ontological and cosmological dimension in order to articulate the cosmological significance of the doctrine of the Trinity in Bavinck. It remains to briefly explore the relationship between the cosmological and soteriological dimensions of the Trinity in Bavinck. And here it is essential to note that the divine act of creation is the beginning, but not the end, of the realization of the counsel of the Triune God in time and space. The realization of the counsel of God not only includes creation but also re-creation. Yet, for Bavinck, while the works of God in the divine economy cannot be isolated from one another, they must be distinguished from one another lest the relationship between nature and grace be confused. In other words, one must distinguish but not isolate the cosmological dimension and soteriological dimension, even as they both find their foundation in the ontological.

As with the cosmological dimension, the soteriological acts of God in the divine economy mirror the relationships *ad intra.* As such, the works appropriated to each of the persons of the Trinity in salvation are not severed from the works appropriated to the persons in creation and preservation. All

---

[56] *RD*, II.408–420.

[57] Bavinck's argument here moves beyond a merely descriptive argument to a prescriptive one concerning the epistemological importance of the doctrine of the Trinity and requires more critical engagement than can be offered here. See Mattson, *Restored to our Destiny*, 44.

the works of God "proceed from the Father, are accomplished by the Son, and are completed in the Holy Spirit."[58] Just as creation proceeds from the Father, so too re-creation proceeds from the Father. Just as the Son is the mediator of creation, so too is he the mediator of re-creation. He is the one "suited for the incarnation."[59] Just as the Holy Spirit is a gift, a personal immanent cause that gives all things their being and draws them to their end, so too the Holy Spirit is the one who completes the work of re-creation. As Bavinck writes at the beginning of volume 4 of the *Reformed Dogmatics:* "God produces both creation and new creation by His Word and Spirit."[60] The same God who creates is the one who redeems.

Yet, the works of God in creation and re-creation are distinct for Bavinck. Creation is the foundation of God's relationship with the world. It is His first act of revelation and displays His glory. In and through creation, God establishes a relationship with humanity, which is articulated by Bavinck through the conception of the covenant. Furthermore, as Bavinck articulates in his article "Creation or Development," it is at creation that the essence and end of all things are established.[61] The doctrine of creation for Bavinck assures that nature is given an integrity of its own.

Re-creation or redemption does not usurp nature but restores it, reorients it, and directs it to its final end. Grace, then, is not opposed to nature but sin. The soteriological dimension of God's work is founded on and preceded by the work of God in creation.

The chief point of importance here is Bavinck's firm commitment to resist collapsing the soteriological dimension into the cosmological, even as both find their metaphysical ground in the ontological dimension and are the outworking of God's eternal counsel. Collapsing the two, according to

---

58 *RD,* II.319.

59 *RD,* III.276: "the Son was the one suited for the incarnation. In the divine being he occupies the place between the Father and the Spirit, is by nature the Son and image of God, was the mediator already in the first creation, and as Son could restore us to our position as children of God."

60 *RD,* IV.33.

61 Bavinck, "Creation or Development." In this article, Bavinck argues against the elevation of evolutionary science to a philosophical worldview. He does not argue against the sciences but against their philosophical claims concerning ontological and metaphysical principles. Furthermore, he argues that it is only within a Christian worldview that one can affirm the development of Creation, which is grounded in the telos that God established for creation.

Bavinck, results in re-creation swallowing up creation. At best, creation merely becomes the stage upon which redemption occurs. At worst, the Fall or the Incarnation becomes ontologically necessary.[62] Certainly, for Bavinck, the Fall and Incarnation are inevitable given God's knowledge and the decrees, but they are not necessary. To err in understanding the integrity and importance of creation is to sacrifice Christian teaching to Gnosticism or Pantheism, whereby creation is diminished and cosmogony becomes theogony. Certainly, creation is the place where re-creation occurs, but according to Bavinck, creation is not merely the stage for re-creation. If it is only a stage, then, grace swallows up nature. God's glory and attributes *are* more clearly and magnificently displayed in re-creation, but it is not the sole display of God's glory. In sum, Bavinck's distinction and differentiation (without separation) of the works of God in creation and re-creation, relies on a distinction of the Trinity in its cosmological and soteriological dimensions. Only when they are properly articulated and connected can the full scope of God's works *ad extra* be maintained.

E. Summary

In concluding Part One, let us highlight a few things. First, the constructive reading offered of Bavinck utilizing his statement concerning the ontological, cosmological and soteriological dimensions of the doctrine of the Trinity underscores the importance of the doctrine of the Trinity in Bavinck's systematic theology. The dogma of the Trinity is the root of all doctrines from creation to re-creation, but who God is, is related but distinguished from what God does in creation and re-creation. Second, for Bavinck, the doctrine of the Trinity has cosmological and soteriological significance. Third, the doctrine of the Trinity shapes and forms the doctrine of creation and re-creation insofar as God's actions in creation mirror His life *ad intra.*

III. ENGAGING MISSIONAL THEOLOGY

While engaging and evaluating Bavinck's systematic project is a valuable pursuit, the main goal of the rest of the paper is to utilize Bavinck as conversation partner in dialogue with Missional Theology. As noted in the introduction, the choice to place Bavinck and Missional Theology in

---

[62] See *RD*, II.424.

conversation is intentional. Bavinck and missional theologians similarly place the doctrine of the Trinity at the centre of theological reflection and seek to develop truly Trinitarian accounts of God's work in the world. Bavinck and many missional theologians also share a concern for God's work in restoring all of creation. Yet, as they do so, they not only differ methodologically but also appropriate the Western theological tradition differently. Furthermore, Missional Theology is a primary example of the contemporary impetus to immediately subsume all doctrine into the doctrine of God in order to solve doctrinal conundrums and cure ecclesiastical action. Therefore, placing Bavinck in conversation with Missional Theology offers an example of the type of sustained engagement that must take place with modern Trinitarian theology.

First, we must identify more precisely what Missional Theology is. As stated in the introduction Missional Theology is a set of academic and popular theological projects that to some degree adhere to the idea that "as God is missional so the church is missional," utilize the term *missio Dei* to refer to God's missional nature, and generate missional praxis from the nature of the Triune God. Arising originally out of the ecumenical context, the impetus for Missional Theology was the need for a new theology of mission in the wake of colonial missions and the decline of Christianity in the West. Drawing from various theological movements, especially the Trinitarian revival, Missional Theology presented itself as a Copernican turn in theology, moving from an ecclesial conception of mission to a Trinitarian one. Given the focus on God's missional nature and action, Missional Theology is often encapsulated by the term *missio Dei.* However, while Missional Theology can be broadly defined as those theological proposals that utilize the *Missio Dei* and affirm the mantra "as God is missional so the church is missional," there are at least two distinct contemporary theological paradigms that utilize the *Missio Dei* and three ways that missional language is used in ecclesial life and theological development.

Theological Paradigms

(i) Cosmological *Missio Dei* Theology: The first missiological paradigm that used the *missio Dei* as an over-arching framework is the cosmological *missio Dei.* Arising during the 1960's and 70's, God's mission is defined as humanization and the eschatological vision of the kingdom, which is characterized by *shalom.*[63] The proponents of this vision of the *missio Dei,* such as the World Council of Churches (WCC) in the 1960's and 70's and Hoekendijk, saw the insights of the *missio Dei* as not only shifting the foundation of mission to doctrine God but also as presenting a renewed vision of the scope of God's mission.[64] What it means for God to be a missionary God is that His mission is tied to His involvement in the world-historical process of humanization and the movement towards *shalom.* Therefore the church's mission is to join these movements. Ecclesiologically, the church is constituted by and called to join God's movements in the world—the primary arena of divine activity.

(ii) Theo-centric *Missio Dei* Theology: Although the cosmological *missio Dei* reigned in the 1960's and 70's, another paradigm emerged that more closely related the mission of God and the mission of the church. This paradigm, represented by thinkers such as Newbigin, Tennent, Van Gelder, Bosch, Guder, Vicedom, Wright, and many others and asks the question: if we understand the *missio Dei* to mean that the Triune God is a missionary God who is the source of all mission, what does that mean for the mission of the church? Theo-centric *missio Dei theology* focuses on God's redemptive mission in the world through Israel, Christ, and the church. In this mission, God seeks to restore His reign and establish His kingdom. The church's mission is to participate in God's mission to establish His kingdom by being sent into the world. Ecclesiologically, the church is constituted by God's mission and is,

---

[63] For example, the WCC report on *The Church for Others* (a report prepared for the Uppsala WCC Conference, 1968) states: "God is constantly active in the world and since it is his purpose to establish *shalom,* it is the Church's task to recognize and point to the signs of this taking place … the whole world is implicated in the death and resurrection of Christ. Hence everything in the world may have a double aspect. Each time a man is imprisoned, tortured or destroyed, death is at work. But each time a man is a true neighbour, each time men live for others, the life-giving action of God is to be discerned. These are signs of the Kingdom of God and of the setting up of *shalom*…. So God as he moves towards his final goal, is using men and women, both inside and outside the churches, to bring *shalom.*" Based on such a vision for the world, the church is to look to the world for its agenda. "It is the world that must be allowed to provide the agenda for the churches." *The Church for Others: Two Reports on the Missionary Structure of the Congregation* (Geneva: World Council of Churches, 1968), 15–23.

[64] See J.C. Hoekendijk, *The Church Inside Out* (Philadelphia: Westminster Press, 1966), 24.

like God, missional by her very nature. Thus, while it shares with the cosmological interpretation the importance of recognizing the cosmic scope of God's kingdom, it does not equate God's mission with the world historical process.[65]

Use of *Missio Dei* in Ecclesial Life & Theological Development:

(i) *Theological Revisionists:* Theological revisionists move mission out of ecclesiology and soteriology and place it in the doctrine of God, and then seek to explain, theologically, the impact this has on the doctrine of the Trinity. Revisionists seek to articulate how God *is* missional in His very being. This includes but is not limited to making mission an attribute of God, mission constituting God's essence as He participates in the world historical process, and mission as being what defines the relationship between the three persons. In sum, *theological revisionists* seek to revise and renew theology based on the insight that God *is* missional. To do so, theological revisionists often draw on the material developed in what is commonly referred to as the Trinitarian revival in the later half of the 20th century. In other words, Barth, Moltmann, Rahner, etc. heavily influence these theological projects. The revisionists can belong to either the cosmological or theo-centric paradigms.[66]

(ii) *Missio Dei* as Model: Affirmative of the movement for the impetus of mission into the doctrine of God, those who use *Missio Dei* as a model do not seek to revise the doctrine of God but rather use the doctrine of God as the model for the church's mission. Missional Theology of this sort does less theological work in the doctrine of God proper, focusing instead on how the

---

[65]See David J. Bosch, *Transforming Mission*, 492; Richard DeRidder, *Discipling the Nations* (Grand Rapids: Baker, 1971), 13; Flett, *Witness of God*, 296; Darrell Guder, "From Sending to Being Sent," in *Missional Church: A Vision for the Sending of the Church in North America*, ed. Guder (Grand Rapids: Eerdmans, 1998), 7; *idem.*, "Practical Theology in Service of the Missional Church," in *Theology in Service of the Church: Essays in Honor of James D. Small*, ed. Charles A. Wiley et al. (Louisville: Geneva, 2013), 16; Lesslie Newbigin, *Open Secret: An Introduction to the Theology of Mission* (1978; Grand Rapids: Eerdmans, 1995), chapter 3; Van Gelder and Dwight J Zscheile, *The Missional Church in Perspective*, 3; Tennent, *Invitation to World Missions*, chapter 3; C.J. Wright, *The Mission of God: Unlocking the Bible's Grand Narrative* (Dower's Grove, IL: InterVarsity Press, 2013), esp. introduction and Part 1; Vicedom, *Mission of God*, 14, 17–26.

[66] A primary example of a Trinitarian Revisionist is Flett, *Witness of God.*

church's life should mirror the divine life.[67] As such, it is common to utilize social models of the Trinity to articulate the church's mission to the world.[68]

(iii) *Missio Dei* as Generic Term: While this is not a particular category of reflection on the *missio Dei,* it is important to mention. Because the phrase has become so common in reference to God and the church's mission, *missio Dei,* for some, has become synonymous with the history of salvation or God's redemptive actions. This has happened as *missio Dei* as a technical term has spread into other, less academic arenas. The *missio Dei* becomes an over-arching metaphor to explain that God is the author of redemption and the church is called to participate in the Spirit's work in drawing people back to God. Mission, here, becomes the new way to describe things like God's work of 'redemption' or even 'evangelism.' When used as an over-arching term, the term often mentions the Triune works of God and His mission, but it does not relate the work of mission back into God's nature.

Given the diversity of Missional Theology, the following engagement is preliminary and cursory. But, as we look at the vast landscape of contemporary Missional Theology and utilize Bavinck to engage in constructive conversation, there are two areas of concern that need to be addressed with regard to some of the ways missional theologians discuss the doctrine of God and consequently, ecclesiology.

If we take Bavinck's ontological, cosmological, and soteriological dimensions as a framework for constructing a truly Trinitarian theology wherein the whole of theology is articulation of who God is and what He does, it becomes clear that Missional Theology—especially in its more revisionary models—tends to collapse the categories. The theological revisionists collapse the soteriological and ontological dimensions of the Trinity with dire results. Even the more moderate usage of mission as a model can collapse the cosmological and soteriological dimensions such that creation is a mere stage upon which salvation takes place.

As more radical Missional Theology moves the mission of God from its soteriological and ecclesiological context into theology proper, it can be

---

[67] A primary example of using *missio Dei* as a model are Newbigin and Tennent.

[68]There are many overlaps here with the social Trinitarian movement in theology. See for example: David E. Bjork, "Toward a Trinitarian understanding of Mission in Post-Christendom Lands," *Missiology: International Review* 27, no. 2 (April 1999).

seen as trying to connect the soteriological and ontological dimensions of Trinity. In other words, seeking to ground God's soteriological works in who He is from all eternity, missional theologians make mission an attribute of God or that which describes the relations between the persons. It provides the connection point between God's inner and outer works. Yet, seen through the lens of Bavinck's necessary-connection-yet-distinction between the soteriological and ontological, it is evident that Missional Theology almost always collapses the soteriological into the ontological.

This becomes particularly problematic because mission, although broadly defined as "purposive sending," tends to also convey a sense of redemptive purpose in missional literature. There is no particular issue with defining God's action in the world as purposive or directed. Nor is there a problem with the idea of God's sending in the world, which is the traditional location for discussing the missions (*missio*) of the persons. However, if mission, defined as purposive-redemptive sending and made an attribute of the divine being, it becomes difficult to maintain the non-necessary nature of creation for God. It also becomes difficult to argue against the necessity of the Fall.

Second, even setting aside the versions of Missional Theology that equate God's mission with the world-historical process,[69] Missional Theology as a theological-ecclesiological project often articulates God's mission as being for the whole world. The church participates in this mission as it loves, worships, and serves a missional God. Echoing Bavinck's articulation of redemption as a type of re-creation, many missional theologians describe God as active in restoring all of creation. However, in seeking to spur the church on to participation in God's mission of restoration by connecting the nature of the church to the nature of God, most such accounts do not adequately articulate a full, Trinitarian account of creation. Thus, God's act of creation is always subsumed under redemptive mission. Or, in Bavinck's terms, the soteriological is collapsed into the cosmological. Creation may be redeemed, but it is primarily presented as a stage upon which redemption occurs. Furthermore, as that which is meant to be fully redeemed is ill-defined or underdeveloped, the church's participation in the mission of God similarly becomes unclear. Furthermore, by making mission what primarily constitutes the church's nature, it becomes difficult to maintain how a church that cannot

---

[69] This approach most obviously, in Bavinck's categories, collapses the cosmological into the ontological. God becomes a part of the cosmological process.

participate in redemptive activities is truly the church.[70]

In closing this brief constructive application of Bavinck's model of the three dimensions, one element of contrast between Bavinck and contemporary Missional Theology should be highlighted: the assessment of the Western theological project. Missional Theology as a whole, following many 20th and 21st century theologians, negatively assesses Western theological development since Constantine. Identifying Christendom as the downfall of the truly missional theology of the early church, missional theologians reject many traditional categories and classifications, particularly in the doctrine of God. Drawing on the Hellenization thesis as well as often uncritically adopting the methodological approach that collapses what God does in the economy with who God is, missional theologians tend to describe the codification and development of theology from Constantine to the 20th century as coinciding with and causing the downfall of mission in the church.[71] Thus, there is very little in contemporary Missional Theology that encourages or exemplifies how to engage with voices from the past. Bavinck, on the other hand, critically draws forward and seeks to revive the Reformed orthodox tradition in which he was raised. Perhaps the framework of ontological, cosmological, and soteriological could provide a different, constructive way forward in the development of Missional Theology that could positively appropriate the insights of the past.

I should stress that I am not against Missional Theology per se nor a description of God as missional or the church as missional. There is some benefit to this language, and some have developed in ways that are attentive

---

[70] A church undergoing intense persecution for example may not be able to participate as fully as another church in God's redemptive mission in the world. In certain missional theologians, such as Flett, this difficulty is slightly overcome as mission is more closely defined as witness to who God is.

[71] The Hellenization Thesis proposes that the Church Fathers corrupted Biblical religion with Greek Philosophy and constructed a concept of God that had little to do with the God of the Bible. Bavinck firmly rejects this thesis: see *RD*, II.279–90. Bavinck's rejection of the Hellenization Thesis is even more apparent when one observes his references to Harnack throughout the *Reformed Dogmatics*. It is clear that Bavinck read and utilized Adolf Van Harnack's *Dogmengeschich*. However, he does not come to the same conclusions regarding the Church Fathers' utilization of Greek philosophical tools and language. For Bavinck, the main triumph of the Fathers was to overcome philosophical speculation, even as they utilized the concepts, tools, and language of Greek philosophy.

to the potential problems highlighted above.[72] Furthermore, there are still issues in contemporary church praxis that must be addressed. However, I am often concerned at the lack of careful distinctions and discussions around talking about God as missional. Bavinck's theology, though not faultless, is helpful to this conversation as he displays how one can systematically develop a truly Trinitarian theology without collapsing every theological element into the doctrine of God proper. In other words, although all of theology is the doctrine of God for Bavinck, logical distinctions and careful articulation of the relationship between who God is and His works are helpful. Such distinctions need not lead to a cold, lifeless, abstract, or bifurcated deity; instead they can aid us articulating a truly Trinitarian theology that can satisfy the heart and the mind. As such, I hope that the cursory conversation between Bavinck's theology and Missional Theology not only illuminates some of the issues within contemporary Missional Theology but also suggests avenues for future engagement with other instances of contemporary Trinitarian theology. For, as theologians seek to do justice to the irreducible Trinitarian nature of Christianity, careful distinctions and categories aid and do not undermine such efforts.

---

[72] See for example, Stephen R. Holmes, "Trinitarian Missiology: Towards a Theology of God as Missionary," *International Journal of Systematic Theology* 8, no. 1 (January 2006): 72–90; and J.A.B. Jongeneel, "The Missiology of Gisbertus Voetius: The First Comprehensive Protestant Theology of Missions," *Calvin Theological Journal* 26 (April 1991): 47–79 where he uses the term *missio Dei* to describe God as the author of creation and redemption.

BIBLIOGRAPHY

Barth, Karl. *Church Dogmatics.* 2nd ed. 14 vols. Edited by T.F Torrance and G.W. Bromiley and translated by G.W. Bromiley. Peabody, MA: Hendrickson Publishers, 2010.

Bavinck, Herman. *Reformed Dogmatics.* 4 vols. Edited by John Bolt. Translated by John Vriend. Grand Rapids: Baker Academic, 2003–2008.

——. *Our Reasonable Faith.* Grand Rapids: Baker, 1977.

——. *Philosophy of Revelation.* London: Longmans, Green, and Co, 1909.

Berkhof, Hendrikus. *Two Hundred Years of Thelogy: Report of a Personal Journey.* Grand Rapids: Eerdmans, 1989.

Bevans, Sephen B. "Wisdom from the Margins: Systematic Theology and the Missiological Imagination." *Australian e-Journal of Theology* 5 (2005):1–18.

Bevans, Stephen B. and Roger P. Schroeder. *Constants in Context: A Theology of Mission for Today.* New York: Orbis Books, 2004.

Bjork, David E. "Toward a Trinitarian understanding of Mission in Post-Christendom Lands." *Missiology: International Review* 27, no. 2 (1999): 231–244.

Bolt, John. *Imitatio Christi. A Theological Analysis of Herman Bavinck's Two Essays on the Imitatio Christi: Between Pietism and Modernism.* Lewiston, NY: Edwin Mellen Press, 2013.

Bosch, David J. *Transforming Mission: Paradigm Shifts in the Theology of Mission.* New York: Orbis Books, 1991.

The Church for Others: Two Reports on the Missionary Structure of the Congregation. Geneva: World Council of Churches, 1968.

Cooke, C.B. "World-Formative Rest: Faithful Cultural Discipleship in a Secular Age." PhD diss., Vrije Universiteit, 2015.

DeRidder, Richard. *Discipling the Nations.* Grand Rapids: Baker, 1971.

Eglinton, James. *Trinity and Organism, Towards a New Reading of Herman Bavinck's Organic Motif.* London: T&T Clark, 2012.

Eitel, Adam. "Trinity and History: Bavinck, Hegel, and Nineteenth Century Doctrines of God." In *Five Studies in the Thought of Herman Bavinck, A Creator of Modern Dutch Theology,* edited by John Bolt, 101–128. Lewiston, NY: Edwin Mellen Press, 2011.

Erikson, Mildred. *Who's Tampering with the Trinity? An Assessment of the Subordination Debate.* Grand Rapids: Kregel Academic, 2009.

Flett, John G. *The Witness of God: The Trinity, Missio Dei, Karl Barth, and the Nature of Christian Community.* Grand Rapids: Eerdmans, 2010.

Fensham, Charles. *Emerging from the Dark Age Ahead: The Future of the North American Church.* Toronto: Clements Academic, 2011.

Guder, Darrell. "From Sending to Being Sent." In *Missional Church: A Vision for the Sending of the Church in North America,* edited by Guder, 1–17. Grand Rapids: Eerdmans, 1998.

——. "Practical Theology in Service of the Missional Church." In *Theology in Service of the Church: Essays in Honor of James D. Small,* edited by Charles A. Wiley et al., 13–22. Louisville: Geneva, 2013.

Harinck, George. "'Something that Must Remain, if the Truth is to be Sweet and Precious to Us': The Reformed Spirituality of Herman Bavinck." *Calvin Theological Journal* 38 (2003): 248–262.

Hastings, Ross. *Missional God, Missional Church: Hope for Re-Evangelizing the West.* Downers Grove: IVP Academic, 2012.

Heideman, E.P. *The Relation of Revelation and Reason in E. Brunner and H. Bavinck,* Part II. Assen, Netherlands: Van Gorcum, 1959.

Heilema, Syd. "Eschatological Understanding of Redemption." ThD diss., Wycliffe College, Toroto, 1998.

Hirsch, Alan. *The Forgotten Ways: Reactivating the Missional Church.* Grand Rapids: Brazos, 2007.

Holmes, Stephen R. "Trinitarian Missiology: Towards a Theology of God as Missionary." *International Journal of Systematic Theology* 8, no. 1 (2006): 72–90.

——. *Quest for the Doctrine of the Trinity: The Doctrine of God in Scripture, History, and Modernity.* Downers Grove: IVP Academic, 2012.

Jenson, Robert. *Systematic Theology, Volume 1: The Triune God.* New York: Oxford University Press, 1997.

Jongeneel, J.A.B. "The Missiology of Gisbertus Voetius: The First Comprehensive Protestant Theology of Missions." *Calvin Theological Journal* 26 (1991): 47–79.

Mattson, Brian. *Restored to Our Destiny: Eschatology and the Image of God in Herman Bavinck.* Studies in Reformed Theology 21. Leiden: Brill: 2001.

Kloosterman, Nelson. "A Response to 'The Kingdom of God is Twofold': Natural Law and the Two Kingdoms in the Thought of Herman Bavinck by David VanDrunen." *Calvin Theological Journal* 45 (2010): 165–76.

Moltmann, Jürgen. *The Crucified God.* Translated by R.A. Wilson and John Bowden. New York: Harper and Row, 1974.

Mowry LaCunga, Catherine. *God for Us: The Trinity and Christian Life.* New York: HarperCollins, 1991.

Newbigin, *Open Secret. An Introduction to the Theology of Mission.* 1978; Grand Rapids: Eerdmans, 1995.

Oborji, Fancis Anekwe. *Concepts of Mission: The Evaluation of Contemporary Missiology.* New York: Orbis Books, 2006.

Oliphant, Scott. "Bavinck's Realism, The Logos Principle, and *Sola Scriptura.*" *Westminster Theological Journal* 72 (2010): 359–90.

Rahner, Karl. *The Trinity.* Translated by Joseph Donceel. New York: Herder and Herder, 1970.

Roxburgh, Alan J. and M. Scott Boren. *Introducing the Missional Church: What it is, Why it Matters, and How to Become One.* Grand Rapids: Baker Books, 2009.

Tennent, Timothy C. *Invitation to World Missions: A Trinitarian Missiology for the Twenty-First Century.* Grand Rapids: Kregel Publications, 2010.

Van Gelder, Craig. *The Ministry of the Missional Church: Community Led by the Spirit.* Grand Rapids: Baker, 2007.

Van Gelder, Craig and Dwight J Zscheile. *The Missional Church in Perspective: Mapping Trends and Shaping the Conversation.* Grand Rapids: Baker Academic, 2011.

Stetzer, Ed and David Putnum. *Breaking the Missional Code: Your Church Can Become a Missionary in Your Community.* Nashville: B&H, 2006.

Van den Belt, Henk. *Autopistia: The Self-Convincing Authority of Scripture in Reformed Theology.* Leiden, Netherlands: Leiden University Press, 2006.

VanDrunen, David. "The Kingship of Christ is Twofold: Natural Law and the Two Kingdoms in the Thought of Herman Bavinck." *Calvin Theological Journal* 45, no. 1 (2010): 147–64.

Van Til, Cornelius. "Bavinck the Theologian." *Westminster Theological Journal* 24 (1961): 48–64.

Vicedom, Georg. *Mission of God: An Introduction to the Theology of Mission.* Translated by Gilbert A. Thiele and Dennis Hilgendorf. Saint Louis: Concordia, 1965.

Volf, Miroslav. *After Our Likeness: The Church as the Image of the Trinity.* Grand Rapids: Eerdmans, 1997.

Wright, C.J. *The Mission of God: Unlocking the Bible's Grand Narrative.* Dower's Grove, IL: InterVarsity Press, 2013.

Zizioulas, John D. *Being as Communion: Studies in Personhood and the Chruch.* London: Darton, Longman, and Todd, 1985.

VI:
BIBLICAL INSPIRATION AND THE DOCTRINE OF GOD, WITH ATTENTION TO THE EXAMPLE OF JOHN WEBSTER

Timothy G. Harmon, University of Aberdeen

ACCORDING TO 2 Timothy 3:16, "All Scripture is inspired by God" (NRSV). Many—prompted by this verse—have queried just what it means that the Bible is inspired. James Burtchaell, in his superb 1969 monograph, *Catholic Theories of Inspiration Since 1810: A Review and Critique*, compiled one of the most searching contemporary catalogues of the sundry theories that have come about from inquiries into the topic of biblical inspiration. Toward the end of this study, Burtchaell voices his frustration, exclaiming, "too much ink" has been "spilled" on the topic; "too many men struggled for too many years to such meagre advantage. It is discouraging … scant parturition has come forth from so many mountains in labor."[1] In reading this, it is good to keep in mind that Burchaell limited his research to only Roman Catholic theories over an approximate one-hundred-and-fifty-year time frame. Imagine his distress if he had undertaken a study of all theories produced over some two-thousand years of Christian history (not even accounting for Jewish approaches to inspiration)![2] While my consideration of biblical

---

[1] James T. Burtchaell, *Catholic Theories of Inspiration Since 1810: A Review and Critique* (Cambridge: Cambridge University Press, 1969), 281.

[2] For larger-scale accounts of the development of the doctrine of inspiration (from antiquity through modernity), see: W. Rohnert, *Die Inspiration der heiligen Schrift und ihre Bestreiter* (Leipzig: Verlag von Georg Böhme, 1889); Wilhelm Koelling, *Die Lehre von der Theopneustie* (Breslau: Verlag von Carl Dülfer, 1891); Christian Pesch, *De inspiratione sacrae scripturae* (Friburgi Brisgoviae: Herder, 1906); Sebastianus Tromp, *De Sacrae Scripturae Inspiratione* (Rome: Apud Aedes Universitatis Gregorianae, 1953); A. Bea, *De Scripturae Inspiratione. Quaestiones Historicae et Dogmaticae* (Rome: Pontificum

inspiration has been nowhere near as comprehensive, I can nonetheless identify with Burtchaell's exasperation: the topic is vast, unwieldy, and sustained study of it is frequently repaid by increased perplexity rather than clarity.

Still, inspiration is not a doctrine that may be summarily dismissed for being difficult. It is, after all, a biblical doctrine (even apart from reference to 2 Tim. 3:16), and, furthermore, one that significantly informs Christian faith and practice. As such I would commend continued efforts to find ways of responsibly confessing this doctrine. Still, I believe that some change in emphasis is warranted. Scott Swain, in a recent statement, seems to indicate that it may be more fruitful to focus on the fact *that* the Bible is inspired, rather than the question of *how* it was inspired.[3] I don't completely disagree with this. It is likely the case that too much attention has been given to the mechanics of inspiration—especially considering that the Bible itself tells us very little about how it was inspired. Still, I would like to suggest not just a move from *how* to *that*, but to *who*. In doing so, I am operating out of a conviction that one's view of God, both in Himself and as he is toward us, is the most significant factor in how one understands the doctrine of biblical inspiration.

In this essay, I explore some of the implications of what it means not just for the Bible to be inspired, but inspired *by God*. In other words, I am here focusing on the linkage between the doctrine of biblical inspiration and the doctrine of God, with attention given to the bearing of the latter upon the former.[4] And, beyond just arguing for the import of the doctrine of God,

---

Institutum Biblicum, 1935); and A. Bea, *De Inspiratione et Inerrantia Sacrae Scripturae* (Rome: Pontificum Institutum Biblicum, 1954).

[3] Scott R. Swain, *Trinity, Revelation, and Reading: A Theological Introduction to the Bible and Its Interpretation* (New York, NY: T&T Clark, 2011), 68–69.

[4] Some other recent attempts to explicitly consider the bearing of the doctrine of God upon the doctrine of Scripture, other than that of John Webster which will be discussed later in this essay, are as follows: Telford Work, *Living and Active: Scripture in the Economy of Salvation* (Grand Rapids: Eerdmans, 2001); David S. Yeago, "The Spirit, the Church, and the Scriptures: Biblical Inspiration and Interpretation Revisited," in *Knowing the Triune God: The Work of the Spirit in the Practices of the Church*, ed. J.J. Buckley and David S. Yeago (Grand Rapids: Eerdmans, 2001); Kevin J. Vanhoozer, "Triune Discourse: Theological Reflections on the Claim That God Speaks, Parts 1&2," in *Trinitarian Theology for the Church: Scripture, Community, Worship*, ed. Daniel J. Treier and David Lauber (Downers Grove: InterVarsity Press, 2009); Timothy Ward, *Words of Life: Scripture as the Living and Active Word of God* (Downers

I am trying to make the case that classical theism uniquely supplies resources for construing inspiration in a way that avoids a number of contemporary pitfalls regarding the nature of and divine action relative to the Bible.[5] The essay includes four parts. First, I define what I mean by "biblical inspiration." Second, I work through a number of difficulties with the core confession that the doctrine of inspiration exists to explicate, namely that "Holy Scripture is the Word of God." Third, I demonstrate how the resources of classical theism can be used to resolve difficulties with inspiration. Fourth, I highlight the example of John Webster.

WHAT IS BIBLICAL INSPIRATION?

Inspiration is notoriously hard to pin down—and this is true of the doctrine as much as the term. The early church supplied no definitive statement on it. While there is rich engagement with the concept of inspiration by those such as Origen, Theodore of Mopsuestia, and Augustine, their treatments are varied, and tend to deal more with the *that* of inspiration than with the *how*. When the manner of inspiration is addressed, it is often through use of a biblical metaphor, such as that of belching or scribal activity (see Psalm 44:1, LXX). Medieval accounts are not any more consistent, and they tend to take inspiration for granted, focusing on *sacra doctrina*, rather than detailing the origin or nature of Scripture as a source of doctrine. It was not until the post-Reformation era that, what Robert Jenson terms the "tradition's only doctrine of inspiration sufficiently developed to serve as a model and foil" was produced.[6] Indeed, seventeenth-century scholasticism offered the most widely-accepted and clearly-articulated version of the doctrine. Still—even if there was relative uniformity among post-Reformation formulations of inspiration, standardization of the doctrine did not endure. Between the

---

Grove, IL: IVP Academic, 2009); Denis Farkasfalvy, *Inspiration and Interpretation: A Theological Introduction to Sacred Scripture* (Washington D. C.: The Catholic University of America Press, 2010); and J. Todd Billings, *The Word of God for the People of God* (Grand Rapids: Eerdmans, 2010).

[5] A recent essay that similarly seeks to demonstrate the import of classical theism for the doctrine of Scripture is: Steven J. Duby, "Free Speech: Scripture in the Context of Divine Simplicity and Divine Freedom," *Irish Theological Quarterly* 82, no. 3 (2017): 197–207.

[6] Robert W. Jenson, "A Second Thought About Inspiration," *Pro Ecclesia* XIII, no. 4 (Fall 2004): 396.

eighteenth century and today, conceptions of inspiration have been fluid, and the available options can appear endlessly diverse.

In sifting through contemporary perspectives, three streams, elements of which are often blended together, are particularly noteworthy. The first stream finds accord with the traditional post-Reformation position. Here, inspiration involves divine action corresponding to the writing of the biblical texts, which then engendered unique characteristics in these texts. Inspiration is thus correlated with biblical production, biblical properties as a result, or both. The primary function of the doctrine is to account for the Bible's singularity. Friedrich Schleiermacher is an apt representative of the second stream, wherein inspiration is a more general divine influence upon the early church.[7] Here, inspiration is not strictly tied to biblical production, and the Bible's properties are given little attention. Inspiration, while present in a heightened way in the early church, can be experienced today as well. Inspiration, then, is less about the Bible's singularity, and more about human experience of the divine. The third stream is represented by Karl Barth, for whom inspiration is primarily a way of describing God's free revelatory action through the text.[8] For Barth, inspiration is not confined to any one component of this divine self-disclosure; rather it includes the then and there as well as the here and now. As such, the illumination of the reader or hearer of the text is included in the idea of biblical inspiration. While Barth did uphold the Bible's singularity, the function of inspiration, in his account, has

---

[7] In his own words, inspiration is simply "the influence of the Holy Spirit on the official activities of the Apostles." Inspiration does not "mean that the sacred writers . . . were informed of the content of what they wrote in a special divine manner." In other words, inspiration is not to be correlated with revelation. Rather, inspiration is involved in "all thinking, so far as it pertains to the Kingdom of God." The difference, then, between the inspiration of the Apostles and that involved in "the common life of Christians" is one of degree. With ordinary Christians, there are only "isolated traces" of inspiration. However, with the Apostles, inspiration admitted of "scarcely any weakening or alteration," due to their proximity to Jesus Christ. Friedrich Schleiermacher, *The Christian Faith*, trans. H. R. Mackintosh and J. S. Stewart (London: T&T Clark, 1999), 598–600.

[8] As he puts it, "This self-disclosure in its totality is *theopneustia*, the inspiration of the word of the prophets and apostles . . . The circle which led from the divine benefits to the apostle instructed by the Spirit and authorized to speak by the Spirit now closes at the hearer of the apostle, who again by the Spirit is enabled to receive as is necessary." Karl Barth, *Church Dogmatics*, ed. G. W. Bromiley and Harold Knight, trans. G. W. Bromiley and T. F. Torrance (Peabody, MA: Hendrickson Publishers, 2010), I, no. 2, 516.

less to do with explaining why the Bible is unique, and more to do with describing the unique action of God that occurs through the Bible.

To simplistically sum up the three streams identified above: the post-Reformation approach focuses on the text itself; Schleiermacher's emphasis is on the community wherein the text was produced; and Barth's accent is on God's self-revelation through the text. As mentioned above, aspects of these streams can be found in many contemporary approaches to inspiration. Conservative and evangelical treatments—such as those that appeal to the work of B. B. Warfield—tend to identify with the first stream. However, over the past several years, some conservatives have become sympathetic to the emerging "theological interpretation of Scripture" movement, which has been influenced by the third stream. In the run-up to Vatican II, Karl Rahner and others advanced social theories to inspiration, which, due to their understanding of inspiration as a charism present in the primitive Christian church, shared much in common with the second stream. Liberal theories of inspiration—such as William Abraham's student-teacher model, where inspiration is construed as influence—may also be identified with this second stream. Other recent theories—such as those of Paul J. Achtemeier, Sandra M. Schneiders, and Stephen B. Chapman—incorporate, in various ways, elements of all three streams, effectively defining inspiration as any divine activity related to the text.[9]

As is evident in the (quite selective) outline above, there are manifold ways inspiration can be defined. Because of this, it is important to specify what one means by "inspiration" in order to avoid equivocation. Doing so is not just a matter of identifying with one of the streams presented above, as all three capture a valid aspect of the biblical teaching regarding God's self-revelation. The question of which definition to use, then, is more about pairing certain terms with certain concepts in a system of doctrine. This is not to flatten out real differences between the approaches. Instead, it is merely to say that within a system of doctrine different terms can be used to identify the same biblical concepts. The term "inspiration" is not a strictly

[9] Such theories are often embraced by those sympathetic to a canonical hermeneutic, and are seeking to account for divine disclosure in and through the Bible, construed broadly enough to include a protracted and variegated process of composition and reception.

biblical one.[10] And so, the matter to be determined is which concepts one will choose to pair with this term—if the term is to be retained.[11] Here, I am using the term in way that generally accords with the traditional doctrine of biblical inspiration, which I define as: *that part of the Christian doctrine of Scripture which explicates the Bible's singularity in relation to all other creaturely texts as a consequence of its divine origin.* In doing so, it addresses both biblical production (causes/authorship) and biblical properties (nature/attributes).[12] These two items can be viewed as respectively correlating with the two main *loci classici* for the doctrine of biblical inspiration, 2 Peter 1:21 and 2 Timothy 3:16.[13]

---

[10] The English term inspiration is sourced in the Latin verb *inspiro*. In the Vulgate, a participial form of this term was used to render the Greek term θεόπνευστος (*omnis scriptura divinitus inspirata*) in 2 Timothy 3:16. The Latin verb from which it is sourced can be used to convey two basic ideas: (1) to stimulate, influence, or give rise to and/or (2) to breathe or blow into. In both senses, the verb takes an object. The English verb 'inspire' conveys the same basic two ideas, except that with the second, it is often taken to refer to in-breathing (inhalation) rather than out-breathing (expiration). The range of uses of the English noun inspiration is even more variegated. It can be used to describe the act of stimulation or breathing (whether in or out), a subject ('he is an inspiration'), or an object ('I had an inspiration').

[11] For a recent example of one who believes the term is misleading, and ought to be modified (to "spiration"), see A.T.B. McGowan, *The Divine Authenticity of Scripture: Retrieving an Evangelical Heritage* (Downers Grove, IL: IVP Academic, 2007).

[12] As will be evident later in my summary of John Webster's approach to inspiration, some believe that the proper topic of inspiration is biblical production, rather than biblical properties. However, even if this is the case, production and properties are intimately related, and it is one of these two topics (or both) that are in view in almost every classical treatment of every inspiration.

[13] In 2 Timothy 3:16, θεόπνευστος is a *hapax legomenon* in the Bible that appears to have been formed from the words θεὸς (God) and πνέω (to blow or breathe), with the verbal adjective ending τος. The term can be taken as either a passive verbal adjective (the majority position) or an active verbal adjective (the minority position). If the former, the idea conveyed by the term is that the Bible is divinely breathed product; if the latter the idea is that God is breathing by means of the Bible. Either way, this term seems to have little to do with biblical production. If the majority interpretation is correct, then it is primarily a term that informs our understanding of biblical properties. The biblical term that, classically, has been understood as referring to the Bible's production is found in 2 Pet. 1:21: φερόμενοι, from the verb φέρω, which denotes carrying or moving—and in context describes God as the subject acting upon human objects. In context, 2 Pet. 1:21 states that the Holy Spirit acted (ὑπὸ πνεύματος ἁγίου) to carry/move (φερόμενοι) human creatures, with the result being that they spoke (communicated verbally) from God (ἐλάλησαν ἀπὸ θεοῦ ἄνθρωποι).

THE CHARACTER OF THE BIBLE AS THE WORD OF GOD

Above, I defined the doctrine of biblical inspiration as that which exists to explicate the Bible's singularity through addressing biblical production (causes/authorship) and/or biblical properties (nature/attributes). I'll come back to the matter of biblical production a bit later. For now, I want to focus on the Bible's properties (its nature/attributes), through considering some ways in which the doctrine of God has been appealed to in order to describe the Bible's character as the Word of God. One of the more patent ways this has taken place is through the notion that if the Bible is *God's* Word, then it must reflect God's character. As such, it is thought, divine perfections can quite straightforwardly be predicated of Scripture. Matthew Barrett provides a recent example of this logic, when he writes: "Scripture is flawless because its divine author is perfect."[14] This logic is also found in the fairly common assertion that because God cannot lie (Titus 1:2), Scripture cannot err. A related move is one wherein predicates of God's *Word* are predicated of the Bible. Regarding the idea of biblical veracity, some appeal to John 17:17 ("thy word is truth").[15] In a like manner, some cite Hebrews 4:12 ("the word of God is living and active") and Psalm 119:89 ("Your word, LORD, is eternal") and conclude that the Bible is living, active, and eternal.

Already, I think it should be evident that there are problems with the sorts of moves made above. What does it even mean to attribute life, activity, and eternality to the Bible? Things get even more problematic when other divine perfections are considered, and the same logic used above is followed. What of God's infinity, sovereignty, omnipotence, omnipresence, omniscience, and immutability? May these be predicated of Scripture? If not, how does one decide which divine perfections may be predicated of Scripture, and which may not? Perhaps, one could appeal only to God's so-called communicable attributes (e.g., holiness, wisdom, truthfulness, goodness, and so on). Doing so would remove some problems (eternality, for example, would no longer be predicated of Scripture). However, not all

---

[14] Matthew Barrett, *God's Word Alone: The Authority of Scripture* (Grand Rapids: Zondervan, 2016), 270. Later, Barrett rightly—in my view—affirms, "*the doctrine of Scripture is inherently located within the doctrine of God*" (271). However, he seems to mistakenly assume that just because this is Scripture's proper doctrinal location, this means that divine perfections may be simply converted into biblical predicates.

[15] See, for example, Barrett, *God's Word Alone*, 264.

difficulties would disappear. For example, God's communicable attributes are sometimes delineated in a way that includes items such as patience, justice, wrath, and jealousy. It seems hard to say exactly how these items would be predicated of the Bible. In addition, there are attributes that are often predicated of the Bible that would make little sense if predicated of God (e.g., sufficiency—which acknowledges that, though the Bible's instruction is not comprehensive, it includes what is needed to accomplish its intended ends).

In my opinion, before too quickly correlating or converting divine perfections and biblical attributes, it is wise to pause and affirm that the Bible is not God, but a created thing. It was composed by humans, through fairly ordinary processes such as memory, oral transmission, inscription using conventional writing instruments and media, and editorial activity.[16] Along with its composition, the biblical texts were transmitted through human means, prior to being received as Christian Scripture.[17] Indeed, the biblical texts are characterized by many of the sorts of things true of creaturely things: they are material not immaterial; they came about through external means, rather than being wholly self-sufficient; they are composite, not simple; they are temporal, coming into existence in time, and involve change (if even only the change that took place in their composition process), not unoriginated, eternal, or immutable. This being the case, especially from the perspective of classical theism (wherein God simply *is* His perfections—so divine perfections cannot be predicated of creaturely things, without qualification), we ought to hesitate before facilely ascribing divine predicates of the Bible. Even John Frame, who is less than convinced of classical theism, acknowledges: "It is important … to distinguish the word of God itself, which is purely divine, from the created media through which the word comes to us … The Creator-creature distinction in Scripture is fundamental and nonnegotiable."[18]

---

[16] One could argue that there are portions of the Bible composed immediately by God—such as the Decalogue (see Exodus 31:18). Still, at the very least, the giving of the Decalogue involved creaturely media (the stone tablets).

[17] For a recent overview of the various factors involved in the Bible's composition, transmission, and reception, see: Paul D. Wegner, *The Journey from Texts to Translations: The Origin and Development of the Bible* (Grand Rapids: Baker Academic, 1999).

[18] John M. Frame, *The Doctrine of the Word of God: A Theology of Lordship, Volume 4* (Phillipsburg, NJ: P&R Publishing, 2010), 48. Hodge and Warfield make a similar point when they write, "The only really dangerous opposition to the Church doctrine of inspiration comes … from some false view of God's relation to the world."

So then, in what sense can the biblical texts be confessed to be the Word of God, if they are creaturely? Many different solutions have been offered. Some have appealed to the category of analogy, positing that the Bible is like the Word of God, in some way (e.g., God reveals himself through it). Others have sought to distinguish between different referents of the Word, such as the fourfold Protestant orthodox distinction between the eternal, incarnate, external, and internal Word (in which the Bible comes under the third category), or Barth's threefold distinction between the Word revealed, written, and proclaimed. The category of testimony can also be deployed, wherein Scripture is not God's Word *per se*, but in so far as it points beyond itself to God. In addition, philosophical distinctions can be made, such as that between matter and form, wherein the creaturely attributes of the Bible correlate with the former, and its divine attributes with the latter.[19] The confession has also been explained sacramentally, as a creaturely sign that participates in the divine, or mediates the divine presence. Along with this, some have appealed to resources supplied by the fields of linguistics and the philosophy of language—such as speech act theory—to elucidate the relation between Scripture and God's Word. Others have paired this with a sort of textual adoption, wherein Scripture is God's Word in the sense that He appropriates or deputizes it for His purposes. Finally, some seek to differentiate between Scripture and the Bible, correlating the Word of God with the former, but not the latter.

There is much that is laudable in the above attempts to clarify the confession that the Bible is the Word of God. While some of the solutions offered may be more convincing than others, the point here is this: recognition of the need to carefully distinguish and relate God and the Bible is imperative—regardless of which solution one employs. This will be dealt with in greater detail below, where I demonstrate how classical theism can help us to confess that the Bible is the Word of God in a way that comports with the biblical testimony about God and creation. However, before doing so, I want to underscore again the creatureliness of the Bible—for I do not believe we can rightly understand its singularity as Holy Scripture, in any

---

Archibald Hodge and B.B. Warfield, *Inspiration* (Eugene, OR: Wipf and Stock, 2008), 9.

[19] Other significant philosophical distinctions that can be made include those between the *verbum* ἄγραφον and *verbum* ἔγγραφον (the unwritten and written Word), and the *logos endiathetos* and *logos prophorikos* (the Word within and the uttered Word).

Christian sense, until we first acknowledge it to be creaturely. This does not mean following someone like Samuel Taylor Coleridge, who famously and scandalously announced in his *Confessions* that the Bible was to be viewed as a book like any other—if even the greatest of all books. Rather, I contend that it is a book like no other, for it is the Word of God—and I resonate with Gaussen's ruminations below:

> To what book … would you liken it? … After trying other books … listen to it … from its first to its last page [it combines] with its majestic unity the indefinable charm of human-like instruction … extending over forty centuries…. But behold, at the same time, what unity, and, lo! what innumerable and profound harmonies in this immense variety! … "Is it possible that a book at once so sublime and so simple can be the work of man?" was asked of the philosophers…. And all its pages have replied, No – it is impossible; for everywhere, traversing so many ages, and whichever it be of the God-employed writers that holds the pen, king or shepherd, scribe or fisherman, priest or publican, you everywhere perceive that one same Author.[20]

And yet, while uniquely of divine origin, the Bible is still a created thing—something material, temporal, and composite. So then, while it may seem especially pious to univocally ascribe divine predicates of the Bible (in the name of upholding a high view of Scripture), statements about the Bible that describe it as anything other than creaturely are instead ruinous—for, if the classical view of divinity is correct, they lead one to idolatrously call that which is not God, "God." A truly high view of Scripture, in my thinking, is one that retains the Creator-creature distinction, acknowledges the Bible as belonging to the latter category, and then thinks well about how to relate the Bible to God in a way that expresses its genuine singularity.

CLASSICAL THEISM AND THE BIBLE

Above, I said that the doctrine of inspiration explicates the Bible's singularity in relation to all other creaturely texts as a consequence of its divine origin (it

---

[20] Louis Gaussen, *Theopneustia*, trans. David Scott (Edinburgh: Johnstone & Hunter, 1850), 55–7.

is the Word of God), and it does so through engagement topics, biblical production (causes/authorship) and/or bib (nature/attributes). In the previous section, I dealt briefly w difficulties that attend the latter category—specifically, the question the Bible can be confessed as "the Word of God" while being creaturely. I indicated that while there are various possible ways of doing so, the common denominator that undergirds any successful explanation is the careful distinction and relation of God and the Bible—which is a specific instance of a more general concern, namely the proper distinction and relation of God and creation. Along these lines, I stated that the Bible's singularity cannot be rightly understood without first acknowledging that it is a created thing, and suggested that doing so is tied to a right recognition of God's singularity.

Here, I submit that there are two primary types of problems that result when God and creation are not properly distinguished and related, and that classical theism offers resources for avoiding these difficulties. The first kind of error stems from a lack of distinction between God and creation (e.g., as with pantheism, or perhaps ontotheology—depending on how one construes it). Here, God and creation are in some way identified (rather than related), allowing for the possibility that the Bible is divine. The second kind of error comes about from a lack of relation between God and creation. Here, God and creation are not just distinct—they also operate independently (e.g., as with deism, and certain strands of dualism). Such understandings of the Creator-creation distinction tend to view the Bible in almost exclusively creaturely terms. These two types of errors do not only impact how one thinks about biblical properties, but also biblical production: the first type of error leads one to view divine and human action as competitive in the Bible's production process; the second tends to view biblical production as a wholly creaturely endeavor.

So then—assuming agreement that the two perspectives identified in the paragraph above are sub-Christian, how can the errors associated with them be avoided? In classical treatments of the doctrine of Scripture, doing so was a function of attention to theology proper (God's life in Himself) and the economy (God's life turned outward to that which is other than Himself). It was understood that these broad doctrinal categories supply the conceptual means whereby God and the Bible can be properly distinguished and related—allowing one to affirm, "Holy Scripture is the Word of God," in a way that does not inappropriately identify God with or isolate him from his eation in general or His written Word in specific. Within theology proper, concepts such as aseity, simplicity, immutability, eternality, and the idea that God is pure act (without potentiality) are fundamental. These, traditionally, have been taken as glosses on the divine Name (see Exodus 3:14), helping to explain what is meant when one confesses it. Important entailments here include the ideas that God's being cannot be separated from His action (said another way, His essence just is His existence, and vice versa), and that His nature cannot be separated from his perfections (thus, God does not so much exercise His perfections, as He just *is* them). The only real distinction that can be made when it comes to God's life in Himself is that between the three persons of the Trinity, on the basis of relations of origin (processions): the Father generates, the Son is generated, and the Spirit is spirated from the Father (and the Son). These processions then inform the divine missions, and in these missions the work of the divine persons is inseparable.

In classical theism, the above view of theology proper provides the lens for understanding all that is not God. Classically, a right view of theology proper enabled one—by means of doctrines of creation (especially *creatio ex nihilo*) and providence—to construe creaturely being as infinitely distinct from yet intimately related to divinity, and creaturely action as compatible rather than competitive with divine action.[21] One of the ways this was done was through speaking of the relation between God and creation as mixed (logical on one side, and real on the other), rather than reciprocal.[22] To put it simply, a logical relation is one in which the term does not change in relation to the other, while a real relation is one in which the term does change in relation to the other. Mixed relations take place when two terms are not of the same ontological order—as is the case with Creator and creature, wherein the former is necessary and the latter is contingent. Thus, the relation between God and creation is mixed: God has a logical relation to creation, while creation has a real relation to God. This way of understanding the relation between God and creation allows for God to remain wholly

---

[21] For an excellent primer on how classical theism enables one to do so, see Kathryn Tanner, *God and Creation in Christian Theology: Tyranny or Empowerment?* (Minneapolis, MN: Fortress Press, 1988).

[22] See John Webster, "*Non Ex Aequo*: God's Relation to Creatures," in *God Without Measure: Working Papers in Christian Theology, Volume I, God and the Works of God* (London: Bloomsbury T&T Clark, 2016), 115–26. This was originally published in *Within the Love of God. Essays on the Doctrine of God in Honor of Paul Fiddes*, ed. A. Moore and A. Clarke (Oxford: Oxford University Press, 2014), 95–107.

transcendent in His self-sufficiency (and thus simple, immutable, eternal, and so on), while yet immanent with His creation, in a qualified sense.

How, then, might classical theism help one to confess, "Holy Scripture is the Word of God"? Perhaps most importantly, it does so through clarifying what this confession *cannot* mean, based on the Creator-creature distinction. For example, because God is simple, it cannot mean that God is Scripture (unless "Holy Scripture" is a predicate of divinity), nor that Scripture is God. Nor, on the basis of divine immutability, can it mean that the Bible becomes the Word of God, if by that, one means that the Bible, in some way, becomes divine, or takes on divine perfections. Nor, if God is pure act, can God's act of speech be differentiated from His nature.[23] But can classical theism help to *positively* confess Scripture as God's Word? I believe that the answer is yes, and one example—that of John Webster—will be provided in the following section. Let me also say that the example of Chalcedon is instructive here. While, on the whole, the incarnational analogy is best avoided (among other things, it ignores the fact that the incarnation is *sui generis*),[24] the Chalcedonian definition nonetheless demonstrates that a classical conception of deity need not be reworked in order to confess the most profound theological mysteries.

But if classical theism supplies a long-established means whereby knotty doctrines such as the doctrine of inspiration may be—if not fully untangled—at least confidently confessed, then why are such means given short shrift in contemporary theology as a whole, let alone in treatments of Scripture? While this is not the place to give a full-scale argument for classical theism's historic pedigree and biblical basis, nor a comprehensive recounting of its decline narrative, Richard Muller's 1983 essay, "Incarnation, Immutability, and the Case for Classical Theism," is worth considering briefly.[25] In this essay, Muller references a 1979 essay by Clark Pinnock, who voices a "complaint against the theological and philosophical synthesis that

---

[23] Kevin Vanhoozer seems to suggest this, when he writes, in order to explain how it is that the Bible is God's Word, that "speech is neither wholly me nor is it wholly other than me." On this basis, he applies the incarnational analogy to the Bible, positing that just as in Christ there are "two natures in one person," in Scripture there are "two voices in one text" (Vanhoozer, "Triune Discourse," 40).

[24] For an incisive critique of this analogy, see Lewis Ayres and Stephen E. Fowl, "(Mis)reading the Face of God: *The Interpretation of the Bible in the Church*," *Theological Studies* 60 (1999): 513–28.

[25] Richard A. Muller, "Incarnation, Immutability, and the Case for Classical Theism" *Westminster Theological Journal* 45 (1983): 22–40.

stood unshaken from the time of the early fathers, through the middle ages and the Reformation, into the period of Protestant scholasticism, and down to the beginning of the nineteenth century."[26] Pinnock himself uses the term "classical theism" in this essay to refer to this synthesis—one wherein doctrines such as divine immutability, impassibility, and eternality were regnant. While Pinnock advocates divergence from such doctrines on biblical grounds, Muller labors to show the influence of German idealism, and the shift from an ontology of being to one of becoming, on Pinnock's perspective. Another influence, says Muller, is Adolf von Harnack's Hellenization thesis. Per Muller, an admixture of these two influences has resulted in "a profound critique against virtually all pre-Kantian views of the divine attributes in the name of the gospel"—a critique exemplified by but not unique to Pinnock.[27] Muller goes on to argue that this critique falters, and he seeks to demonstrate that classical theism not only has the weight of traditional precedence, but further, accords with the teaching of Scripture. There is not space here to make a detailed case for why Muller's argument is more convincing than Pinnock's. At the very least, I want to suggest that Muller ought to be consulted prior to accepting Pinnock's narrative (which seems to have been embraced by many conservative evangelicals) *tout court.*

Along with the reasons Muller proffers, I would like to suggest two additional factors contributing to classical theism's present disfavor in my own conservative evangelical context. One factor is related to the use of language. D. Stephen Long provides an incisive assessment of the current situation, when he writes, "Modern theology finds itself swinging between two equally unpalatable poles."[28] One such pole is the tendency toward univocal language (the notion that "our language signifies God just as it is"), and the other toward equivocal language (the notion that our language "cannot signify God").[29] Classical theism navigates between these two poles,

---

[26] Muller, "Incarnation, Immutability, and the Case for Classical Theism," 22. Here, Muller is referring to Clark Pinnock, "The Need for a Scriptural, and Therefore a Neo-Classical Theism," in *Perspectives on Evangelical Theology*, ed. Kenneth Kantzer and Stanley Gundry (Grand Rapids: Baker, 1979), 37–42.

[27] Muller, "Incarnation, Immutability, and the Case for Classical Theism," 24.

[28] D. Stephen Long, *Speaking of God: Theology, Language, and Truth* (Grand Rapids: Eerdmans, 2009), 15.

[29] Long, *Speaking of God*, 16.

positing that our language for God is analogical.[30] Thus, when we call something in creation good, it is good in a way that is similar to the way in which God is good, but it is not exactly the same. God is infinitely good, while all creaturely goods are finite. God does not receive good, but is the eternal source of all creaturely goods. With God, good, while a distinct attribute (but not a separate part), is nonetheless coterminous with God. Thus, good is not something God occasionally chooses to be or act upon. Rather, because God is pure act, there is no potential for God to be or act good; He simply *is* good. However, contemporary evangelicals have tended to eschew the notion of analogical language in favor of univocal language. One reason for this—I think—is a desire to uphold the truth of the Bible, coupled with employment of a correspondence theory of truth, and the assumption that correspondence entails univocal language (which it does not).

A second factor contributing to classical theism's present disfavor is that it construes God (and, correspondingly, creation) in a way that is an affront to modern sensibilities. This is something picked up on by Kathryn Tanner, who writes that, in the contemporary era, classical accounts of divinity (here she is specifically referencing classical notions of divine agency) are taken to "imply a coercive tyranny that must block a creature's … capacity for free self-determination."[31] The commonly-accepted contemporary idea is that divine and human agency are inversely rather than directly proportionate: as divine agency increases, creaturely agency decreases, and vice versa. Thus, to make room for human freedom, divine agency must in some sense decrease. James Dolezal identifies an associated feature of modern theology, namely the idea that "God is involved in a genuine give-and-take relationship with His creatures"—or what he terms, "theistic mutualism" (or, "theistic personalism").[32] So then, in the contemporary climate, there is buy-in to the

---

[30] Thus, when we call something in creation good, it is good in a way that is similar to the way in which God is good, but it is not exactly the same. God is infinitely good, while all creaturely goods are finite. God does not receive good, but is the eternal source of all creaturely goods. In addition, with God—unlike creatures—good, while a distinct attribute, is nonetheless coterminous with God. Thus, good is not something God occasionally chooses to do. Rather, because God is pure act, there is no potential for God to act good or not; He simply *is* good.

[31] Tanner, *God and Creation in Christian Theology*, 2.

[32] James E. Dolezal, *All That Is In God: Evangelical Theology and the Challenge of Classical Christian Theism* (Grand Rapids: Reformation Heritage Books, 2017), 2.

notion of real reciprocal relationship and interaction with God, along with a desire to preserve creaturely freedom. While classical theism deals with these topics, the solutions it provides—such as mixed relations—are often viewed as unpalatable. For evangelicals, this appears to be linked to the earlier-mentioned embrace of univocal language, which leads to reading certain passages in a way that seems to require a reciprocal relation between God and creation (e.g., Exodus 32:14).

THE EXAMPLE OF JOHN WEBSTER

So far in this essay, I have defined the doctrine of inspiration as that which explicates the Bible's singularity in relation to all other creaturely texts as a consequence of its divine origin. Further, I have argued that this singularity cannot be rightly understood without first properly distinguishing and relating God and creation. I set forth the facile conversion of divine perfections and biblical attributes as a negative example, and suggested that classical theism supplies the resources needed to avoid this misguided practice. Here, in this section, I set forward John Webster as a salutary model of how to take seriously the import of the doctrine of God upon the doctrine of Scripture. In doing so, I focus on his mature treatment of inspiration, and show how it relies upon a classical understanding of theology proper, which then informs how he understands the Creator-creature distinction and relationship. Further, I highlight the way in which Webster focuses on select divine perfection (i.e., knowledge and goodness) as a means of explicating biblical inspiration. This move, I believe, is one we can learn from: rather than simply correlate a given divine perfection with a biblical attribute, Webster carefully demonstrates what that divine perfection has to do with the Bible and its inspiration.

John Bainbridge Webster (1955–2016) was a British theologian who is known, among other things, for his theological method.[33] While initially

[33] Regarding Webster's theological method, see John Webster "Discovering Dogmatics," in *Shaping a Theological Mind: Theological Context and Methodology*, ed. Darren C. Marks (Aldershot: Ashgate Publishing Company, 2002), 129–36; *idem*, "Theological Theology," in *Confessing God: Essays in Christian Dogmatics II* (London: T&T Clark, 2005), 11–31. This was originally published as *Theological Theology: An Inaugural Lecture delivered before the University of Oxford* on 28 October, 1997 (Oxford: Clarendon Press, 1998); *idem*, "Biblical Reasoning," in *The Domain of the Word: Scripture and Theological Reason* (London: Bloomsbury T&T Clark, 2012), 115–32, original

schooled in a more critical approach, Webster later came to be an advocate of what he termed "positive Christian dogmatics," which involved prioritizing confession over criticism.[34] Moving on from criticism, Webster sought to gain a better understanding of historical theology. Through this exercise, he came to appreciate the value of dogmatic orientation—that is, seeking to gain an understanding of individual doctrinal loci in view of their interconnections and as parts of a whole. In tracing these connections, Webster believed that the proper starting point is contemplation of God's perfect life in himself. All other doctrines are subordinate, and must be carefully ordered to theology proper, in order to avoid the distortion brought about by disorder and disproportion. Webster knew well the diligence and patience required for this work, and he committed himself to it. Further, he championed this work in an era and in a context where its validity and value had been, to a significant degree, overlooked or dismissed.

Webster's effort to orient all doctrines to theology proper is exemplified in his several treatments of the doctrine of Scripture. This is especially evident in his essays on Scripture written during the final decade or so of his career, when, in preparation for a planned multi-volume systematic theology, Webster focused on matters of prolegomena, along with key material aspects of Christian dogmatics' "double theme" of "theology proper and economy."[35] However, even in earlier essays on Scripture and its interpretation, Webster highlighted the import of the doctrine of God upon the doctrine of Scripture. For example, in his 1998 essay, "Hermeneutics in Modern Theology: Some Doctrinal Reflections," which leans into Barth and

---

published in *Anglican Theological Review* 90 (2008), 733–51; *idem*, "Principles of Systematic Theology," in *The Domain of the Word: Scripture and Theological Reason*, 133–49, originally published in *International Journal of Systematic Theology* 11 (2009): 56–71; Darren Sarisky, "Theological Theology," in *Theological Theology: Essays in Honour of John Webster*, ed. R. David Nelson, Darren Sarisky, and Justin Stratis (London: Bloomsbury T&T Clark), 1–15; Ivor J. Davidson, "John," in *Theological Theology: Essays in Honour of John Webster* (New York: Bloomsbury T & T Clark, 2015), 17–36; and John Webster, "What Makes Theology Theological?," in *God Without Measure: Working Papers in Christian Theology, Volume I, God and the Works of God* (London: Bloomsbury T&T Clark, 2016), 213–24. This was originally published in the *Journal of Analytic Theology* 3 (2015): 17–28.

[34] Webster, "Discovering Dogmatics," 130–131.

[35] John Webster, "On the Theology of Providence," in *The Providence of God: Deus Habet Consilium*, ed. Francesca Aran Murphy and Philip G. Ziegler (London, UK: Bloomsbury T&T Clark, 2009), 159.

away from scholasticism—a stance that is nearly the opposite of the one he would adopt later on, Webster underscores the fact that a properly Christian description of the Bible proceeds "under the aspect of divinity' (*sub specie divinitatis*)."[36] Still, it is in his later constructive work that the sensibility articulated in this earlier essay was given its most decisive expression.

Over the course of his career, Webster provided three significant treatments of the doctrine of biblical inspiration: in his 2003 monograph, *Holy Scripture: A Dogmatic Sketch*[37], his 2012 essay, "The domain of the Word,"[38] and his 2015 essay, "On the Inspiration of Holy Scripture."[39] All three show Webster laboring to orient the Bible to the doctrine of God. However, these treatments are far from uniform (even if, in a number of ways, they are complementary). A shift is evident in his 2012 essay, "The domain of the Word." In the preface to the volume this essay is contained in, Webster writes:

> Readers of earlier volumes … may notice some changes of emphasis and idiom in the present collection: more consideration is paid to patristic and mediaeval authors and to their heirs in post-Reformation scholastic theology, and more is expected of the theology of the creation and of the Spirit. Perhaps most of all, I have found my attention arrested by the preponderance of God's infinitely deep, fully realized life in giving an account of the substance of Christian faith.[40]

While Webster did indeed, in his later work, give less attention to modern figures such as Jüngel and Barth and more attention to scholastic figures such

---

[36] John Webster, "Hermeneutics in Modern Theology: Some Doctrinal Reflections," in *Word and Church: Essays in Christian Dogmatics* (Edinburgh, UK: T&T Clark, 2001), 47. Originally published in *Scottish Journal of Theology* 51 (1998): 307–341.

[37] John Webster, *Holy Scripture: A Dogmatic Sketch* (Cambridge: Cambridge University Press, 2003). In particular, see pages 5–41.

[38] John Webster, "The domain of the Word," in *The Domain of the Word: Scripture and Theological Reason* (London: Bloomsbury T&T Clark, 2012), 3–31.

[39] John Webster, "*ὑπὸ πνεύματος ἁγίου φερόμενοι ἐλάλησαν ἀπὸ θεοῦ ἄνθρωποι*: On the Inspiration of Holy Scripture," in *Conception, Reception, and the Spirit: Essays in Honor of Andrew T. Lincoln*, ed. J. Gordon McConville and Lloyd K. Pietersen (Eugene, OR: Cascade Books, 2015), 236–50.

[40] Webster, *The Domain of the Word*, ix.

as Anselm and Aquinas, it is the last part of the above statement that gets at what Webster perceives to be the ground of these changes, namely a more fulsome grasp of the significance of the doctrine of God—in particular God's perfect life in himself.

In my view, the trajectory set in "The domain of the Word" is most fully realized in Webster's essay, "On the Inspiration of Holy Scripture." In it, he lays out his most mature, systematic, and explicitly theocentric presentation of the doctrine of inspiration, sourced in "the doctrine of God the loving teacher who conducts ignorant creatures to knowledge of himself, and so to happiness."[41] In *Holy Scripture: A Dogmatic Sketch*, Webster had attended to "God's revelatory activity," that is, "the self-presentation of the triune God, of which the text is a servant."[42] However, while underscoring the importance of giving priority to divine movement in construing one's doctrine of Scripture and its inspiration, Webster did not give much space to explicitly detailing the nature and/or attributes of the God who is the agent of this movement.[43] In "The domain of the Word," Webster emphasized God's rule, which is "constituted by the communicative presence of the risen and ascended Son of God who governs all things."[44] While not ignoring God's revelatory activity, this essay situated it within a broader landscape where Jesus Christ reigns, and in which the doctrines of creation and providence are given sustained reflection. Still, the accent in this essay was on the economy, rather than theology proper.

In contrast with these former treatments of inspiration, "On the Inspiration of Holy Scripture" explicitly demonstrates the way in which attention to theology proper can serve to inform one's doctrine of Scripture. Webster begins his essay with a primer on method, outlining the material and formal considerations that must be addressed in developing a doctrine of Scripture.[45] After this, Webster proceeds to explicate these considerations in

---

[41] Webster, "*ὑπὸ πνεύματος ἁγίου*," 238.

[42] Webster, *Holy Scripture: A Dogmatic Sketch*, 6.

[43] Webster, *Holy Scripture: A Dogmatic Sketch*, 14.

[44] Webster, "The domain of the Word," 3.

[45] The material considerations he identifies are: location, origin, nature, ends, and uses. The first of these has to do with Scripture's location within the economy. The second addresses matters related to Scripture's causes or authorship; it is here that the doctrine of inspiration is directly attended to. The third topic deals with Scripture's properties or attributes, in view of its place in the economy, and its origin—including the fact that it was composed under divine inspiration. The fourth

greater detail, beginning with the first material topic, Scripture's location in the economy. However, prior to giving direct attention to the economy, Webster first turns to theology proper. In doing so, he focuses on God's knowledge and his goodness. With each of these, Webster highlights the way in which they set God apart from His creation, as informed by doctrines such as divine aseity and simplicity: God is the source of all knowledge—both of himself and His creatures; His knowledge is simple, and likewise eternal and singular—God does not acquire bits and pieces of information over time, nor is His knowledge fragmented in any way.

God's goodness explains why there is such a thing as creaturely knowledge, and why there are creatures at all. God does not create out of need or lack, but rather, *ex nihilo*, out of absolute benevolence. To His creatures, God gives, sustains, and directs knowledge, for the sake of "intelligent fellowship with the creator."[46] Thus, all creaturely knowledge is not only divine-sourced, but purposeful. Creation is, in Webster's words, "a realm of benevolent divine instruction and creaturely acquisition of knowledge."[47] Sin brings ignorance. However, God does not abandon His creatures. Rather, He works reconciliation through revelation: the Word is sent by the Father in the Spirit to instruct ignorant creatures, to the end of fellowship with God. Scripture, then, is situated within this economy as a gracious instrument of divine instruction.[48] It is in this context that the function of biblical inspiration is properly seen, namely explicating the way in which Scripture carries out its role, through attention to its causes or authorship. As Scripture's primary cause, God employs secondary causes, namely the prophets and apostles, whom God calls, sanctifies, and equips so

---

concerns the purpose or telos of Scripture. Here, the question of what Scripture exists for is posed. The fifth topic then regards the actual employment of Scripture, in accord with its ends. The formal considerations are: comprehensiveness, material order, and proportionality. As to the first, what Webster is getting after is the notion that, in the explication of a doctrine of Scripture, one must not be myopic, but rather, must have the whole in view. Second, not only the proper identification and relation of components is significant, but also their ordering. Third, care must be given so that doctrinal components are not unduly inflated or deflated.

[46] Webster, "*ὑπὸ πνεύματος ἁγίου*," 239.

[47] Webster, "*ὑπὸ πνεύματος ἁγίου*," 240.

[48] While it indeed is such an instrument, it is not the only one. Along with Scripture, Webster references assembly of the saints for worship, participation in the ordinances, and church government.

that "they become fitting instruments of divine teaching."[49] Inspiration, then, is the personal action of the Holy Spirit, in keeping with divine processions and missions, that moves these instruments so that they come to be used in God's work of benevolent instruction.

Such are the main contours of Webster's treatment of inspiration in "On the Inspiration of Holy Scripture." Along with what I have adumbrated above, Webster has much to say about the mechanics of inspiration, and when he does, correlates of classical theism such as mixed relations and compatibilism are appealed to. However, without detailing these, what I hope is evident in this sketch is the way in which, for Webster, the doctrine of God shapes how he apprehends everything else. In the particular instance presented here, Webster approaches biblical inspiration through consideration of God's wisdom and goodness—allowing classical dogmatic theology to delimit and direct his efforts. In so doing, more than providing a definitive statement on inspiration (there are facets of his approach that I do not follow),[50] Webster is teaching us how to take seriously the import of theology proper for any given theological loci. And, if any one lesson can be learned from Webster it is this: all theological inquiry proceeds *sub specie divinitatis*. The beautiful thing about a doctrine like divine simplicity—which Webster embraced—is that it allows one to contemplate a single doctrinal locus in so many different ways. Above, Webster selects the perspective of divine knowledge and goodness, and supplies a rich meditation of how these perfections inform the doctrine of Scripture—one wherein "God the loving teacher" by means of Holy Scripture, "conducts ignorant creatures to knowledge of himself, and so to happiness."[51] However, one could just as easily select attributes such as divine presence and sovereignty (which Webster gave greater attention to in *Dogmatic Sketch* and "The domain of the Word"), and explore Scripture in relation to these, as an instrument of God's self-presentation and rule.

Finally, I want to point out two particularly salient features of Webster's treatment of inspiration—especially in view of the content provided in the first three sections of this essay. First, Webster—through a

---

[49] Webster, "*ὑπὸ πνεύματος ἁγίου*," 242–43.

[50] Webster, following Augustine, believed that theology, *in via*, is discursive, and thus never static, but always developing.

[51] Webster, "*ὑπὸ πνεύματος ἁγίου*," 238.

classical understanding of theology proper—avoids the sorts of errors detailed earlier in this essay. His presentation is informed by a firm Creator-creature distinction, and yet he is able to relate the creature to the Creator in a profoundly intimate way. He does so through appeal to the language of divine missions, creation, and providence—along with more conventional appeals to the language of reconciliation. As to missions, inspiration, while an undivided work of the Trinity, is specially ascribed to the person of the Spirit. Creation and providence, then, supply the means to confess that the Spirit moves the biblical authors—not extrinsically, against their will, but intrinsically, in keeping with their creaturely design and calling—so that the words they write are ἀπὸ θεοῦ—from God (see 2 Peter 1:21). Creation and providence, however, are not independent of, but ordered to God's work of reconciliation. In this work, the Bible is no mere repository of information, but an instrument for directing creatures to their proper end: fellowship with the Trinity.

Second, although Webster does not treat biblical properties as a component of the doctrine of inspiration proper, he nonetheless addresses the nature of Scripture. For him, the Bible is *not* just a book like any other, apart from its use (either by God or within the church). Rather, as he puts it: Scripture is "a text that possesses certain properties … by virtue of the role it plays in the triune God's outer work in which he loves creatures by instructing them."[52] Along with existing for a specific end, these properties exist because of a particular origin, namely divine authorship, which, for Webster, is another way of talking about God's primary causality. Part of this causality is providing the human biblical authors the *res* and *verba* of the biblical texts—the contents of Scripture, and the precise words by which these contents are conveyed.[53] Certain properties may be predicated of these

---

[52] Webster, "*ὑπὸ πνεύματος ἁγίου,*" 241.

[53] Webster anticipates objections to verbal inspiration, appealing to the classical notion of non-competitive divine and human causality: "To say that God … supplies both content and word, is not to espouse an account of the authorship of Scripture that opposes its integral human authorship. It is, rather, to what *kind* of human authorship is exercised by the prophets and apostles, by tracing how it came to be and what is its end. Divine authorship is not partial or contributory; biblical inspiration is not joint authorship. Such conceptions once again envisage God as one of a string of causes, not as incommensurable first cause.… To say that those moved by the Spirit spoke from God is to say that Scripture arises from no violation of the literary integrity of its writers, but the opposite: ἀπὸ θεοῦ indicates both the sovereign

words, such as: "veracity, sufficiency, perspicuity, efficacy, canonicity, and authority."[54] And yet, these properties are not true of Scripture because some seem to correlate with divine perfections (and not all, of course, do). Rather, these properties accord with Scripture's divinely-determined "ambassadorial or ministerial" function, in which it "bears to us the divine Word."[55] It is in this way, then, that one can make a case for an attribute such as biblical veracity; Scripture is true, because veracity accords with Scripture's purpose in the economy, and God has perfectly fit Scripture for its purpose.[56] This may at first seem like a trivial distinction—but I believe it to be a significant one.

CONCLUSION

In this essay, I have considered what it means for the Bible to be inspired *by God.* I began by stating that while the doctrine of biblical inspiration is difficult, it ought not to be dismissed. However, I recommended a change in emphasis in ongoing efforts to construe the doctrine; while the fact and mechanics of inspiration are important, the most significant factor in how one understands the doctrine of biblical inspiration is, I said, the doctrine of God. As such, I commended paying close attention to the bearing of the doctrine of God upon the inspiration of Scripture. Further, in considering the doctrine of God, I maintained that classical theism uniquely supplies resources for construing inspiration in a way that avoids a number of contemporary pitfalls regarding the nature of and divine action relative to the Bible.

In the first part of this essay, I defined the doctrine of inspiration as that part of the Christian doctrine of Scripture which explicates the Bible's singularity in relation to all other creaturely texts as a consequence of its

---

origin and moving power of their authorship, and its genuinely human phenomenality" ("*ὑπὸ πνεύματος ἁγίου*," 249).

[54] Webster, "*ὑπὸ πνεύματος ἁγίου*," 237.

[55] Webster, "*ὑπὸ πνεύματος ἁγίου φερόμενοι*," 248. Webster believes that resistance to such a notion (whether out of a desire to uphold either Scripture's authentic humanity or divinity) is rooted in a "loss of confidence in the explanatory power of appeal to first and final causes."

[56] This leads to the question of what one means by biblical veracity or truth—which is a complex topic. Whether termed, "veracity," "truth," "inerrancy," or "infallibility," the issue is not so much the term, but how one defines that term.

divine origin. In the second part of the essay, I critiqued two ways the doctrine of God is appealed to in order to describe the Bible's character, and said that before correlating or converting divine perfections and biblical attributes, it is wise to pause and affirm that the Bible is a created thing. In the third part of this essay, I discussed two ways that an inadequate view of the Creator-creature distinction and relationship negatively impact one's understanding of biblical inspiration, and argued that classical theism offers resources for avoiding these difficulties. Finally, in the fourth part of this essay, I set forth the example of John Webster. In particular, I looked at his 2015 essay, "On the Inspiration of Holy Scripture."

My hope, in bringing this essay to a close, is—whether or not you are convinced that classical theism best explicates the Creator and all things in relation to Him, that you have been provoked to think more deeply about the import of the doctrine of God upon the doctrine of Scripture. Considering this connection, I believe, is not a stage to move past. If, indeed, all things—including all doctrines—acquire increased clarity over time, through the patient and prayerful contemplation of God's perfect life in Himself, then dogmatics is not finally about compiling or appealing to a reified compendium of doctrine, but rather, ongoing reflection upon God by means of His Word and Spirit. But this is not an undertaking to be done in isolation, but rather, in the assembly of the saints—those present with us today, and those who have gone before us.

And so, with the above thoughts in mind, it is fitting to conclude this meditation on Scripture with the following words, with which Webster concludes his final essay on the doctrine of Scripture and its inspiration. These words—an excerpt from the collect for the Second Sunday in Advent from the *Book of Common Prayer*—express well the saint's proper attitude toward Scripture:

> Blessed Lord, who hast caused all holy Scriptures to be written for our learning; grant that we may in such wise hear them, read, mark, learn, and inwardly digest them, that by patience, and comfort of the holy Word, we may embrace, and ever hold fast the blessed hope of everlasting life, which thou hast given us in our Saviour Jesus Christ. Amen.[57]

[57] John Webster, "*ὑπὸ πνεύματος ἁγίου*," 250.

BIBLIOGRAPHY

Ayres, Lewis and Stephen E. Fowl. "(Mis)reading the Face of God: *The Interpretation of the Bible in the Church*." *Theological Studies* 60 (1999): 513–28.

Barth, Karl. *Church Dogmatics*. Edited by G. W. Bromiley and Harold Knight, and translated by G. W. Bromiley and T. F. Torrance. Peabody, MA: Hendrickson Publishers, 2010.

Barrett, Matthew. *God's Word Alone: The Authority of Scripture*. Grand Rapids: Zondervan, 2016.

Bea, A. *De Scripturae Inspiratione. Quaestiones Historicae et Dogmaticae.* Rome: Pontificum Institutum Biblicum, 1935.

——. *De Inspiratione et Inerrantia Sacrae Scripturae.* Rome: Pontificum Institutum Biblicum, 1954.

Billings, J. Todd. *The Word of God for the People of God.* Grand Rapids: Eerdmans, 2010.

Burtchaell, James T. *Catholic Theories of Inspiration Since 1810: A Review and Critique*. Cambridge: Cambridge University Press, 1969.

Davidson, Ivor J. "John." In *Theological Theology: Essays in Honour of John Webster*, edited by R. David Nelson, Darren Sarisky, and Justin Stratis, 1–16. London: Bloomsbury T&T Clark.

Dolezal, James E. *All That Is In God: Evangelical Theology and the Challenge of Classical Christian Theism*. Grand Rapids: Reformation Heritage Books, 2017.

Duby, Steven J. "Free Speech: Scripture in the Context of Divine Simplicity and Divine Freedom." *Irish Theological Quarterly* 82, no. 3 (2017): 197–207.

Farkasfalvy, Denis. *Inspiration and Interpretation: A Theological Introduction to Sacred Scripture.* Washington D.C.: The Catholic University of America Press, 2010.

Frame, John M. *The Doctrine of the Word of God: A Theology of Lordship, Volume 4*. Phillipsburg, NJ: P&R Publishing, 2010.

Gaussen, Louis. *Theopneustia.* Translated by David Scott. Edinburgh: Johnstone & Hunter, 1850.

Hodge, Archibald and B.B Warfield. *Inspiration.* Eugene, OR: Wipf and Stock, 2008.

Jenson, Robert W. "A Second Thought About Inspiration." *Pro Ecclesia* XIII, no. 4 (2004): 393–98.

Koelling, Wilhelm. *Die Lehre von der Theopneustie.* Breslau: Verlag von Carl Dülfer, 1891.

Long, D. Stephen. *Speaking of God: Theology, Language, and Truth.* Grand Rapids: Eerdmans, 2009.

McGowan, A.T.B. *The Divine Authenticity of Scripture: Retrieving an Evangelical Heritage.* Downers Grove, IL: IVP Academic, 2007.

Muller, Richard A. "Incarnation, Immutability, and the Case for Classical Theism." *Westminster Theological Journal* 45 (1983): 22–40.

Pesch, Christian. *De inspiratione sacrae scripturae.* Friburgi Brisgoviae: Herder, 1906.

Pinnock, Clark. "The Need for a Scriptural, and Therefore a Neo-Classical Theism." In *Perspectives on Evangelical Theology*, edited by Kenneth Kantzer and Stanley Gundry, 37–42. Grand Rapids: Baker, 1979.

Rohnert, W. *Die Inspiration der heiligen Schrift und ihre Bestreiter.* Leipzig: Verlag von Georg Böhme, 1889.

Sarisky, Darren. "Theological Theology." In *Theological Theology: Essays in Honour of John Webster.*

Schleiermacher, Friedrich. *The Christian Faith.* Translated by H. R. Mackintosh and J. S. Stewart. London: T&T Clark, 1999.

Swain, Scott R. *Trinity, Revelation, and Reading: A Theological Introduction to the Bible and Its Interpretation.* New York: T&T Clark, 2011.

Tanner, Kathryn. *God and Creation in Christian Theology: Tyranny or Empowerment?* Minneapolis, MN: Fortress Press, 1988.

Tromp, Sebastianus. *De Sacrae Scripturae Inspiratione.* Rome: Apud Aedes Universitatis Gregorianae, 1953.

Vanhoozer, Kevin J. "Triune Discourse: Theological Reflections on the Claim That God Speaks, Parts 1&2." In *Trinitarian Theology for the Church: Scripture, Community, Worship*, edited by Daniel J. Treier and David Lauber, 25–78. Downers Grove: InterVarsity Press, 2009.

Ward, Timothy. *Words of Life: Scripture as the Living and Active Word of God.* Downers Grove, IL: IVP Academic, 2009.

John Webster. "Hermeneutics in Modern Theology: Some Doctrinal Reflections." In *Word and Church: Essays in Christian Dogmatics.* Edinburgh: T&T Clark, 2001; originally published in *Scottish Journal of Theology* 51 (1998).

——. "Discovering Dogmatics." In *Shaping a Theological Mind: Theological Context and Methodology*, edited by Darren C. Marks, 129–36. Aldershot: Ashgate Publishing Company, 2002.

——. "Theological Theology." In *Confessing God: Essays in Christian Dogmatics II*, 11–32. London: T&T Clark, 2005; originally published as *Theological Theology: An Inaugural Lecture delivered before the University of Oxford* on 28 October, 1997. Oxford: Clarendon Press, 1998.

——. *Holy Scripture: A Dogmatic Sketch.* Cambridge: Cambridge University Press, 2003.

——. "Biblical Reasoning." In *The Domain of the Word: Scripture and Theological Reason*, 115–32. London: Bloomsbury T&T Clark, 2012; originally published in *Anglican Theological Review* 90 (2008): 733–51.

——. "Principles of Systematic Theology." In *The Domain of the Word: Scripture and Theological Reason*, 133–49; originally published in *International Journal of Systematic Theology* 11 (2009): 56–71.

——. "The domain of the Word." In *The Domain of the Word: Scripture and Theological Reason*, 3–31. London: Bloomsbury T&T Clark, 2012.

——. "*ὑπὸ πνεύματος ἁγίου φερόμενοι ἐλάλησαν ἀπὸ θεοῦ ἄνθρωποι*: On the Inspiration of Holy Scripture." In *Conception, Reception, and the Spirit: Essays in Honor of Andrew T. Lincoln*, edited by J. Gordon McConville and Lloyd K. Pietersen, 236–52. Eugene, OR: Cascade Books, 2015.

——. "What Makes Theology Theological?" In *God Without Measure: Working Papers in Christian Theology, Volume I, God and the Works of God*, 213–24.

London: Bloomsbury T&T Clark, 2016; originally published in the *Journal of Analytic Theology* 3 (2015): 17–28.

——. "*Non Ex Aequo*: God's Relation to Creatures." In *God Without Measure: Working Papers in Christian Theology, Volume I, God and the Works of God*, 115–26. London: Bloomsbury T&T Clark, 2016; originally published in *Within the Love of God. Essays on the Doctrine of God in Honor of Paul Fiddes*, edited by A. Moore and A. Clarke, 95–107. Oxford: Oxford University Press, 2014.

——. "On the Theology of Providence." In *The Providence of God: Deus Habet Consilium*, edited by Francesca Aran Murphy and Philip G. Ziegler, 158–78. London: Bloomsbury T&T Clark, 2009.

Wegner, Paul D. *The Journey from Texts to Translations: The Origin and Development of the Bible*. Grand Rapids: Baker Academic, 1999.

Work, Telford. *Living and Active: Scripture in the Economy of Salvation*. Grand Rapids: Eerdmans, 2001.

Yeago, David S. "The Spirit, the Church, and the Scriptures: Biblical Inspiration and Interpretation Revisited." In *Knowing the Triune God: The Work of the Spirit in the Practices of the Church*, edited by J.J. Buckley and David S. Yeago, 49–93. Grand Rapids: Eerdmans, 2001.

VII: ENCOUNTER WITH THE TRIUNE GOD IN THE REFORMED LITURGY FOR THE LORD'S SUPPER: EUCHARISTIC PRAYER OR COMMUNION ORDER?

Christopher Dorn, Independent Scholar

THE EUCHARISTIC PRAYER (or Great Prayer of Thanksgiving) is the Christian church's expression of thanksgiving over the bread and wine at the Lord's Supper. In it the Father is praised and thanked, the Son is remembered for His saving acts through which God reconciled the world to Himself, and the Holy Spirit is invoked to bless the gifts of the bread and wine so that they may become for those who receive them the communion in the body and blood of Christ.

The Communion Prayer mandated for use in the Order for the Sacrament of the Reformed Church in America (RCA) provides an example of a contemporary Eucharistic Prayer, and will serve as the focus of the first part of this essay. Suffice it to say here that it shares with many other Eucharistic Prayers this basic Trinitarian structure. In this respect, they together conform to the classic Eucharistic Prayers of the fourth and fifth centuries, on which they were modeled when churches worldwide undertook to revise their liturgies for the Lord's Supper under the impetus of the liturgical and ecumenical movements of the twentieth century.

The basic ecumenical consensus on the Eucharistic Prayer as the privileged form for the celebration of the Lord's Supper is reflected in the document *Baptism, Eucharist and Ministry* (BEM), which the World Council of Churches' Commission on Faith and Order approved at Lima, Peru in 1982 for transmission to member churches.[1] BEM's formulation of the Trinitarian content of the Lord's Supper can be seen to have been drawn for the most part from the classic Eucharistic Prayers that member churches had already by that time adapted for their own use: The Lord's Supper involves thanksgiving to the Father, memorial of Christ, invocation of the Spirit, communion of the faithful, and anticipation of the kingdom. Translated into more than forty languages, BEM remains the most outstanding text of the modern ecumenical movement. Responses to BEM from more than 190 churches fill six volumes, indicating the high level of interest then in the subjects that it treated.[2]

In many confessionally Reformed churches, however, we are witnessing today a retreat from the liturgical consensus represented by BEM. It may be objected that since many of these churches did not at all participate in these movements, it hardly makes sense to speak of a retreat, so far as they are concerned. Nevertheless, it may also be possible to attribute this divergence in part to the current "(re)confessionalization" of these Reformed churches, at least as far as I have witnessed it in my region among congregations in the Presbyterian Church in America, Evangelical Presbyterian Church, the Orthodox Presbyterian Church, the United Reformed Churches in North America, among others. Not only does this find expression in a return to the sources of classic Reformed orthodoxy, including Calvin, the Reformed confessions of the sixteenth and seventeenth centuries, and the Puritan divines. It is also evident in the ongoing use of liturgies for the Lord's Supper patterned after the sixteenth-century Reformed communion orders.[3]

Compelling arguments can be made for the rejection of a Eucharistic Prayer in favor of a classic Reformed communion order as a framework for a Reformed liturgy for the Lord's Supper, and I will attempt to review some of these later in this essay. The question, however, is whether this rejection

---

[1] Faith and Order Paper No. 111 (Geneva: World Council of Churches, 1982).

[2] *Churches Respond to BEM: Official Responses to the Baptism, Eucharist and Ministry Text* (vols. 1–6), ed. Max Thurian (Geneva: World Council of Churches, 1986–88).

[3] For the complications that the co-existence of the ecumenical and confessionally Reformed Eucharistic traditions have introduced into the manner in which Reformed congregations worldwide celebrate the Lord's Supper, see F. Gerrit Immink, *The Touch of the Sacred: The Practice, Theology, and Tradition of Christian Worship*, trans. Reinder Bruinsma (Grand Rapids: William B. Eerdmans Publishing Company, 2014), 224–6.

comes at too high a cost. If the liturgy for the Lord's Supper ought to reflect, model, or even mediate and enact an encounter between the Triune God and his covenant people as they assemble at the Lord's Table, then it is important to ask whether and how far the classic Reformed communion order satisfies this requirement. My analysis will suggest that it does not go far enough. I then examine critically the theological rationale for the defense of the Reformed communion order on the basis of sixteenth-century Reformation concerns. I argue that these do not decisively rule against the use of the Eucharistic Prayer. However, if confessionally Reformed churches remain unconvinced, it may nevertheless be possible to reconceive the classic communion order in a way that resolves the difficulties the preceding analysis will have uncovered. I conclude with a suggested model that may help the confessionally Reformed churches to recover a more robust Trinitarian conception of the celebration of the Lord's Supper.

THE COMMUNION PRAYER[4]

In his now classic *Eucharist in the West*, the late liturgical theologian Edward J. Kilmartin advances the hypothesis that the developed Eucharistic Prayer has its antecedents in the covenant prayers of the Jewish people.[5] An analysis of the structure common to these prayers reveals that it consists generally in (1) thankful recognition of the fidelity of God in initiating and maintaining the covenant; and (2) confident petition to God to restore and build up the covenant people with a view to the final fulfillment of the covenant.

In view of this basic "anamnetic-epicletic"[6] structure, Kilmartin proposes that the Eucharistic Prayer articulates a theology of covenant

---

[4] The Communion Prayer is in large part a translation of several formulae from the Eucharistic liturgy of the Reformed Church in France (ERF), which is found in the *Liturgie de l'Eglise réformée de France*, first published in 1950 and then in a revised edition in 1963. For an extended discussion of the process by which the committee arrived at the decision to adopt the majority of this French liturgy to serve as the prototype of the Communion prayer for the RCA, see my *The Lord's Supper in the Reformed Church in America: Tradition in Transformation* (New York: Peter Lang, 2007), 108–121. For the literary and theological analysis that appears below, see 167–75.

[5] *The Eucharist in the West: History and Theology*, ed. by Robert J. Daly, S.J. (Collegeville: The Liturgical Press, 1998), 333, 340, 355.

[6] With regard to the claim that the Eucharistic Prayer has an "anamnetic-epicletic" structure, it may be helpful here at the outset to define the two liturgical terms contained in the expression. *Anamnesis* can designate that section of the Eucharistic

modeled on that of the covenant into which God entered with Israel. But in the developed Eucharistic Prayers of the fourth and fifth centuries, this theology is patterned after the trinitarian activity of God in establishing the new covenant in Jesus' blood. God enters into relationship with the new people of God from the Father, through the Son, and in the Holy Spirit. For this reason, the Christian petition for the fulfillment of the covenant relationship (the goal of eucharistic praying) is ordered to a twofold communion in the Holy Spirit with Christ (and through him with the Father), on the one hand, and with the ecclesial body of Christ in the unity of this same Spirit, on the other. It remains now to examine whether and in what manner the worshiping assembly that offers the Communion Prayer is seeking this very goal. To facilitate the analysis, I reproduce the text of the prayer here:

> The Lord be with you.
> **And also with you.**
> Lift up your hearts!
> **We lift them up to the Lord.**
> Let us give thanks to the Lord our God.
> **It is right to give our thanks and praise.**
>
> Holy and right it is, and our joyful duty to give thanks to you at all times and in all places, O Lord our Creator, almighty and everlasting God! You created heaven with all its hosts and the earth with all its plenty. You have given us life and being, and preserve us by your providence. But you have shown us the fullness of your love in sending into the world your Son, Jesus Christ, the eternal Word, made flesh for us and for our salvation. For the precious gift of this mighty Savior who has reconciled us to you we praise and bless you, O God. With your whole Church on earth and with all the company of heaven we worship and adore your glorious name.

Prayer that recalls God's saving acts; it can also refer in the more restricted sense to that part of the prayer after the institution narrative ("On the night on which he was betrayed, he took bread...") that begins "remembering, we therefore...." *Epiclesis* can mean "petition" generally, but it typically refers to the invocation of the Holy Spirit on the bread and wine of the Lord's Supper and/or the people who share them.

**Holy, holy, holy Lord, God of power and might,
heaven and earth are full of your glory.
Hosanna in the highest!
Blessed is he who comes in the name of the Lord.
Hosanna in the highest!**

Most righteous God, we remember in this Supper the perfect sacrifice offered once on the cross by our Lord Jesus Christ for the sin of the whole world. In the joy of his resurrection and in expectation of his coming again, we offer ourselves to you as holy and living sacrifices.

Together we proclaim the mystery of the faith:

**Christ has died!
Christ is risen!
Christ will come again!**

Send your Holy Spirit upon us, we pray, that the bread which we break and the cup which we bless may be to us the communion of the body and blood of Christ. Grant that, being joined together in him, we may attain to the unity of the faith and grow up in all things into Christ our Lord. And as this grain has been gathered from many fields into one loaf, and these grapes from many hills into one cup, grant, O Lord, that your whole Church may soon be gathered from the ends of the earth into your kingdom. Even so, come, Lord Jesus!

[The Lord Jesus, the same night he was betrayed, took bread; and when he had given thanks, he broke it and gave it to them, saying, "Take, eat; this is my body which is given for you: do this in remembrance of me."

After the same manner also, he took the cup when they had supped, saying, "This cup is the new testament in my blood: this do, as often as you drink it, in remembrance of me."

The bread which we break is the communion of the body of Christ.

> The cup of blessing which we bless is the communion of the blood of Christ.][7]

It is clear that in the Communion Prayer the assembly speaks to God both in thankful memory and in petition that God strengthen it in the covenant relationship with a view to its eschatological fulfillment. In the opening thanksgiving (or "preface"), the assembly expresses its recognition of the Father's goodness and love through giving thanks for the gifts of creation and life, which the Father preserves by His providence. But it renders praise to the Father especially for "sending into the world [His] Son, Jesus Christ, the eternal Word." In contrast to many of its counterparts, however, the Communion Prayer does not subsequently elaborate on the saving acts that God accomplished through Jesus Christ; it is content rather to sum these up by reciting the Nicene principle for the whole economy of salvation: "made flesh for us men and for our salvation." Closer analysis of this Christological section of the preface, however, reveals the awareness that the mission of the Word has two dimensions: one relative to human beings (Jesus Christ the Lord is the experiential manifestation of the "fullness of the [Father's] love for human beings"); the other relative to God (Jesus Christ the Lord, "who became man for us men and for our salvation," is the agent of the implied acts by which he has "reconciled" the assembly to God).

In the confidence that arises from the recognition that this "mighty Savior" has reconciled it to God, the assembly can dare to claim that its worship has communion with the "whole Church on earth and with all the company of heaven who cry, 'Holy, Holy, Holy!'"

The memorial proclamation of the saving intervention of God through Jesus Christ naturally leads to joyful petition for fulfillment of the covenant relationship established in Jesus. Before the *epiclesis*, however, there appears an *anamnesis*-offering formula: commemorating the "perfect sacrifice once offered on the cross by our Lord Jesus Christ for the sin of the whole world," the worshippers express their desire to offer themselves to the Father "in the joy of his resurrection and in expectation of his coming again" as "holy and living sacrifices."[8]

---

[7] The full text of the Communion Prayer can be found at http://images.rca.org/docs/worship/lordsday.pdf, 12–14.

[8] The *anamnesis*-offering formula is conventional in contemporary Eucharistic Prayers, but in the Communion Prayer it diverges from the majority of its counterparts with regard to the immediate context in which it stands. In most

The offering serves as a bridge to the invocation of the Holy Spirit to transform the worshippers so that their desire to participate in the saving acts summarized in the memorial acclamation ("Christ has died…) may be realized. The Spirit is understood to mediate Christ to the worshippers, so that they may enjoy communion in the body and blood of Christ and with one another now and later in the kingdom of the Father still to come. To this end, the assembly asks the Father to send the Holy Spirit upon it in the expectation that the confirmation and completion of the covenant relationship will be signified and sealed in sacramental communion.

An analysis of the epicletic section in the Communion Prayer, accordingly, reveals the desire of the community (1) to obtain communion in the body and blood of the Lord under the mode of the actions of breaking the bread and blessing the cup; (2) to become what it has received (that is, anticipating the reception of the sacramental body of Christ, it seeks to become the ecclesial body of Christ); and (3) to participate in the kingdom fully realized when the Lord Jesus comes again and the "whole Church [is] gathered from the ends of the earth into [this] kingdom." In these words adapted from *Didache* 9.4, we see an expansion of the *epiclesis* into an eschatological perspective: the community seeks to be transformed into the ecclesial body of Christ, "grow[ing] up in all things into him who is the Head, even Christ our Lord," in the hope of what has still to be achieved. In other words, the community expects to experience in sacramental communion with Christ and with members of His body the anticipation of the joy of the Kingdom.

Eucharistic Prayers, the formula typically follows the institution narrative, which ends with the memorial command ("Whenever you drink it, do this in remembrance of me…"). The *anamnesis*-offering formula then appears as a response of obedience to Jesus' command that the meal be celebrated in memory of him ("Remembering, therefore, we offer to you…"). In the Communion Prayer, however, this formula is free-standing and the institution narrative, instead of being incorporated into the prayer itself, is appended to it. For the problems that this disjunction between the institution narrative and the *anamnesis*-offering formula creates for the internal coherence of the prayer and for the movement of the liturgy of the Lord's Supper generally, see my *The Lord's Supper in the Reformed Church in America*, 169–72.

THE TRINITARIAN DYNAMIC OF THE COMMUNION PRAYER

In the Communion Prayer, communion with Christ (and in and with Him reconciliation with the Father) is mediated by the Holy Spirit through the faith of the community expressed in a memorial proclamation of the saving acts of Jesus Christ. The worshippers open themselves to the Father's descending movement (*katabasis*) toward them through Jesus Christ, a movement recreating and renewing the covenant people, precisely through their own ascending movement (*anabasis*) toward God in prayer and petition. To enlarge on this point even further, we may observe that through the prayer there is a "binding" and "actualization" of the covenant relationship in which the self-offering of the Father through the Son in the Holy Spirit finds response in the self-offering of the worshippers to the Father in thanksgiving for Jesus Christ with whom they enjoy communion through the Spirit. In this perspective, the Communion Prayer conveys a dialogical understanding of the Lord's Supper, in which the divine *katabasis* in word and sacrament is the enabling condition for the human *anabasis* in praise, thanksgiving, and petition. The association of these two movements in this liturgy for the Lord's Supper reflect, model, or even mediate and enact the divine communication of life and the participation of the worshippers in the gift of this new life. It bears repeating that this is the goal of the liturgical celebration, the content of the act of communion.

Arguably, failure to articulate the mystery of this communion in explicitly Trinitarian terms represents a failure to respond adequately to the demand the Apostle Paul laid down in his account of the institution of the Lord's Supper. To the cup saying, "do this, as often as you drink it, in remembrance of me" (1 Cor. 11:25), Paul added, "for as often as you eat this bread and drink this cup, you proclaim the Lord's death until he comes" (v. 26). Proclamation of the death of Christ of course already occurs in the rehearsal of the institution narrative, but it cannot be limited to it. Proclaiming it adequately demands situating it within the broader context of salvation history, on which it depends for its meaning. In this connection, Wolfhart Pannenberg interprets the significance in early Christian Eucharistic celebrations of the readings from the prophets (Old Testament) and the "memoirs of the Apostles" (New Testament).[9] "In this way, recollection of

[9] Cf. Justin Martyr, *The First Apology*, 67.
http://www.ccel.org/ccel/schaff/anf01/Page_186.html

Jesus and his death included what God did under the old covenant and brought to light its prophetic function relative to the coming of the person of Jesus and his history within God's saving work on behalf of the human race."[10] The readings thus enlarged the scope of the *anamnesis* of Christ's death to include the "totality of salvation history that culminated in the death and resurrection of Jesus Christ."[11] Only then does it become possible to see that in the "fullness of time, God sent his Son, born of a woman, born under law, to redeem those under the law, that we might receive adoption to sonship" (Gal. 4:4–5). And the Trinitarian structure of the experience of this salvation finds concentrated expression in the verse that follows: "Because you are his sons, God sent the Spirit of his Son into our hearts, the Spirit who calls out *Abba* Father" (v. 6). If the liturgy of the Lord's Supper, not to mention worship generally, does not enable and guide this response on the part of the worshippers, then it is in danger of losing its distinctively Christian character. It thereby puts worshippers at risk of failing to recognize that they assemble in the Holy Spirit to worship God the Father through Jesus Christ. The consequences for Christian orthodoxy, as well as the spiritual health of the churches, can only be fatal sooner or later.

THE TRINITY AND THE CLASSIC REFORMED COMMUNION ORDER

The image with which John Calvin introduces his doctrine of the Lord's Supper in Book IV, Chapter 17 of the 1559 edition of the *Institutes* implicitly situates the sacrament within a Trinitarian context: what is happening at the Lord's table is nothing less than the gathering of a household, where the Father graciously receives worshippers not only as servants but as sons and daughters. He demonstrates His fatherly care for His offspring by nourishing them at a spiritual banquet, in which Christ attests Himself as lifegiving bread.[12] Later Calvin asserts that the souls of the worshippers are truly refreshed by the eating of His flesh and the drinking of His blood thanks to

---

[10] *Systematic Theology*, vol. 3, trans. Geoffrey W. Bromiley (Grand Rapids: Eerdmans, 1998), 333.

[11] *Systematic Theology*, 334.

[12] *Institutes of the Christian Religion*, ed. John T. McNeill, and trans. Ford Lewis Battles (Philadelphia: Westminster, 1960), 2:1359–1360.

the Holy Spirit, who imparts to them the things signified by the sacrament, despite the distance and separation between them and Christ.[13]

It remains to be seen, however, whether this Trinitarian conception of the Lord's Supper finds adequate articulation in the Reformed communion order, which constitutes the classic framework for the Reformed liturgy for the Lord's Supper, both among the Reformed churches at the time of the Reformation and the confessionally Reformed churches at the present time. To determine an answer to this question, it will be helpful to provide an outline of the communion order found in the *Forme des Prieres* that John Calvin compiled for Geneva in 1542.

Prayer for Worthy Reception
Institution Narrative from 1 Corinthians 11:23–29
Fencing of the Table
Self-Examination
Comfortable Words
Exposition of the Meaning of the Sacrament
Reformed *Sursum Corda*
Distribution accompanied by a sung Psalm or Scripture Readings
Post-communion Psalm or Prayer of Thanksgiving

A communion order of this sort used in the fledgling Reformed churches probably derived in most cases from a vernacular paraliturgical service popular in the territories of Southwest Germany and the Swiss city states.[14] In the communion order outlined above the institution narrative (drawn from 1 Cor. 11:23–29) serves as the biblical warrant for the celebration and, after the prayer for worthy reception (also known as the prayer of humble access), introduces the entire order. The penitential sections, consisting in the excommunication, the self-examination, and the comfortable words, follow. These can be seen as a response to the Pauline admonition to everyone "to examine himself" lest he "eat and drink condemnation to himself" (vv. 27–29). Then comes a long exposition of the meaning of the Last Supper, in accord with Calvin's conviction that the institution narrative is no liturgical formula enunciated by the priest, but rather "a living preaching which edifies its hearers … and reveals its

[13]*Institutes*, 2:1370.

[14] Cf. my *The Lord's Supper in the Reformed Church in America*, 5.

effectiveness in the fulfillment of what it promises."[15] There follows the Reformed *Sursum Corda* in which the worshippers are exhorted to seek Christ on high where He dwells "in the glory of his Father," and not in the "earthly and corruptible elements" as if He were "enclosed in the bread or wine." The order resumes with the distribution of the bread and the wine, accompanied either by the singing of a Psalm or Bible verses recited by the minister. The post-communion thanksgiving concludes the service, and the assembly is dismissed with a blessing.[16]

It is not necessary to analyze the texts of the formulae indicated here to conclude that the fundamental aim of the Lord's Supper celebrated within the framework of this communion order is to ensure a fruitful reception of the sacrament. For Calvin and his Reformed co-religionists generally this necessitated a detailed exposition of the meaning of the institution narrative, with emphasis on the moral disposition necessary for access to the table, as well as an explanation of the proper relation between the sign (bread and wine) and signified (body and blood of Christ). Parenthetically, it is worth noting that in contrast to what we have seen in our analysis of the Eucharistic Prayer, communion in the body and blood of Christ is not mediated by the eucharistic *action* of the worshipping assembly. Rather the worshippers are nourished by the *reception* of Christ's gifts, as he accomplishes in them inwardly all that He shows them outwardly by the visible signs of bread and wine. In this perspective, the proper place for thanksgiving is *after* the consumption of the elements.

The forms for the administration of the Lord's Supper in the confessionally Reformed churches in the United States today do not depart from this basic pattern and outlook. A brief glance at those found in the directories for worship of the Orthodox Presbyterian Church and the Presbyterian Church in America, for example, will suffice to confirm this observation.

In the framework adopted by the former, the minister begins the celebration with the reading of the institution narrative drawn from either 1 Corinthians 11:23–29 or one of the Gospel accounts of the Last Supper (Matthew 26:26–29, Mark 14:22–25, or Luke 22:14–20). The form provides for an exposition of the meaning and nature of the sacrament, after which

---

[15] *Institutes*, 2:1416.

[16] English translation in Bard Thompson, *Liturgies of the Western Church* (New York: World Publishing, 1961), 197–210.

follow the invitation and the fencing of the table. The minister may proceed next to the act of exhorting the assembly with the Reformed *Sursum Corda*. He concludes this part of the celebration with a prayer for worthy reception. Then, taking up the bread at the table, the minister introduces the fraction by repeating the institution narrative. The bread is broken, and the elements are distributed and consumed. The celebration concludes with a prayer of thanksgiving and a parting blessing.

In the guidelines for the celebration prescribed for the latter, there are no real differences worth mentioning, with the exception of the omission of an explicit fencing of the table. In the last analysis, one can conclude that both maintain fidelity to the essential shape of the sixteenth-century Reformed communion order.

But in returning to the object of our investigation, we have again to confront the question: Is the Lord's Supper as framed by the Reformed communion order conceived as a Trinitarian event? Perhaps a tentative answer is that in the Reformed communion order it is not as conspicuously so as implied in Calvin's theology of the Lord's Supper outlined in the *Institutes*. Both the prayer for worthy reception and the post-communion thanksgiving are directed to the Father, but no explicit language about the role and activity of the Holy Spirit in uniting worshippers with Christ (and through Him with the Father) and with one another is thematically developed anywhere, as it is in the Communion Prayer. Arguably the relative neglect of the Spirit in these terms is a major culprit in the obscuring of the Lord's Supper as an unambiguously Trinitarian event. This observation in itself, however, may not necessarily convince confessionally Reformed churches to abandon the Reformed communion order in favor of a Eucharistic Prayer. The reasons for which they may still be reluctant to do so will emerge from a closer examination of the arguments against the use of the latter in the Reformed liturgy for the Lord's Supper.

REFORMED ARGUMENTS AGAINST THE USE OF A EUCHARISTIC PRAYER

We can observe that the basic difference between the Reformed communion order and the Eucharistic Prayer consists in the fact that the former is primarily an exhortation addressed to the worshipping assembly in the name of God while the latter is a prayer addressed to God in behalf of the assembly. The confessionally Reformed churches can insist against the latter that the former is the proper framework for a Reformed liturgy for the Lord's Supper on the basis of at least two objections.[17] First, to address a prayer repeatedly to God to act for the renewal of the covenant relationship implies that Christ's past sacrifice is insufficient; it evidently has not removed the consciousness of sin from the members of the assembly who commemorate it in the sacrament, despite the explicit teaching of the Epistle to the Hebrews to the contrary.[18] The Eucharistic Prayer, then, deprives the worshippers of the assurance of their salvation. To address the institution narrative (and exposition of its meaning) to the assembly, on the other hand, underscores the finality of this past sacrifice. Nothing more has to be done by the worshippers except to receive the gift and promise of Christ in faith, which expresses itself through sincere thanksgiving.

Second, even if the finality of Christ's sacrifice is affirmed, to address a prayer to God still implies that the "activation" of this past sacrifice for the assembly in the present depends on its own liturgical activity. This appears to deny that Christ alone is able to save on the basis of His own saving acts. Put otherwise, it seems to express that it is not the case that Christ alone is ceaselessly active for salvation. The rite that Christ instituted as a memorial of His saving death and resurrection, then, no longer remains *only* His own when it is celebrated, but belongs *also* to the assembly. It follows then that the assembly thereby cooperates with Christ in its own salvation, suggesting a "Pelagianizing" or "synergistic" concept of grace.[19] Thus the use of a Eucharistic Prayer fatally compromises the central Reformation principles,

---

[17] For the following, see Rowan Williams' synopsis of the objections that Reformed theology has raised against the concept of the Eucharistic Prayer in *Eucharistic Sacrifice—Roots of a Metaphor*, Grove series no. 31 (Bramcote: Grove Books, 1982), 3–4. For an extended discussion of the objections to the Eucharistic Prayer on the basis of an interpretation of Reformation principles, see Oliver K. Olson, "Contemporary Trends in Liturgy Viewed from the Perspective of Classical Lutheran Theology," *Lutheran Quarterly* 26 (May 1974): 110–157; and "Liturgy as Action," *Dialog* 14 (1975): 108–113. See also Donald Macleod, "Calvin into Hippolytus?" in *To Glorify God: Essays on Modern Reformed Liturgy*, eds. Bryan Spinks and Iain Torrance (Edinburgh: T&T Clark, 1999), 255–67.

[18] Cf. esp. 9:6–10:14.

[19] For an elaboration of this objection, see the restatement of the classic Reformed doctrine of the sacraments by G.C. Berkouwer in his *The Sacraments*, trans. Hugo Bekker (Grand Rapids: Eerdmans, 1969). For Berkouwer, the problem against which the Reformers contended consists in the ordering of the sacrifice and its application in terms of "possibility" and "realization." "The creating of the 'possibility' is a decisive *conditio sine qua non* for salvation, but it is not decisive for salvation itself. Between the possibility and the realization lies the decisive act of the Church" (270).

solus Christus, sola gratia, sola fidei. On the basis of these principles, therefore, it is necessary to reject not only the idea that there is a need to supplement this once for all sacrifice with prayer to make it effective, but even the idea that there is a need to make it anamnetically present in the liturgical celebration.

These objections reflect the high theological stakes involved for the combatants in the sixteenth-century Eucharistic controversies. The first objection illustrates the challenge that confronted the Reformers and their Roman opponents to distinguish and relate properly the past saving event of Christ and the present mode of His saving action now. Alasdair Heron has correctly observed that either one of two options presented themselves. Either one insisted that what is past is complete and what follows must be sharply distinguished in order to safeguard the unique and unrepeatable character of the former, or that what is past lives continually in the present. According to Heron, the danger of the first is that of losing the connection between the past and the present, while the danger of the second is that of failing to distinguish them adequately, thereby obscuring the "once for all" character of the perfect sacrifice of Christ for sins.[20]

The second objection reflects the Reformation conflict over the interpretation of the meaning of a sacrament. Again Heron has shown that either one maintained that a sacrament designates the action of God as mediated through the action of the church, or that a sacrament denotes a sign that accompanies a word addressed to faith. The danger of the first is that of an identification of the action of God with that of the church; the danger of the second is that of a reduction of the sacrament to a "naked sign" in which God is no longer conceived to act directly.[21]

REPLY TO THE ARGUMENTS

Our first response to these objections is to make the simple observation that to address prayer to God to act in the Lord's Supper does not necessarily imply the insufficiency of Christ's sacrifice; it can also be seen to express the insufficiency of the worshipping assembly to make the salvation accomplished by Christ there and then (*illic et tunc*) effective for itself here and now (*hic et nunc*). "It is the Spirit that gives life; the flesh is of no avail" (Jn

---

[20] Alasdair I.C. Heron, *Table and Tradition* (Philadelphia: Westminster Press, 1983), 153.

[21] Heron, *Table and Tradition*, 155.

6:63). It is precisely with this problem of forging the link between past and present that the doctrine of the saving activity of the Holy Spirit is concerned, as Calvin famously posed it.[22] In this regard, as liturgical theologian Jean Jacques von Allmen has pointed out, it has to be acknowledged that the "mystery and energy" of the Lord's Supper is not at the disposal of the assembly that celebrates it, but must always be sought in prayer.[23]

Nor does it follow from this attitude of dependence on prayer that the members of the assembly are thereby deprived of the assurance of salvation. To be sure, the Spirit is free to act when and where he chooses (*quando et ubi deus vult*), but the assembly has the assurance that its prayer will be answered in the words of Jesus Himself, who promised that God would give the Spirit to those who ask for Him (Lk. 11:13). And if this still does not satisfy the objection, one may finally ask whether in the Reformed perspective there is any material difference between the *epiclesis* before communion in Christ's body and blood and the prayer for illumination before the hearing of the proclaimed word.

The Holy Spirit is intimately involved in history to actualize in the church and world God's act of reconciliation and redemption in Jesus Christ. In this perspective, it is important also to affirm that the Spirit not only directs the worshipping assembly back to the past sacrifice of Christ so that it may nourish itself on His body and blood through the working of that same Spirit in the present. He also always opens it up to a future eschatological fulfillment which each celebration of the Lord's Supper anticipates. In the Lord's Supper, then, we have not only to do with Christ's past and present, but with past, present and future converging in him, making him the ground, accompaniment, and goal of our histories, indeed of all histories.

---

[22] Cf. Calvin's classic statement of this problem in the *Institutes*: "First, we must understand that as long as Christ remains outside of us, and we are separated from him, all that he has suffered and done for the salvation of the human race remains useless and of no value for us. Therefore, to share with us what he has received from the Father, he had to become ours and to dwell within us.... It is true that we obtain this by faith. Yet since we see that not all indiscriminately embrace that communion with Christ which is offered through the gospel, reason itself teaches us to climb higher and to examine into the secret energy of the Spirit, by which we come to enjoy Christ and all his benefits" (1:537).

[23] Jean-Jacques von Allmen, *The Lord's Supper* (Cambridge: The Lutterworth Press, 1969), 31.

In this light, one will appreciate that in each celebration of the Lord's Supper, the assembly commemorates the saving acts of Jesus Christ in the tension between the "already" and "not yet." In the words of Dutch Reformed theologian A. van de Beek, worshippers are not "parachuted behind the Christological eschaton" when they celebrate the Lord's Supper.[24] God's people have already been saved, but in hope (Rom. 8:24). God's people have already the "guarantee of the Spirit" (Eph. 1:13–14), but they do not yet possess the "glorious freedom of the children of God" (Rom. 8:21). For this reason, God's people continue to assemble to pray, as they "groan inwardly while eagerly awaiting their adoption as children" (Rom. 8:23). In this activity, they are helped by the Spirit, who "intercedes for the saints in accordance with the will of God" (Rom. 8:27). In these terms the reality of the past, present, and future dimensions of salvation can be seen to provide warrant to the worshipping assembly for addressing God continually to act on behalf of the church and world. One may recall here that Jesus taught His disciples to *pray* to the Father for the coming of the kingdom (Matt. 6:10; Lk. 11:2). Indeed, in the *epiclesis* of the Communion Prayer, as we have already seen, we can discern the assembly's perception that the process whereby it "attains to unity of the faith" and "grows up in all things into Christ [its] Lord" is ordered to the coming of the kingdom. In sum, celebrating the sacrament of its unity is an activity that must be repeated and renewed, because what the assembly is in the present is not yet what it shall be in the future when, together with the church universal, it will at last have been made perfect by the transforming power of the Holy Spirit and gathered into God's kingdom at the *parousia* of Christ. "Even so, come, Lord Jesus!"

CONCLUSION

Whether or not these brief observations succeed in allaying the suspicions among the confessionally Reformed churches about the use of a Eucharistic Prayer as a framework for a Reformed liturgy for the Lord's Supper is an open question. Nevertheless, if these churches remain disinclined to adopt it for reasons outlined above, they should at least be aware of the problems attending the use of a classic Reformed communion order. One of these, as I have attempted to argue, is that in it the Lord's Supper as a Trinitarian event

---

[24] *Why? On Suffering, Guilt, and God*, trans. John Vriend (Grand Rapids: Eerdmans, 1990), 301.

of encounter between God and His covenant people does not receive as adequate a liturgical expression as it does in the Eucharistic Prayer.

In view of this problem, we may ask in the last analysis whether it is possible to reorganize the elements of the Reformed communion order to make more explicit this Trinitarian event of encounter. Space allows us to provide only one example of a revised order:

> Exposition of the Meaning of the Sacrament
> Institution Narrative
> Distribution
> Prayer for Worthy Reception
> Communion
> Post-Communion Psalm or Prayer of Thanksgiving

Here the theme of the love of the Father revealed in the sending of the Son into the world to save sinners is spelled out explicitly in the first element, which serves appropriately to introduce the celebration. This theme in turn receives confirmation in the institution narrative, in which the incarnate Son announces His intention to offer up His life to restore or renew the covenant between God and His people. The bread and the wine are then distributed to the worshippers, who receive the sacramental signs as they are seated in the pews. They refrain from consuming them until the minister offers the prayer for worthy reception. For this purpose, we suggest as a model the prayer found in the Form for the Holy Supper contained in the Church Order of the Palatinate, which Frederic III (1515–1576) had commissioned and published in Heidelberg in 1563. This form was translated for Dutch Protestant refugees who had settled there, and subsequently became the communion order mandated for use in the Reformed Church in the Netherlands and later in America.[25] We reproduce the prayer below:

> O most merciful God and Father, we beseech thee that thou wilt be pleased in this Supper, in which we celebrate the glorious remembrance of the bitter death of thy beloved Son Jesus Christ, to work in our hearts through the Holy Spirit, that we may daily, more and more, with true confidence, give ourselves up unto thy Son Jesus Christ, so that our afflicted and contrite hearts, through the power of

[25] Cf. *Lord's Supper in the Reformed Church in America*, 11–37.

> the Holy Spirit, may be fed and comforted with his true body and blood; yea, with him, true God and true Man, that only heavenly bread; and that we may no longer live in our sins, but he in us, and we in him, and thus truly be made partakers of the new and everlasting covenant of grace; that we may not doubt that thou wilt forever be our gracious Father, never more imputing our sins unto us, and providing us, as thy beloved children and heirs, with all things necessary, as well for the body and the soul. Grant us also thy grace, that we may take upon us our cross cheerfully, deny ourselves, confess our Savior, and in all tribulations with uplifted heads expect our Lord Jesus Christ from heaven, where he will make our mortal bodies like unto his most glorious body and take us unto himself in eternity.[26]

Here the Father is asked to act upon the hearts of the worshippers by the Holy Spirit in the Supper. The object of the petition is twofold: first, that the Spirit may work to the end that the worshippers may be conformed in obedience to Christ and in perfect trust in the Father; and second, that they may be fed and comforted with the true body and blood of Christ to the end that they may participate in the new covenant of grace with a view to its eschatological fulfillment.

Participation in this covenant is signified and sealed in the corporate act of eating and drinking. Having been nourished at the Lord's Table, the assembly then can offer up praise and thanksgiving to the Father for the gift of His Son, which they have appropriated in and by the Holy Spirit.

As already stated, the foregoing serves as only one example. The intent is to so arrange the elements that the katabatic-anabatic dynamic according to which the mutual encounter between the Trinitarian God and His covenant people takes place in the celebration of the Lord's Supper is adequately reflected and expressed. Whether they adopt a Eucharistic Prayer or a Reformed communion order, Reformed pastors and worship leaders will certainly want to be guided by this intention as they prepare their liturgies for the Lord's Supper.

---

[26] http://images.rca.org/docs/worship/AlternateOrder1792.pdf, 5. Accessed April 6, 2018.

BIBLIOGRAPHY

Berkouwer, G.C. *The Sacraments.* Translated by Hugo Bekker. Grand Rapids: Eerdmans, 1969.

Calvin, John. *Institutes of the Christian* Religion. 2 vols. Edited by John T. McNeill, and translated by Ford Lewis Battles. Philadelphia: Westminster, 1960.

Churches Respond to BEM: Official Responses to the Baptism, Eucharist and Ministry Text. Vols. 1–6. Edited by Max Thurian. Geneva: World Council of Churches, 1986–88.

Dorn, Christopher. *The Lord's Supper in the Reformed Church in America: Tradition in Transformation.* New York: Peter Lang, 2007.

Daly, S.J., Robert J., ed. *The Eucharist in the West: History and Theology.* Collegeville: The Liturgical Press, 1998.

Heron, Alasdair I.C. *Table and Tradition.* Philadelphia: Westminster Press, 1983.

Immink, F. Gerrit. *The Touch of the Sacred: The Practice, Theology, and Tradition of Christian Worship.* Translated by Reinder Bruinsma. Grand Rapids: William B. Eerdmans Publishing, 2014.

Baptism, Eucharist, and Ministry. Faith and Order Paper No. 111. Geneva: World Council of Churches, 1982.

Macleod, Donald. "Calvin into Hippolytus?" In *To Glorify God: Essays on Modern Reformed Liturgy*, edited by Bryan Spinks and Iain Torrance, 255–67. Edinburgh: T&T Clark, 1999.

Olson, Oliver K. "Contemporary Trends in Liturgy Viewed from the Perspective of Classical Lutheran Theology." *Lutheran Quarterly* 26 (1974):110–157.

——. "Liturgy as Action." *Dialog* 14 (1975): 108–113.

Thompson, Bard. *Liturgies of the Western Church.* New York: World Publishing, 1961.

Van de Beek, A. *Why? On Suffering, Guilt, and God.* Translated by John Vriend. Grand Rapids: Eerdmans, 1990.

Von Allmen, Jean-Jacques. *The Lord's Supper.* Cambridge: The Lutterworth Press, 1969.

Pannenberg, Wolfhart. *Systematic Theology.* Vol. 3. Translated by Geoffrey W. Bromiley. Grand Rapids: Eerdmans, 1998.

Williams, Rowan. *Eucharistic Sacrifice—Roots of a Metaphor.* Grove Series No. 31. Bramcote: Grove Books, 1982.

VIII:
CLASSICAL THEISM IN A WORLD COME OF AGE

Joseph Minich, University of Texas at Dallas

INTRODUCTION: THE ABSENCE OF GOD

"IMAGINE there's no heaven. It's easy if you try." John Lennon's 1971 hymn of progressivist secular globalism is famous for its attempt to imagine an end of earthly history without reference to heavenly or infernal postulates. And yet, commentators usually miss the significance of the line "It's easy if you try." Arguably, hundreds of years from now, if this song is preserved in the annals of the Western musical canon, future historians will dissertate far more on the line, "It's easy if you try," than on "Imagine there's no heaven." "It's easy if you try" captures a feature of the late modern West that is definitive.[1] It is, in fact, easy to imagine a cosmos without Heaven, Hell, or God. And indeed, it is sometimes difficult to imagine one with them. This is not universally true, but it is strikingly (which is to say relevantly) true. Of course there are many exceptions, but the frequency with which modern persons sense that their faith is held onto by a sheer act of will distinguishes what, for us, is a common *pistic* condition from that of most of our ancestors—for whom God's reality was woven into the immediate fabric of the cosmos. But for all the endless commentary that has been spilled on this development, I suggest a fairly simple "felt" reason for the state of affairs. To wit, God is absent. Certainly, there are lots of metaphysical arguments demonstrating His existence and lots of ink has been spilled inferring His

---

[1] Here I agree with Charles Taylor's summary of the modern conditions of belief in *A Secular Age* (Cambridge: Belknap, 2007).

necessity or probability from the phenomenon of nature.[2] And there are even attempts to say that persons have directly encountered God—several of which presumed encounters resulting in swanky book deals. But, in point of fact, for the most part, the ordinary experience of the average person is that they do not see God. They do not hear God. He is not immediate, nor claims to His "presence" particularly public in their verifiability (as say, for instance, was the assassination of President Kennedy in 1963). To be sure, God has rarely been "present" in the above sense—and this felt absence has generated all sorts of theodicies, eschatologies, and reflections on suffering (from Job, to the Psalms, to the poetry of Franz Wright). What is unique in our situation is that this felt absence is *metaphysically*, rather than just existentially, unbearable. Somehow, the fact that I don't immediately experience God, that His manifestation is not public and verifiable, is an argument against His existence.[3] For our ancestors, this might cause a crisis of faith in God's character or goodness, but to un-think God from the basic metaphysical furniture of the cosmos was unimaginable. And it needs to be noted that this likely had little to do with the persuasive charm of natural theology. As useful as its arguments are, it would perhaps be overstating their ancient (which is not to deny their modern) role in establishing the faith of the ordinary person. But they *have*, arguably, taken on a much larger function for modern persons—the field of "apologetics" and "natural theology" commonly serving to render religious claims both plausible and persuasive.

Getting back to Lennon, the third verse of his hymn calls us to "Imagine no possessions. I wonder if you can." Note the contrast here with the first verse. On the one hand, it is easy to imagine a cosmos which is depopulated of all divine agency, but it is a challenge to imagine the *future* that Lennon hopes for. Once again, this is precisely in contrast with our ancestors. Imagining no heaven or religion was impossible. But imagining no countries or possessions, sharing all the world, and the brotherhood of man, was extremely plausible—indeed, a common eschatological hope. The reason this future could easily be so imagined was that it, presumably, was promised in

---

[2] Most recently and competently by Edward Feser, *Five Proofs for the Existence of God* (San Francisco: Ignatius, 2017).

[3] This argument tends to function more as a matter of instinct against larger background assumptions about reality, but it has been given explicit philosophical utterance in J.L. Schellenberg's recent *The Hiddenness Argument: Philosophy's New Challenge to Belief in God* (New York: Oxford University Press, 2017).

the revealed will of a God whose being and power were not in question. Remove God from the "cosmic imaginary" (as Taylor might put it), and you lose the future as well. Now, Lennon's implied sense of turmoil concerning the historical *now* is as old as mankind itself, but the feeling of "metaphysical turmoil" belongs to us more specifically. Certainly you sense birthpangs of it in Donne's "Tis all in pieces, all coherence gone, all just supply, and all relation." Arguably (and it is not particularly important for my purposes to tell a clean linear narrative), in the late 19th and early 20th centuries, we witness a moment wherein reality in general is felt to be an object of anxiety (at least among the educated)—whether it be in *The Education of Henry Adams* or Walter Lippmann's later *A Preface to Morals*.[4] Lennon's 60's and 70's, then, might be seen as the moment in which these sentiments are democratized and popularized rather than initiated.[5] It is, therefore, important to note that the whole period ranging from the seventeenth until the twentieth century—in which the "future" runs away from us—also happens to be the era in which *history* becomes a science (a subject in which there are "laws"—the study of which will presumably make that future more clear).[6] To reiterate, then, the future seems elusive at precisely the moment that God and His world are. Let us consider this further.

THE ABSENCE OF HISTORY AND THE ABSENCE OF GOD

Purportedly we want to address the topic of atheism and of God's absence directly—not to mention classical theism. Why "digress" with a discussion of history or of "the future?" In charting this course, I am influenced by the work of Jacques Ellul, in his under-studied *Hope in Time of Abandonment*. Ellul writes,

---

[4] See Daniel H. Borus, *Twentieth-Century Multiplicity 1900–1920* (Lanham: Rowman & Littlefield, 2009). An important study of this period is James Turner, *Without God, Without Creed: The Origins of Unbelief in America* (Baltimore: The Johns Hopkins University Press, 1985).

[5] Important statistics can be found in Hugh McLeod, *The Religious Crisis of the 1960's* (New York: Oxford University Press, 2007), 212.

[6] A classic survey is Karl Löwith, *Meaning in History* (Chicago: The University of Chicago Press, 1949). A more recent survey can be found in Ernst Breisach, *Historiography: Ancient, Medieval, and Modern* (Chicago: The University of Chicago Press, 2007).

> The silence of God means the absence of history. Nothing could be more vainly presumptuous, more ridiculously sad, more profoundly unimpressive, more crucially impertinent, than to say that 'man makes his history.' Man heaps up nonsense and absurd action. He strings pearls, in other words events, without order or standard. Man reveals himself in his inconsistencies and in his conformities. With his blind and exuberant activism he certainly constructs nothing, especially not history. He creates successive empires and conquers the moon. He kills, then dies. Caught in a Brownian movement, he agitates furiously. He attributes great importance to what he's about to do and to live, only to discover later on that it was worthless.... Only a completely abstract philosopher could believe in a progressive incarnation of The Idea, in liberation through transition to a classless society, and that such a thing is history. One would have steadfastly to turn his back on the content of lives, of societies, of activities, of events, of politics, on their content and on their reality, to believe that it makes any sense, and that history is made in this way by a piling up of human results. As long as there is no fixed reference point outside this flow, outside this sequence, there is no history. As long as there is no intervention of a factor which is radically other, there can never be anything but combinations of like with like, lacking any possibility of the attribution or the discovery of meaning.[7]

For Ellul, then, the absence of God and modern disorientation (for he speaks of historical disorientation as one of many disorientations) are twin features of the same phenomenon. His own suggestion, that these are evidences of God's abandonment, is idiosyncratic. Drawing on a significant portion of biblical revelation, his case is worth considering, but we need not accept his diagnostic to maintain that he has rightly intuited the relationship between divine and historical absence(s). The God-drained universe is a universe of futural disorientation.

Another diagnostic emphasizes man's abandonment of God rather than God's abandonment of man. Some, indeed, have traced our sickness to the abandonment of classical theism as such. David Bentley Hart's recent and controversial, *The Experience of God*, is one such example. Largely a defense of

---

[7] *Hope in Time of Abandonment* (1973; Eugene: Wipf and Stock, 2012), 89–90.

classical theism, Hart attempts to capture our abandonment of the metaphysical structures which allegedly warrant the classical view of God. He writes,

> Martin Heidegger … was largely correct in thinking that the modern West excels at evading the mystery of being precisely because its governing myth is one of practical mastery. Ours is, he thought, the age of technology, in which ontological questions have been vigorously expelled from cultural consideration, replaced by questions of mere mechanistic force: for us, nature is now something 'enframed' and defined by a particular disposition of the will, the drive toward dominion that reduces the world to a morally neutral 'standing reserve' of resources entirely subject to our manipulation, exploitation, and ambition. Anything that does not fit within the frame of that picture is simply invisible to us. When the world is seen this way, even organic life—even where consciousness is present—must come to be regarded as just another kind of technology. This vision of things can accommodate the prospect of large areas of ignorance yet to be vanquished (every empire longs to discover new worlds to conquer), but no realm of ultimate mystery. Late modernity is thus a condition of willful spiritual deafness. Enframed, racked, reduced to machinery, nature cannot speak unless spoken to, and then her answers must be only yes, no, or obedient silence. She cannot address us in her own voice. And we certainly cannot hear whatever voice might attempt to speak to us through her.[8]

For Hart, atheism *wilfully* forgets what the word "God" even means. God is not a being among beings, a first domino in a series of efficient causalities. And indeed, it is precisely a sort of late modern technological posture that attunes us to the world in such a way that material and efficient causality simply *are* what it means, for us, that a thing is "real." This comportment, however, progressively evaporates a sense of the more fundamental meaning of "being," being-as-such, existence-as-such, that

[8] David Bentley Hart, *The Experience of God: Being, Consciousness, Bliss* (New Haven: Yale University Press, 2013), 311–12. Hart is, of course, drawing on Martin Heidegger's classic essay, "The Question Concerning Technology," originally published in 1954.

within which any things are what and as they are at all. For Hart, to know what we talk about when we talk about God is to render God (Being-qua-being, the ground of beings) simply inescapable. Divine absence, then, is actually a symptom of the willful move away from classical theism.

If Hart relates the phenomenon of divine absence to the decline of classical theism, Herman Bavinck moves beyond Ellul in relating specifically *classical* theism to the problem of history's elusiveness. In his magisterial *The Philosophy of Revelation*, Bavinck interacts extensively with attempts to discover the laws and meaning of history within the movement of history imminently. He writes,

> The confession of the unity of God is the foundation for the true view of nature and also of history. If this be denied, we must either abide by the multiplicity of reality, by a pluralism of monads and souls, spirits or 'selves,' demons or Gods; or because man can never find satisfaction in such a multiplicity, we have to search in the world itself for a false unity, as is done by monism in its various forms, and then all differentiation is sacrificed to this false unity. The souls of men then become parts and phenomena of the one world-soul, and all created things become *modi* of the one substance. Only, then, when the unity of all creation is not sought in the things themselves, but transcendentally (not in a special, but in a qualitative, essential sense) in a divine being, in his wisdom and power, in his will and counsel, can the world as a whole, and in it every creature, fully attain its rights. A *person* alone can be the root of unity in difference, of difference in unity. He alone can combine in a system a multiplicity of ideas into unity, and he alone can realize them by his will *ad extra*. Theism is the only true monism.[9]

Note that, for Bavinck, it is not just that history needs a reference point outside of itself, but a reference point which lacks the composition that obtains in history specifically and finitude generally. Let us "imagine" for a moment, then, that Hart and Bavinck are correct. It would seem natural that our instinct might be to evaluate these affairs negatively—lamenting the bygone age when God was clear, the future was secure, and we didn't have

---

[9] Herman Bavinck, *The Philosophy of Revelation* (London: Longmans, Green, and Co, 1909), 136 (emphasis in original).

to traffic around in all this reality-numbing technology. This is, of course, pure nostalgia. What is more, it is a *non-historical* posture. If one believes that the future is secure in God's plan, it might be worth asking what this current stage is meant to accomplish within the divine will. And here, whether we agree or not with his particular interpretation, Ellul is asking precisely the right sort of question. What is *God* up to?

THE ABSENCE OF MAN TO HIMSELF

Before we can answer this, however, it is important to consider what we're actually trying to achieve and to which historical motions these considerations belong. What we want, presumably, is to address the modern person for whom divine absence is a metaphysical crisis and for whom the future is elusive. But to give depth to these two dimensions, I would argue that we must do more than merely attempt to describe a cosmic imaginary or attempts to de-problematize the future. Man does not negotiate his relationship to these things outside his concrete, immediate, and practical life—but largely in and by means of them.[10] As such, we will get at these questions best if we are wise with respect to the situation in which the persons asking the questions find themselves. In my judgment, then, there is a third key dimension of the history to which we belong that warrants careful consideration. This is the ascendancy of the late modern technological/economic order, which includes both the massive quantity of modern technologies as well as the extensive and qualitative manner in which they mediate to us a relationship of control between our active wills and our passive selves/world.[11] This control, nevertheless, has tended to grown in direct proportion to our alienation from our own labor, from one another, and from the world in itself.[12] This, of course, echoes Hart's inflection of Heidegger, but here I am not emphasizing this condition as a *willful* posture

---

[10] I do not mean here to pit the material over against the ideal or vice versa as the determining factor. Rather, I mean to emphasize that our relation to both is specific, finite, historical, conditioned, and concrete.

[11] An important recent contribution is David Edgerton, *The Shock of the Old: Technology and Global History Since 1900* (New York: Oxford University Press, 2011).

[12] The most important theorist of this phenomenon remains Jacques Ellul, on whose corpus see Jacob Van Vleet, *Dialectical Theology and Jacques Ellul: An Introduction Exposition* (Minneapolis: Fortress, 2014).

but as the default settings into which we are born—a condition which is, then, difficult to see clearly and critically without significant effort.

An enormous amount has been written about such alienation, and it would be a bit laborious to rehearse it here.[13] As well, my own thoughts can only be tentative, suggestive, and incomplete, but the claim I'd want to make is this: The decline of classical theism and the modern inflection of the quandary of divine absence arguably share a common root—namely—a tacit relationship to the world, presumably grounded in God, as (in whole or in part) devoid of agency. God is not tacit because agency is not tacit in being as such. The placement of God in the furniture of the cosmos, then, is shifted from His classical place as the Being grounding beings to one in which the "divine" is inferred from marks of agency (i.e. divine fingerprints) in phenomena that might presumably be interpreted as otherwise than agentic (certain aspects of reality apparently counting as more compelling on this score than others).

Let me try to unpack this. To the extent that human beings are *engaged* in self-possessed labor, and are forced to navigate around other agents as well as the activity of the world itself—to this extent the whole cosmos tacitly "manifests" as agentic.[14] Our most primal experiences are of being spoken to, of wonder at each new object with which we must learn to cope, and of learning to cooperate with other persons whose will and being are different than our own. In such a sense of the world, divine agency is not even an inference, but the immediately understood reality within which all other agencies are united—the Agency which transcendentally grounds all others. The world feels very different when most of my experiences of it are mediated by technologies which render it a world "for me"—when I do *not* have to navigate around it, when my relationships with others are mediated simply by my will (moving, unfriending on Facebook, changing jobs, etc) rather than by necessary confrontation and cooperation, and when even my own labor is more or less absorbed within a system of mechanized exchanges (thereby foreclosing the kinds of cultivation that make a person feel as though

---

13 The classic statement is, of course, Karl Marx's *Economic and Philosophical Manuscripts of 1844*. Several helpful studies can be found in Alex Callinicos, *The Revolutionary Ideas of Karl Marx* (Chicago: Haymarket Books, 2012), and Amy Wendling, *Karl Marx on Technology and Alienation* (New York: Palgrave Macmillan, 2009).

14 In this emphasis on "engagement," I am influenced by Richard Sennett's *The Craftsman* (New Haven: Yale University Press, 2009).

they are actually making some small piece of the world different). Here we can situate the common sensibility that even one's own agency is ultimately a gear in a machine, an aimless body of impulses and promptings which we do not ultimately *possess*—but in which we *are possessed* in selves and a-histories behind which there is no final Actor. We often experience our own selves as something in which we are "carried along." Of course, this is all artifice suspended atop nature, but it is dominating and comprehensive artifice—easily rendering the impression that our itching and unrestful faculties of heart and mind have been scratched when they have rather been numbed.

Trying to rope in this third practical dimension, then, is no triviality. Again, if the goal is to speak to actual humans, it is worth noting that while our neighbors might be instinctually averse to the philosophical abstraction (a felt imposition in the world which seems "real" to them) which often attends discussions concerning "the existence of God," they are certainly not numb to their felt alienation from themselves and from one another. And so arguably, by navigating toward our dismissiveness of these other realities through this more immediately felt terrain, we begin to chart a path home.[15]

THE JOURNEY HOME: PREPARATORY MEASURES

Here I find myself contending against any account of our condition which locates primary emphasis on philosophical movements, whether it be

[15] Let it be noted that these are precisely the sorts of anxieties which so many philosophically dismissive projects are attempting to tranquilize. In its reliance upon nature-suspending technologies, modern progressivism can imagine a "future" (a history) in which alienation is presumably evaporated, in which agency is achieved. Nevermind the well-attested incoherencies of each of these (often trans-humanist) projects. What drives them is not attunement to being, but relief to our alienation from it. In any case, that their actively pursued destination is but a parody of what their natures craves can perhaps be more easily exposed when we ask, "What happens after you've achieved the brotherhood of man, the lack of possessions, the omega point, the fusing of consciousness, laser vision, etc?" It's a fascinating question, and while this blank space can be populated sentimentally by words like "love" or "community," very often these are attempts to dignify visions of the good life that don't substantively move us beyond "being free" or "not being told what to do" or "chilling out." But this is only to overcome one alienation with another—an alienation of man from his projects solved by an alienation of man from his natural end—to wit, the enjoyment of the infinite in the mirror of finitude. The latter is arrived at when limits are conceived of as the good that they are, and when the transcendence of human nature would be seen as the loss that it is.

nominalism's parity of being, Cartesian skepticism, or political voluntarism. Certainly these systems and instincts aren't un-related to anything I'm seeking to address, and each could be appropriated in tension with classical theism. But even apart from these movements, the alienation which I'm attempting to identify occurs and therefore re-shapes the instincts *about* and comportment *to* being that makes classical theism plausible and "natural" in the first place. I am thinking specifically of whatever practical features of the world render the world itself silent, broken into thinking subject and silent object (experientially rather than philosophically). Whatever metaphysics we have, this is what the common experience of the world is like. Hume's fact/value distinction isn't first a philosophy, but a way in which the world "seems" to us. Lessing's "accidental truths of history" which stand across a wide ditch from the "necessary truths of reason" already sound the birth-pangs of a race alienated from its own sense of belonging (in relation to which more primal phenomenon, reason*ing* is a second-order activity). It is perhaps difficult for late modern man to imagine what the (practically) cosmic primacy of *volk* or blood or nation might have been like—a sense of heritage, civilization, and connection to land which was instinctively indistinguishable from the realm of necessary truth. Recent political events, indeed, are perhaps vengeance on our inability to grasp this. Conversely, there is danger in our ignorance since we fail to note the modern surrogates of these impulses as just that—potentially violent late modern forms of belonging. In any case, the point I am emphasizing is that this is largely a practical, rather than an intellectual, shift. And for ministerial purposes—let it again be noted that in whatever manner we hope to address moderns, we will have to address ones who live in *this* world.

And yet to be involved in pioneering this effort ordinarily reverses the practical/intellectual order. Numbed to reality, the arguments for theism (while not formally changed) can function for us in a way that they did not for our ancestors. They rather help the mind to recognize that reality's historically accidental *absences* can distort what the mind more essentially grasps. Explicitly conscious of this, we can begin to notice that, in fact, we still actually and practically live and move around in the old boring metaphysical structures unawares. We might then be motivated to more *strategically* and consciously mold our behaviors, our daily liturgies, and our habits to form souls which instinctually "feel" that the world is the way which our minds are persuaded that it is.[16] Here one brings together intellectual persuasion concerning classical theism with practical comportment to this reality in adoration, prayer, liturgy—"wonder" being the fitting posture of the heart towards this object of the mind. This wonder spills over into wonder at the echoes of God in His creation as finitude raises the soul to God.[17]

And yet, we're not quite ready to navigate home. I have just summarized anxieties and therapies that exist not only in various branches of Christendom, but even outside of them. And what stands out to me is that while this line of thought does get at the metaphysical (and to some extent practical) dimension of our historical and practical alienation, it does not get at the *historical* dimension of our historical alienation. We are easily left with a sense that history can have meaning, but perhaps little (beyond the generic) sense of what that is. And this, it must be noted, is dangerous. There have been many compelling critiques of modern materialism, defenses of classical theism, and celebrations of virtue or spiritual practices which nevertheless had their *telos* in some Pharisaical—which is to say idolatrous—project. The recovery of ancient traditions can most certainly function in this manner, as can the reduction of historical meaning to one's belonging to a certain *volk*. Indeed, our hearts are deceptive (Jeremiah 17:9), and we must recognize our distinctive vulnerabilities. To the extent that ecclesio-centric projects, for instance, attempt to recover a "belonging" which is a kind of Christian "identity politics," one fears that we have not yet fully transcended our disorientation—but have rather internalized it more profoundly. Like a gardener who lacks the fitting sense of belonging to the *human* project, we might have some competent tools, knowledge of how to use them, and even accomplish some of the immediate tasks of cultivation (planting, growing food). But to garden is to unleash potential which exceeds my immediate use,

---

[16] Here, I am of course drawing on James K.A. Smith's "cultural liturgies" project, initiated in *Desiring the Kingdom: Worship, Worldview, and Cultural Formation* (Grand Rapids: Baker Academic, 2009)—with the caveats that I have made here in my article, "Class(ic)ifying Jamie Smith," located at https://calvinistinternational.com/2013/05/27/classicifying-jamie-smith/.

[17] See Kenneth Schmitz, *The Recovery of Wonder: The New Freedom and the Asceticism of Power* (Montreal: McGill-Queens University Press, 2005).

to push into the realm of the uncultivated. And so it is with history. As such, it is worth thinking through this historical dimension more carefully.[18]

Of first importance, then, it must be stated that we *are* involved in our history before we understand it. Or, Ellul's alternative formulation is that our generation is "in the grip of the absence of history in a world which is nothing but history."[19] What I want to emphasize here, once again, is that we live in a primal comportment to the human project which is prior to our distorted intellectual/spiritual inflection of it. And so part of our task in recovery is to avoid some clash of narratives (the Christian versus the Islamic versus the Marxist versus the …)—as though the Christian "narrative" is just one right next to others, one which just so happens to be true. This isn't false, but it mis-states things. There is, in fact, a single collective history to which we belong and to which humans are either more fittingly or unfittingly attuned. Indeed, many non-Christians are caught up in human history in a way that challenges those whose belonging to the Christian faith is a myopic belonging—indistinguishable from a sense of one's ethnicity or a set of enculturated gestures. This is important to emphasize because the modern project in relation to which we feel some large degree of tension is also *itself* an inflection of the project that just *is* the human project. It is distorted, but what is desired in an idol is a parody of man's natural end. And if we fail to relate to humans as involved in the same project which just *is* the human project, we will perhaps (to that extent) fail to articulate Christ as the Desire (and the *telos*) of the nations.[20]

---

[18] See Robert Pogue Harrison, *Gardens: An Essay on the Human Condition* (Chicago: The University of Chicago Press, 2008) in conversation with his more recent, *Juvenescence: A Cultural History of Our Age* (Chicago: The University of Chicago Press, 2014).

[19] Jacques Ellul, *Hope in Time of Abandonment* (1973; Eugene: Wipf and Stock, 2013), 17.

[20] Note again what I said above (footnote 15) about progressivism. On the one hand, it is attractive precisely to the extent that it cultivates a sense of "common-ness" in which people can be corporately engaged, but it cashes out in something shallow. It inflects the meaning of the historical process—but fails to capture its end. And arguably, this is a felt anxiety for those engaged in it. In its transhumanist variety, for instance, there is both excitement and anxiety concerning what happens when we transcend our bodies, when we inhabit particles, when we achieve some degree of immortality. Nevermind whether this is possible or coherent. More immediately, *this project gives us a history*! But it navigates with a single sail (the pursuit of freedom) without getting at our felt alienation from far more than this (to wit, the purpose of

It is, finally, essential to highlight the relationship between the historical and the practical dimensions of our alienation. Human labor is perhaps the most immediate manner in which the human feels himself to be a part of the human project—to history. An individual life of cultivation can give us a sense of individual history,[21] but a tacit sense of belonging to *History* can only be achieved where our sense of individual project and common project intersect. To the extent that our world does not seem like one in which we take some direct part in these larger motions, precisely to that extent will our history remain enigmatic. What is more, it is precisely to that extent that a divine Author will seem but a projection onto the order of things.

So this is our situation. Our individual and historical alienation are bound up with one another—and each are bound up with a cosmos in which the God of classical theism is, more than simply implausible, also inconsequential. And yet there is another side to this story.

---

freedom). The popularity of dystopian and science fiction novels speaks of both our fascination with and anxiety about this future. In its telling, we are still ultimately suspended in laws which are less than agentic and are subject to forces which ultimately transcend any personal control. But, even if we achieve freedom and the transcendence of our limits—what would we do then? What would our project be then? What would our *history* be then? By contrast, if the finite (i.e. the limited!) is suspended in the infinite, we preserve both the stages, seismic shifts, and chapters which constitute the narrative we call history—without collapsing the future into a singularity. There is, in Revelation 22, an everlasting dimension to the human project. Because God is infinite, the finite will always be able to press further into Him, grow in its capacity to know and to love, be able to cultivate His creation "more"—and yet to never scratch the surface of God's gravity. Imagine, if you will, that Handel's *Messiah* is but the music of children. Both this future and our Handelian past can only finally be held together if there is an actual infinite. More boldly, non-historical finitude is difficult to even imagine since the mirror of finitude seems superfluous without a mode of being who enjoys and gives utterance to what is beheld. The classical Christian claim is that this mode of being is man—the mouthpiece of creation.

[21] See Sennet, *The Corrosion of Character: The Personal Consequences of Work in the New Capitalism* (New York: W.W. Norton, 1998), 44.

THE JOURNEY HOME: GETTING OUT THE MAP

For Dietrich Bonhoeffer, the modern absence of God from the world is not a situation to be lamented, but one wherein God Himself calls us to religious maturity. Bonhoeffer writes,

> God as a working hypothesis in morals, politics, or science, has been surmounted and abolished; and the same thing has happened in philosophy and religion (Feuerbach!). For the sake of intellectual honesty, that working hypothesis should be dropped, or as far as possible eliminated.... Anxious souls will ask what room is left for God now; and as they know of no answer to the question, they condemn the whole development that has brought them to such straits. I wrote ... before about the various emergency exits that have been contrived; and we ought to add to them the *salto mortale* (death-leap) back into the Middle Ages. But the principle of the Middle Ages is heteronomy in the form of clericalism; a return to that can be a counsel of despair, and it would be at the cost of intellectual honesty. It's a dream that reminds one of the Song *O wüsst' ich doch den Weg zurück, den weiten Weg ins Kinderland* [commonly translated "Oh, I wish I knew the way back, the way into childhood"]. There is no such way—at any rate not if it means deliberately abandoning our mental integrity; the only way is that of Matt. 18.3, i.e. through repentance, through *ultimate* honesty. And we cannot be honest unless we recognize that we have to live in the world *etsi deus non daretur* [commonly translated "as if God did not exist"]. And this is just what we do recognize—before God! God himself compels us to recognize it. So our coming of age leads us to a true recognition of our situation before God. God would have us know that we must live as men who manage our lives without him. The God who is with us is the God who forsakes us (Mark 15.34). The God who lets us live in the world without the working hypothesis of God is the God before whom we stand continually. Before God and with God we live without God. God lets himself be pushed out of the world on the cross. He is weak and powerless in the world, and that is precisely the way, the only way, in which He is with us and helps us. Matt. 8.17 makes it quite clear that Christ helps us, not by virtue of his omnipotence, but by virtue of his weakness and suffering.

> Here is the decisive difference between Christianity and all religions. Man's religiosity makes him look in his distress to the power of God in the world; God is the *deux ex machine.* The Bible directs man to God's powerlessness and suffering; only the suffering God can help. To that extent we may say that the development towards the world's coming of age outline above, which has done away with a false conception of God, opens up a way of seeing the God of the Bible, who wins power and space in the world by his weakness.[22]

For all the ways in which we might want to counter Bonhoeffer's claims (especially as appropriated by later theologians), particularly fascinating is his sense that mankind has "come of age" and must live "without God" (apparently) in the way a young man must ultimately learn to live without a parent. There are all sorts of ways which this could be modified and contested, but the reflections which follow will perhaps unwittingly vindicate Bonhoeffer as having captured just the right tension (and in just the right image) for modern Christians. In *fact*, we still practically move around in a world wherein we don't have to make explicit reference to God. This is historically remarkable. Our motions throughout the day, week, month, and year can aid in our survival, achieve social success, and even some degree of personal fulfillment with nary a glance beyond the finitude of the finite. Bonhoeffer speaks of modern man as having "come of age."[23] In my judgment, the best way to capture our "age" is to say that we are faced with the malady of young adulthood. Apart from our will (perhaps contra Hart), we have been kicked out of the house of our cultural childhood into a state of both increased dependence and increased independence. Of course, juveniles tend to be more aware of the latter than the former, but our options as it respects our own story are the options of an unhomed juvenile in relation to his own heritage. These options are three. On the one hand, there is the option of a childlike (i.e. uncritical) appropriation of our ancestor's legacy. This option is usually motivated by a longing for the simplicities of

[22] Bonhoeffer, *Letters & Papers From Prison* (New York: Simon & Schuster, 1997), 360–361 (emphasis in original). My reading of Bonhoeffer is significantly dependent upon Richard Bube's essay, "Man Come of Age: Bonhoeffer's Response to the God-of-the-Gaps," *Journal of the Evangelical Theological Society* 14, no. 4 (1971): 203–220.

[23] Cf Harrison's recent reflections, *Juvenescence: A Cultural History of Our Age*, 145–51, that we are both "extremely young" and "extremely old" in the modern America.

childhood. And yet, one can never have childhood back. A child does not have a culpable relationship to their heritage, but those who must necessarily *choose* it to preserve it do. Kant might call this "self-imposed tutelage." Implied in Kant's famous definition of enlightenment is that our freedom is a simple fact and our dependence self-imposed. Turning Kant around, it could be argued that modernity is a state of *other*-imposed agency. Like the forcibly un-homed juvenile, we are free whether we want to be or not, and it is this that the path back to childhood (as Bonhoeffer calls clericalism) can never reckon with. Another path, then, is to entirely reject the project of one's parents. This is the option of much of modernity. It is the alter-ego of the first option and arguably the most common path taken in our culture. Here, whatever is "new" and "future" stands in no need of justification. But beneath the intensity and speed and the distraction and the advent of thing after thing is an underlying anxiety. It can be numbed and ignored, but the market for dystopian and science fiction suggests to us that we waver in a dialectical motion between the uncritical fetishization of the new and a childish, nostalgic relationship to the primitive.

And yet, for Bonhoeffer, this appears to be more an opportunity than a moment about which we ought to be anxious. The opportunity of imposed agency, of un-homed juvenility, is that we can learn to grow up. And so the final option, the wise option, is to stand critically within one's heritage. This is the option of *free* cultivation, of self-possession, of responsible ownership. And this means that whatever prophetic postures we might want to take, whatever disciplines we might want to recover, whatever enchantment we might want to "re"—these must not be a *reaction to* alienation from, but *leadership within* the human task—pushing us forward in the same project in which we and all of our neighbors are distortedly engaged. We are drawn into and drawing towards the reality to which they attempt and fail attunement. Most importantly, we must perform this task in precisely *this* context and in *this* world, which fights against such comportment—whether by intention or accident.

THE JOURNEY HOME PROPER

As we begin to chart a course home, we might have re-tooled our metaphysical ship, re-engaged our historical sails, and untied all our alienated knots, but we cannot sail without wind. We cannot sail without something beyond us which pushes us toward our destination. That wind is a word from beyond. Ellul writes that God "is a God of History, and this discovery about God is Judaism's monumental invention, which has been completely adopted by Christianity. This is the origin of all historical thinking and of History…. God, the World, Time, and History are connected through the Word."[24] God's speech is not merely a post-lapsarian correction to our mis-direction. It is an original feature of man's world. God speaks, and man's attunement to creation and orientation to the future were always meant to exist in concert with that speech. God's speech makes history, and as Ellul claims, speech and words have a distinctive relationship to time—not as an absolute series of moments but as an experienced phenomenon in which we are engaged and in which we develop.[25] We cannot navigate the world without language, and we have no history without it. But as speakers and as responders to speech, we make history. And *God's* speech initiates and drives that history.

The history to which humans belong, then, is one which groans for the revelation which is also its origin. Of course, this has always been the case. But the evaporation of agency, history, engagement (etc) has had the effect of rendering revelation itself implausible, and with it, our own futural orientation. And yet we *remain* our own history. And precisely because we *are* our own history, we cannot help but seek to find revelation in surrogate places—whether it be scientists, technocrats, gurus, or anyone who make sense out of our universal task and end. And so, it is not just the fact of agency but the primary agency of *God* which requires emphasis. The agency of God in history reminds us that the future is not entirely a human achievement. The path from juvenility to adulthood is unpredictable, but for a juvenile to learn wisdom is for him to learn his own potentialities *as well as* his limitations. But limitation will never appear as "good" apart from a strong sense of the manner in which it actually relates to the future which is otherwise forcefully sought in the limit-despising transgressive seizure of history.

How is this related to atheism and/or to classical theism? On the one hand, we can establish the very possibility of history as derivative of classical theism—on the other, we can *announce* and enact the history which reorients us toward the plausibility of classical theism within itself. It seems to me that the latter path is actually an important and under-appreciated one in our

[24] Jacques Ellul, *The Humiliation of the Word* (Grand Rapids: Eerdmans 1985), 55.

[25] See Ellul, *The Humiliation of the Word*, 5–47.

world. Arguably, we have been more successful at restating classical theism and perhaps at addressing our alienation in certain isolated bits. But have we captured our disorientation in respect of the human story itself—the relation of our cultivation to the entire meaning of our species?[26] Apart from making this move, classical theism, philosophy, ecclesiology (etc) can only function as just one more identity in the sea of identities, a superior but functionally private project which can only posture itself to the public world as an imposition. And so, finally, let us briefly consider what a state of imposed agency means in its relationship to three things: 1. The precise shape of the historical hole left in the wake of God's vanishing. 2. How the content of divine speech fills out this gap in precisely the shape of this absence—and therefore illuminates the human project. 3. How this history to which we belong leads the heart and mind to the God who is its ground.

ORIENTED FROM DIVINE SPEECH

And so, first, the evaporation of God is an opportunity because of many idols that have been evaporated with Him. Our being un-homed from the cosmos and from our various traditions has actually demonstrated that most of these traditions are radically contingent and unfit to bear the burden of the human story. This has, of course, happened in other contexts. Just as Augustine treated the tragic fall of Rome as an opportunity for Christians to recognize their chief citizenship in the city of God, modern Christian can recognize, in the heritage-consuming world of modernity, that many of the cultural norms and mores in which we might be tempted to find our ultimate orientation are only a contingent piece of history (able to be removed from the main story).[27] What passes through the historical flame of modernity is nevertheless the essential things of God and His word. But this, then, establishes what constitutes our certain *history*, which cannot perish within it. The accidental truths of history are only formally accidental. They are historically essential, and the necessary truths of reason but the scaffolding atop which they are

---

[26] It is remarkable to note how common it is to publish works which think in this scope. For instance, Robert Wright, *Nonzero: The Logic of Human Destiny* (New York: Vintage Books, 2000).

[27] Two important treatments are Marshall Berman, *All That is Solid Melts Into Air: The Experience of Modernity* (New York: Penguin, 1982), and Zygmund Bauman, *Liquid Modernity* (New York: Polity, 2000).

accomplished. Concerning the manner in which God's revelation actively constructs this history, then, Bavinck writes,

> Revelation gives us a division of history. There is no history without division of time, without periods, without progress and development. But now take Christ away. The thing is impossible, for he has lived and died, has risen from the dead, and lives to all eternity; and these facts cannot be eliminated, —they belong to history, they are the heart of history. But *think* Christ away for a moment, with all he has spoken and done and wrought. Immediately history falls to pieces. It has lost its heart, its kernel, its centre, its distribution. It loses itself in a history of races and nations, of nature and culture-peoples. It becomes a chaos, without a centre, and therefore without a circumference; without distribution and therefore without beginning or end; without principle and goal; a stream rolling down from the mountains, nothing more. But revelation teaches us that God is the Lord of the ages and that Christ is the turning point of these ages. And thus it brings into history unity and plan, progress and aim. The aim is not this or that special idea, not the idea of freedom, or of humanity, or of material well-being. But it is the fullness of the Kingdom of God, the all-sided, all-containing dominion of God, which embraces heaven and earth, angels and men, mind and matter, cultus and culture, the specific and the generic; in a word, all in all.[28]

For this reason, our need for revelation is not an aimless and unstructured impulse which impels us to compare the world's religious literatures, like sailors comparing star-charts to a cloudy sky. Our lack has *shape*! If the revelation of Christ simply *is* our history in its consummate form, for which all history before it was prepared and out of which all history from it lives—then God's speech stands on its own. Understand that I do not mean that it cannot be confirmed by the world into which it speaks. Much the opposite. It makes and sustains this world and necessarily, therefore, aligns with it. But the history which culminates here just *is* human history—of which we are always already a part. God's speech stands on its own, therefore, because (for those who listen to its announcements) it speaks to

[28] *Philosophy of Revelation*, 141 (emphasis in original).

us authoritatively, accurately, illuminatingly, and with power. "'Is not my word like fire,' declares the LORD, 'and like a hammer that breaks a rock in pieces?'" (Jeremiah 23:29)

ORIENTED TOWARD DIVINE MISSION

Second, then, how does this word illuminate the human project as such? It does so by announcing and accomplishing an inescapable end in precisely the *shape* of our lack. The opportunity of cultural juvenility, of our current alienation, is that we can be reoriented to that from which we can never finally be alienated (and which is more easily obscured in other contexts). So, for instance, even in seeking just modes of labor and the opportunity for normal human cultivation—we can avoid an idolatrous relationship to these projects (i.e. putting our final hope in them). This is given to us in the gospel's treatment of our labor and our history. To wit, all of human history is to be given back to God in Christ (1 Corinthians 15:28). All human cultivation ultimately moves between the poles of Genesis 1 and Revelation 22. But added to this original commission, as its redeemed inflection, is the call to cultivate the nations with the gospel. That is, to preach and to make disciples by baptism (Matthew 28:16–20)—to spread Christianity under the King who reigns over heaven and earth. This commission touches all aspects of the creation mandate and reorients it to the end of Christ's kingdom (which was its original aim). Rather than erasing all distinction, nation, *volk*, provincial histories, it actually fulfills them by taking them into itself and even serving them. And yet it does this precisely to the extent that it renders them penultimate and therefore enables them to serve the good of a species which shares a more primal history and a more profound end.

In related fashion, the New Testament speaks in a dual fashion about our penultimate callings. On the one hand, we are called to take freedom if we can achieve it (1 Corinthians 7:21). And yet, we are also called to love and be Christ even to unjust masters (1 Peter 2:18). This is not some insensitive neglect of our dignity and humanity. It is rather the heralding of a calling which cannot be suppressed—to belong to the true history that just is human history. In our life *coram deo*, even injustice is an opportunity to reflect God's character and to unleash a new order of things (i.e. love) into this world. This calling contextualizes all others. We can be unjustly limited in our ability to cultivate the creation commission—but we can never be prevented from the love which re-animates the world and that commission. And yet inasmuch as this love is unleashed in the world, it leaves a more just world in its wake—masters who care about the alienation of their servants, moral sensibilities about human dignity which are the historical legacy of the world Christian movement, etc.[29]

Nevertheless, we need to be careful here. This is a difficult subject. Many persons apparently do what they do for the glory of God but not, apparently, for the kingdom of Christ as such. Muslim eschatology isn't just about a pile of virgins, but also about enjoying the greatness of God. Similar things could be said of Jewish eschatology. And yet, Paul seems to treat both philosophical sophistication and religious piety apart from Christ and His body as mere fleshliness (Colossians 2: 16–23). And indeed, Paul can speak of anything beyond eating, drinking, and being merry as foolishness apart from the promise of Christian resurrection (1 Corinthians 15:32). I confess my own fear of these words. But I want to honor them. I also, however, want to honor a Christ who spoke of those who were "not far from the kingdom of heaven" (a category perhaps echoed in Paul's Mars Hill discourse in Acts 17). I think we can relieve these tensions in the following manner: Inasmuch as anything gets us anything of value but does not get us Christ, we have missed the point of history. We have missed life (John 17:3). It is not that these things aren't good. It is that they are all relative. We were not meant to merely contemplate divine simplicity (which mystifies the mind). We were meant to be caught up in a concrete history—involved with a God who acts and speaks within it—all of which centers around the Christ who holds it all together. And so inasmuch as any tradition captures our end as in God and His glory and His kingdom, it lives in reality. But inasmuch as it fails to see Christ as the one in whom all of these things are fulfilled, it misses the axis upon which it all turns.[30] I don't know what else to make of Paul's statements

---

[29] Perhaps no text in the New Testament highlights this with the precision of Colossians 3, wherein Paul encourages the saints to keep their mind on the "things above" where their "life is hidden with Christ in God." Out of this, like ripples from the epicenter of an earthquake which fixes rather than fragments the world, he unfolds the social implications of this reality. On the impact of Christianity in the development of humanism, see David Bentley Hart, *Atheist Delusions: The Christian Revolution and its Fashionable Enemies* (New Haven: Yale University Press, 2009).

[30] One question which might follow from this is precisely what we mean by "Christ." Is the historical Jesus of Nazareth essential to history? Certainly He is to our *actual* history, but what if there had been no fall? In what sense could we say that Christ is "essential" to history in its character as created rather than in its character as redeemed? Minimally, theologians have often spoken of the Logos as the Mediator

that God "made known to us the mystery of his will according to his good pleasure, which he purposed in Christ, to be put into effect when the times reached their fulfillment—to bring unity to all things in heaven and on earth and under Christ" (Ephesians 1:9–10), that all things were created for Christ—that He might reconcile all things to Himself (Colossians 1:15–20), or in Jesus' claim that eternal life (which is more than just forgiveness) is to know God *and* to know Christ (John 17:3). Straining at a pithy formulation, perhaps we can say that *what the Christian faith shares in common with other faiths stands in intrinsic tension with that wherein they differ. And this is because what is shared in common between them is extrinsically fulfilled and consummated in what is distinctive within the Christian faith.* This distinctiveness is fundamentally historical—including an account of the fall, God's promise to overcome man's guilt and restore the world, and the consummation of that promise in a new Adam. The history of God, man, sacrifice, heroism, war, empire, culture, art, prophet, priest, and king is fulfilled and then unleashed in history as a new

---

between God and man in creation. Maximally, theologians have sometimes spoken of the incarnation as an end of history even apart from the fall. In my judgment, this is a somewhat speculative matter about which theologians may differ. I am inclined toward the maximal position for the following reasons: (A) Paul speaks of common marriage (an institution prior to the fall) as intrinsically related to the relationship between Christ and His church; (B) 1 Corinthians 15:42–49 roots the contrast between Adam and Christ not only in the fall, but also in Adam's pre-fallen state in contrast to its telos in Christ's state of resurrection; (C) It would seem fitting that the state of final blessedness would involve an embodied relationship with a divine Person. This is not because of some ontological gap that needs to be overcome, but because the manner in which we experience meaning and know others is embodied. The longing that the church experiences to embrace Christ is surely more than a longing for a state of mind, but a longing to have the Lamb in our midst—to love and to be loved as we love and are loved. In short, the intrinsic relationship between creation and the incarnation is the intrinsic relationship between creation and God's desire to maximally bless creates in the capacity of their nature to enjoy Him (across not a metaphysical—but rather a modal gap). This is not to replace traditional emphases concerning our final contemplation of the divine, but rather to add to them. Nevertheless, even if this is misguided, two more points are worthy of attention. First, even if the fall is accidental to human nature as such, it is not accidental in God's plan. As such, the centrality of the historical Christ to our *actual* history still underscores what (or Who) we were made for, whether or not this can be derived from our nature considered in isolation from the history of which it is a part. Second, as I have argued above, divine speech begins prior to the fall—begetting and moving history forward. But this is the particular speech of a particular "Person" who just is the Logos. To miss just *this* speech, then, is to step out of the historical current and its center.

power (the Holy Spirit) to love. Christ's telic sense-making of these structures and His resolution of their tensions is manifest in the fact that the Christian movement is truly a world movement. This is fueled, of course, by its addressing our most deeply suppressed need for forgiveness and redemption from sin and guilt—the profound depth of which is uniquely emphasized in the Christian tradition (thus making its history, which is our history, a history of gratuitous redemption).

For all of these reasons, Christian mission is perhaps a unique apologetic in our age. The love of neighbor is not just a calling, but our chief participation in the history to which humanity belongs. Faith and hope will cease, but love will never cease (1 Cor. 13). This is the center of Christian cultivation and of Christian civilization. Living out of the historical event to which human belongs and which is the coming of Christ, this commission, then, is its own apologetic. Bavinck writes, "While unbelief increases in Christian countries, mission plants one congregation of Christ after another in the heathen world. Today, mission is probably the strongest apology for the Christian faith.... Mission shows the power of ... Christ."[31]

CONCLUSION: ARRIVING HOME

How, thirdly and finally, does any of this relate to classical theism and to atheism? This is really one question. Again, the decline of classical theism is related to the rise of atheism—but not because one always "causes" the other. Each are the natural manner in which the world manifests when we have been alienated from it and our history. And we are alienated especially from the latter when we are un-homed in our participation in the human project. These three: our alienation from our labor, our loss of history, and the decline of classical theism, share a history. And what evaporates in our state of imposed agency is any default at-home-ness and engagement in the world. What is demanded, therefore, is a more willful posture toward reality. Recalibrating, we discover the history in which we already participate. The kingdom of God, then, is not a mere surrogate of what has been lost, but the

[31] Cited in de Wit, *On the Way to the Living God: A Cathartic Reading of Herman Bavinck and an Invitation to Overcome the Plausibility Crisis of Christianity* (Amsterdam: VU University Press, 2011), 12 n. 22. Note the self-conscious historical contingency of Bavinck's claim here (i.e., it is "today" that this is the strongest apology for the Christian faith).

primal history which it never was—but which impels us to echo its life into and to cultivate those histories which are suspended in it. A world thus cultivated is a world in which classical theism is plausible and atheism is not—because it is a world in which we are once again at home in our own nature. Only this time, the will had to choose what was recognized by the mind despite felt and sometimes tempting alternatives. In other words, we had to grow up.

BIBLIOGRAPHY

Bauman, Zygmund. *Liquid Modernity*. New York: Polity, 2000.

Bavinck, Herman. *The Philosophy of Revelation*. London: Longmans, Green, and Co, 1909.

Marshall Berman. *All That is Solid Melts Into Air: The Experience of Modernity*. New York: Penguin, 1982.

Bonhoeffer, Dietrich. *Letters & Papers From Prison*. New York: Simon & Schuster, 1997.

Borus, Daniel H. *Twentieth-Century Multiplicity 1900–1920*. Lanham: Rowman & Littlefield, 2009.

Breisach, Ernst. *Historiography: Ancient, Medieval, and Modern*. Chicago: The University of Chicago Press, 2007.

Bube, Richard. "Man Come of Age: Bonhoeffer's Response to the God-of-the-Gaps." *Journal of the Evangelical Theological Society* 14, no. 4 (1971): 203–220.

Callinicos, Alex. *The Revolutionary Ideas of Karl Marx*. Chicago: Haymarket Books, 2012.

De Wit, Willem J. *On the Way to the Living God: A Cathartic Reading of Herman Bavinck and an Invitation to Overcome the Plausibility Crisis of Christianity*. Amsterdam: VU University Press, 2011.

Edgerton, David. *The Shock of the Old: Technology and Global History Since 1900*. New York: Oxford University Press, 2011.

Ellul, Jacques. *Hope in Time of Abandonment*. 1973; Eugene: Wipf and Stock, 2013.

——. *The Humiliation of the Word*. Grand Rapids: Eerdmans 1985.

Harrison, Robert Pogue. *Gardens: An Essay on the Human Condition*. Chicago: The University of Chicago Press, 2008.

——. *Juvenescence: A Cultural History of Our Age*. Chicago: The University of Chicago Press, 2014.

Hart, David Bentley. *Atheist Delusions: The Christian Revolution and its Fashionable Enemies*. New Haven: Yale University Press, 2009.

——. *The Experience of God: Being, Consciousness, Bliss*. New Haven: Yale University Press, 2013.

Löwith, Karl. *Meaning in History*. Chicago: The University of Chicago Press, 1949.

McLeod, Hugh. *The Religious Crisis of the 1960's*. New York: Oxford University Press, 2007.

Minich, Joseph. "Class(ic)ifying Jamie Smith," located at

https://calvinistinternational.com/2013/05/27/classicifying-jamie-smith/

Schmitz, Kenneth. *The Recovery of Wonder: The New Freedom and the Asceticism of Power*. Montreal: McGill-Queens University Press, 2005.

Sennett, Richard. *The Corrosion of Character: The Personal Consequences of Work in the New Capitalism*. New York: W.W. Norton, 1998.

——. *The Craftsman*. New Haven: Yale University Press, 2009.

Smith, James K.A. *Desiring the Kingdom: Worship, Worldview, and Cultural Formation*. Grand Rapids: Baker Academic, 2009.

Taylor, Charles. *A Secular Age*. Cambridge: Harvard Belknap, 2007.

Turner, James. *Without God, Without Creed: The Origins of Unbelief in America*. Baltimore: The Johns Hopkins University Press, 1985.

Van Vleet, Jacob. *Dialectical Theology and Jacques Ellul: An Introduction Exposition*. Minneapolis: Fortress, 2014.

Wendling, Amy. *Karl Marx on Technology and Alienation*. New York: Palgrave Macmillan, 2009.

Wright, Robert. *Nonzero: The Logic of Human Destiny*. New York: Vintage Books, 2000.

ABOUT THE DAVENANT INSTITUTE

The Davenant Institute supports the renewal of Christian wisdom for the contemporary church. It seeks to sponsor historical scholarship at the intersection of the church and academy, build networks of friendship and collaboration within the Reformed and evangelical world, and equip the saints with time-tested resources for faithful public witness.

We are a nonprofit organization supported by your tax-deductible gifts. Learn more about us, and donate, at www.davenantinstitute.org.

Made in the USA
Middletown, DE
11 July 2020

12145162R10146